POST-HYPNOTINS

How to give post-hypnotic sug   ses

ARNOLD FURST

Melvin Powers
Wilshire Book Company

12015 Sherman Road, No. Hollywood, CA 91605

Printed in the United States of America

ISBN 0-87980-119-0

CONTENTS

CONTENTS

Dedication

To

TAKEO OMORI

Chairman of The Board
Tokyo Kikaika Kogyo Co., Ltd.
and
President of
Hypnotism And Psychological Institute

TRIBUTE
To
Lester T. Kashiwa, M.D.

By using hypnosis in his general medical practice and thereby developing many original techniques, Dr. Kashiwa has made a tremendous contribution to the field of hypnotherapy. I wish to express my sincere appreciation for the considerate manner in which Dr. Kashiwa generously contributed many of his case histories which are included in this book. The names of all his patients have been changed for obvious reasons of ethical procedure.

Arnold Furst

CHAPTER ONE

Knowing What To Say

When the physician begins to use hypnosis for therapy he soon discovers that the procedure can be divided into two sections. The first section can be labled 'the induction of hypnosis' and this is naturally the greatest concern of the novice. He waits in impatient anticipation for the first indication of response on the part of his patient. He is greatly interested in the 'depth of the hypnotic state' he has induced and he frequently makes several 'tests' to satisfy himself as well as the subject that he has been successful in his attempt to use this modality. As the hypnotist's experience increases he begins to recognize the importance of the second section which consists of preparing and administering the suggestions or instructions which we will term 'the hypnotic prescription'.

No one ever completely loses a sense of amazement upon recognizing the change in respiration and the other outward indications which reveal that the subject has entered into a 'state of hypnosis'. The hypnotist will tend to adopt two or three induction techniques which best suit his personality and operating conditions. The perfectionist will be interested in learning as many different induction techniques as possible and he will experiment with them on various occasions where an opportunity arises or the circumstances demand a modification of the usual procedures. It is therefore fitting and proper tnat a great number of induction techniques be presented in this book and they will be described in the most careful fashion with the greatest concern given to every detail so that the reader can successfully add these techniques to his daily practice.

The twenty-two rapid induction techniques which originally appeared in CASE HISTORIES IN HYPNOTHERAPY will be included in this volume for the sake of completeness and several additional rapid induction techniques will be found in the second part of this book.

The ability to induce a 'state of hypnosis' is a skill which can be acquired and used by those who are meek and un-assuming as well as those who are dominating and aggressive. Like all skills, proficiency in its use can be gained only from constant practice and experience. It is obvious that some degree of proficiency in the use of hypnosis is necessary before one can apply it to hypnotherapy. The knowledge of suggestions or 'hypnotic prescriptions' devised and used by Dr. Lester T. Kashiwa of The Hawaiian Islands and other practicing physicians will be of great value to those interested in this field. Many 'hypnotic prescriptions' which have been used successfully over a period of ten or more years can be considered as 'time tested' and are of great value in specific instances. Hypnotic prescriptions for acne, alcoholism, arthritis, burns, bursitis, childbirth, enuresis, high blood pressure, hives, homosexuality, impotence, insomnia, masturbation, overweight, premature ejaculation, smoking, stuttering, and removal of warts are included in this book for reference by the practicing hypnotherapist. More important, however, will be the careful consideration of the various factors necessary to the preparation of an effective 'hypnotic prescription'. With this knowledge, the practicioner can cope with the rare and unusual ailments and complaints which might otherwise cause him some degree of embarrassment and frustration.

We can compare the use of hypnosis with the use of the hypodermic injection. Knowing how to insert the hypodermic needle in the patient's vein is a skill which anyone can acquire. Knowing what medication and what amount of that medication should be given to the patient in the particular hypodermic injection is a matter usually decided by the physician in charge of the patient. Thus we can see that hypnosis is also a skill which anyone can learn and it is not enough to be able to hypnotice the patient. It is important to know what to say to the patient after the 'hypnotic state' has been induced.

CHAPTER TWO

The Power Of Positive Expression

So much has been written on the subject of the 'power of positive thinking' it should be almost axiomatic to expect that all parents, teachers and physicians will express their instructions in a positive fashion. Unfortunately, this is not the case and the consequence is that the instructions given often lose much effectiveness.

There is a tremendous compelling force behind negative instructions. Therefore if you are asked to NOT think of this page during the next thirty seconds you will find your attention returning here no matter how conscientiously you direct it elsewhere. A popular college student challenge is for one to ask the other, "Can you describe a circular staircase without using your hands?" As soon as the thought is presented that the description is to be given WITHOUT the use of hands, the compelling force behind 'negative expression' becomes operative and the individual finds himself thinking of the NECESSITY of using his hands.

There is a common 'stunt' used by some stage hypnotists in their public demonstrations. The stage hypnotist hands a person a very full glass of water and acts as though he is holding an imaginary glass of water himself. The performer shakes his hand from side to side and says, "Now don't be nervous. Do not shake your glass of water. Try very hard to keep the water from spilling."

The person holding the actual glass of water promptly begins to splatter water from his glass all over the stage. He receives one suggestion by watching the hypnotist shake the imaginary glass of water. The second suggestion is received by the statement, "Now, don't be nervous." Nervous is the only word in that sentence which is suggested. The third powerful negative suggestion is presented by the statement, "try very hard to keep the water from spilling." The implication is that the person will find it difficult to hold the glass steady even if he does try very hard.

When a parent realizes that the instructions: "Don't be nervous", will tend to cause the child to become nervous, the parent will strive to encourage the child to be calm and self-confident with a few words of praise and reassurance. Whenever a student says to me, "I am nervous and afraid to go out and perform", I take the few moments necessary to give him this formula of reassurance. Putting my arm on the student's shoulder I say, "Now I want you to remember that at one time or another you were able to perform everything correctly during your rehearsals and therefore you have every reason to expect that you will perform correctly at this time." In each instance I have been rewarded by having the student return from his performance with the statement, "It was easy! You know, I had nothing to worry about!"

I am sure that had I expressed the negative thought with the words, "You have nothing to worry about", the child's mind might have countered with this belligerent reaction: "It is easy enough for you to say to me that I have nothing to worry about. You don't have to go out in front of those people. You don't know how many foolish errors I made while I was rehearsing and you don't realize how embarrassed and mortified I will be if things go wrong as I am beginning to feel they might."

When a parent says to a child, "Do not stutter", this simple sentence causes the child to stutter the next time he tries to speak. However, if the parent says with sincerity, "I want you to speak more slowly and more carefully because I know that when you speak slowly and carefully you will speak more properly", this will tend to assist the child in overcoming his speech defect.

Our first rule in preparing an "hypnotic prescription" is that the instructions must be expressed in a positive fashion. Thus we find that the patient who wishes help in breaking his habit of smoking is told, "You will have more will-power and self-control."

If the hypnotherapist attempted to assist the patient in overcoming the habit of smoking by giving him a series of 'negative instructions' he might say, "You will find that the idea of smoking will be repulsive and cigarettes will taste vile and putrid and they will make you cough and your eyes will burn and tear and the inhaling of the cigarette fumes will cause you to become nauseous and vomit." These 'negative instructions' will have only a temporary effect and after a period of days or weeks the patient will be curious to see if these unpleasant and abnormal reactions to cigarettes still remain. A friend told me that after he had been hypnotized and told that cigarettes would have an unappealing bitter taste, he continued to smoke for several weeks before he was able to enjoy his cigarettes as before. But he did continue to smoke and he was able to eventually overcome the negative suggestions given to him by the hypnotist.

Let us imagine the thoughts a snowball might have as it is being rolled up a hill. "This is a very unusual position for me to be in", the snowball is thinking, "I wonder how soon the force of gravity will overcome the thrust that caused me to be going UP this hill instead of DOWN as I know I should be going?" Our thoughts are similar when a hypnotist tels us that we will find cigarette smoking unpleasant and distastful since we know from our past experience that cigarette smoking can be very relaxing and enjoyable. We wonder how long this artificial situation can endure since it is going counter to the 'laws of nature' as we understand them.

When the snowball is rolled down a hill it might have these thoughts, "Here I go down the hill and the further down the hill I travel the larger I get and the larger I get the faster I travel down the hill and so I can see that I am likely to get larger and travel faster as I continue and I therefore I have every reason to expect that I will go further and further down the hill." When we find 'some degree of improvement' in our condition as the result of positive instructions given to us by the hypnotist, we can accept the fact that, like the snowball going down the hill, we are making some progress and going in the right direction and therefore we have every reason to expect the improvement to continue.

CHAPTER THREE

Refer Only To The Future

This second rule for preparing hypnotic prescriptions is nothing more than the logical extension of the idea of positive expression offered in the previous chapter.

As long as the hypnotist is giving the subject instructions for his future behavior and conduct, the subject remains passive and accepts them. To mention mistakes the patient may have made in the past invites the possibility of a mental challenge and rejection.

Often when we see a person who is overweight we tend to jump to the conclusion that the individual overeats. Sometimes this is the case, but on the other hand, the obesity may be caused by a glandular disorder. A fifteen year old boy was examined by his family physician and told that his condition was due to his "eating too much". The boy objected with the logical explanation that he was much bigger than the other boys in his class and needed more food to "fill his huge stomach".

No one enjoys being told they acted un-wisely in the past and often we can rationalize and explain our conduct so that it appears that our particular situation and circumstances allowed for us to have acted in one fashion only.

We all want to be accepted and understood. When the hypnotist says to the subject, "I can see how this condition developed and it was through no fault of yours", the patient feels kindly toward the therapist and mentally vows to make every effort to bring about the changes suggested since he then wishes more than ever to please the individual who is so anxious to assist him in bringing about the improvement which they both desire.

I have noticed that some people think it is sufficient to admit their errors and misconduct and by so doing, dismiss them completely. They say, "Oh yes, I am always late for my appointments" and thus indicate that others are expected to accept them with this short-coming since they have no intention to correct their behaviour.

The fact remains that what happened in the past can not be altered and nothing can be gained by dwelling upon that which is beyond recall.

The hypnotic session can be kept brief and happy with an optimistic air when all instructions are considered to be "post-hypnotic". Keep in mind the warning expressed in the following couplet.

Of all words spoken or written by pen
The saddest are these, "It might have been".

CHAPTER FOUR

One Thing At A Time

Ten years ago I felt it was wise to have a brief discussion with the patient and discover the various problems which could be helped or improved by the hypnotic suggestions. It seemed that by putting all the problems together this would give the hypnotist the advantage of added motivation and improve his chances as far as successfully hypnotizing the subject during the initial session.

With experience I have learned that the hypnotist should expect some degree of success during the initial hypnotic session without "added motivation" and the reasons for treating one problem at a time are many and overwhelming.

First of all the hypnotic sessions should be kept as brief as possible. Aside from the economic fact that the physician can afford to spend a limited amount of time with each patient is the more important fact that when the hypnotic session is short and the instructions given are not repeated, the patient is able to accept the idea that his problem will respond to hypnotic treatment since the therapist was so "off handed" with the treatment. Elsewhere in this book mention is made of the "brush-off technique" which is another term used to describe a terse giving of the hypnotic prescription for added effectiveness.

When I was asked to hypnotize an individual who wanted to stop smoking and drinking I agreed to give the hypnotic prescription for smoking to the person at the first session and invited him to return at a later date for us to consider his problem of alcoholism. When this arrangement was followed the patient did stop smoking but never did find time to return to me so that I could treat his problem of excessive drinking. I know that it is easy for a smoker to respond to hypnosis but the alcoholic often has a deep-rooted problem which creates a need for him to escape from reality and often he will resist hypnosis rather than lose this avenue of escape.

When the patient comes to his physician with an assortment of complaints it is possible for the doctor to be selective and offer to treat the ailment which he feels is most likely to respond to the hypnotic prescription he has used successfully in the past. The added confidence the practitioner will gain must be imparted, to some extent, to the subject and it will be a "plus factor" for the initial hypnotic session.

If four or five different prescriptions are given during one session there is a risk that one of the prescriptions might be rejected and then the patient is likely to report that the entire "hypnotic treatment" was a failure. It is far better to single out one complaint, speak directly regarding it and finish the prescription with "general suggestions" indicating that the patient wil find some degree of improvement in all matters which trouble him.

When the physician treats one complaint at a time he has an excellent excuse to invite the patient to return for another hypnotic session. The physician wants the patient to return so that he can observe the rate of improvement, but he does not dare explain this to the subject for this presents the negative suggestion that the rate of improvement might not be fast enough and that there is a possibility of failure, to some degree. When the patient returns to have an entirely different matter discussed, the therapist has the opportunity to examine his records, observe the improvement and modify the treatment, if necessary.

We will find that most patients enjoy the experience of the hypnotic sessions and they will welcome the opportunity to return.

CHAPTER FIVE

Make A Contribution

When a person comes to a hypnotist with a problem he will often insist that the condition has existed over some period of time and "he has tried everything" and the implication is that all things being equal, the problem will remain. By making a contribution or the adding of some new thought or idea, the hypnotist changes the situation and thereafter "all things do not remain equal" and the individual can accept the idea that matters will be different in the future.

I can best explain this rule by giving some examples from the "time-tested prescriptions" which will be found in this book.

When a young man came to me and explained that he was contemplating suicide because his fiance broke their engagement, I told him that he was going to meet a young lady who would be much more wonderful than anyone he had ever known before. I promised him that he could not imagine anyone like her and he would have to go to parties and dances and social gatherings in order to meet this extraordinary girl.

When a person asks to stop smoking the basic suggestion given to him is that he will have increased will-power and self-control. Then as a "contribution" I explain that by smoking one creates an irritation and thus the more one smokes, the more one wishes to smoke. Conversely it is also true that the longer a person goes without smoking the less need the person has to smoke. Then it is possible to suggest that as each hour passes following the hypnotic session the individual will have less need and less desire to smoke.

The pregnant woman who is receiving hypnotic suggestions for childbirth is told that she will recognize the difference between the feeling of pain and the feeling of pressure. The hypnotist promises her that she will feel pressure when her baby is delivered but it will not make her uncomfortable since she can withstand a great deal of pressure.

The individual suffering from a condition of arthritis is told that he has a calcium deposit between his bones. He is then told that a drop of lubrication will be secreted in the future each time he moves the affected arm or leg. He is told that the very minute drop of secretion will tend to cover the calcium deposit and thus remove any possibility of friction or discomfort. You will note that care is taken to omit the use of the word . . . "pain", whenever possible. Whenever it is desired to alleviate a painful condition, the patient is told he will feel more rested and more comfortable.

The basic instructions to a person who stutters or stammers is that he will speak more slowly and more carefully in the future. Then the contribution is made as follows: "You know that you have no difficulty when you sing and that is because singing is simply speaking with a rhythm. In the future you can practice speaking correctly by speaking with a rhythm. You can tap with your finger on the table, in the privacy of your room, and you can speak as follows. 'One, two, three, four. I will speak more slowly and more carefully'. By speaking one word with each tap of your finger you will be able to establish a rhythm and as you practice speaking with a rhythm you will become aware of your ability to speak properly".

A condition of insomnia is often brought about by a "fear of failure". The individual begins to worry and fret as he tosses and turns in bed and as it gets later he thinks of his need for rest and sleep and becomes more upset and unhappy as he realize that he should be sleeping since he has such a demanding day ahead of him and he will be needing all of his strength. The hypnotherapist tells the patient with insomnia that the medical men doing research regarding sleep have discovered that when we lie in bed with our eyes closed we receive 80 per cent of the benefits that we would derive from being asleep. In this way we can remove much of the "fear of not sleeping" and the patient is more likely to relax and follow the other hypnotic instructions given as part of the prescription.

I have found that over 90 per cent of all sexual problems are due to a "fear of failure" and so many problems can be helped by pointing out an advantage which might be gained from the problem. I have found this to be a good contribution to make when young college students ask me to help them overcome the habit of masturbation. Like the prescription for smoking, I suggest that the subject have more will-power and more self-control in the future. Then I explain that the act of masturbation can be used as a form of training similar to the muscular training that one receives from working in a gymnasium. The individual can train himself to have increased endurance and the ability to interrupt the sex act at will. The idea that the act of masturbation might be used constructively will act as a deterrent.

CHAPTER SIX

General Beneficial Instructions

The final three rules for the preparation of all hypnotic prescriptions are always grouped together and are sometimes the basis for the complete prescription when the therapist is at a loss for more specific instructions.

The most important rule in this category is that there will be some degree of improvement. This is necessary since each patient responds in an individual manner depending upon his background, training and previous experience and pre-conceived ideas regarding hypnosis. To promise a complete change or "cure" would be inviting failure since this condition is often temporary and not likely to have a permanent lasting effect.

The body must heal itself according to it's capabilities and limitations. "Some degree of improvement" allows for a wide variance in the amount of responce which the patient can expect.

Often the subject will report a complete and 100 per cent removal of his problem or complaint. This the practitioner must accept with a gracious air while trying to conceal his inner suprise and exaltation. Frequently the improvement will be slow and very slight at first. On these occasions the hypnotist is pleased that he gave the following instructions as part of the hypnotic prescription. "You will notice the improvement, no matter how slight it will be at first, and you will be well pleased with the amount of improvement you will notice. The improvement will be progressive and so as each day goes by your condition will improve more and more and thus you and I can be sure that it will be lasting and permanent."

When the physician concludes the hypnotic prescription in this fashion he can look forward to having all his patients return with a satisfactory report. Often the only complaint is that the rate of improvement is "too slow" and then it is easy for the hypnotist to deny any requests for additional hypnotic treatment with the honest explanation that one short hypnotic session is best and that since the patient has noticed the slight improvement we know that the improvement will continue with each passing day and then be more lasting. As long as the improvement continues there can be no deterioration or return to the former condition.

When the patient insists for a more rapid improvement or a second session . . . "just to make sure", the therapist can agree to modify the treatment with suggestions that the subject may resort to "self-hypnosis" if a need for immediate attention arises in the future. The subject is told that he need only close his eyes and turn his palms upwards and he will then feel as heavy and tired as he feels during the hypnotic session and he will then feel a degree of immediate improvement due to his state of relaxation.

The most difficult part of hypnotic treatment is for the hypnotist to restrain himself and control his urge to ask the patient any questions regarding the results from the hypnotic session. If the physician puts forth any questions regarding the effectiveness of the treatment he makes the subject aware that there was a degree of un-certainly involved and raises doubts in his mind as to the amount of the improvement he felt.

CHAPTER SEVEN

Summary

Rules For Preparing A Hypnotic Prescription

1. Prescription must be expressed in positive fashion.

2. Refer only to the future.

3. Make your prescription for one thing at a time.

4. Make a contribution of a new thought or idea.

5. Promise the subject there will be some degree of improvement.

6. Explain that the improvement will be progressive and will increase with each passing day.

7. Tell the subject he will notice the improvement, no matter how slight it may be at first.

8. Tell the subject he will be well pleased with the amount of improvement he will notice.

CHAPTER EIGHT

Prescriptions Used For Children

It is often difficult to suggest the use of hypnosis to old patients of several years standing and generally speaking, some unexpected development or an entirely new ailment is needed before the doctor can begin such treatment. It was only by accident that Dr. Lester T. Kashiwa, resident physician of The Maui General Hospital in The Hawaiian Islands, discovered Lindia's problem was psychosomatic and thus received permission from her parents to give her some hypnotic suggestions which eventually cured her condition.

Hives

Name: Lindia
Age: 7 years, old in 1954
Complaint: Hives

History: Dr. Kashiwa had been treating seven year old Lindia for three years for a condition of hives which had failed to respond to the many types of medication which had been prescribed for her.

One afternoon, Lindia was interested in watching a television program in the wating room when she and her parents were called into the doctor's office. Lindia began to cry and scream because she did not want to leave the program she had been viewing. However, she was forced to accompany her parents who told the doctor she was feeling well at that moment but had suffered a most severe attack of hives the previous night. As Dr. Kashiwa began to examine the crying child he noticed a rash of hives begin to appear all around her neck. This sudden appearance made Dr. Kashiwa suspect the condition was psychosomatic and entirely due to the child's frustration and anger over being forced to leave the television program she had been enjoying. Dr. Kashiwa explained this to the parents and told them he was sure he could treat the condition by the use of hypnosis now that he knew what brought it on. The parents agreed readily since all else had failed.

Dr. Kashiwa spoke to Lindia and told her it would be easy for him to remove the hives by the use of hypnosis because he now realized the hives had not been caused by any of the food she had eaten but rather had been caused by the fact she did not want to leave the television program. He told her the hives appeared when she had been forced to do things against her will and in the future she would have the power to make the hives go away as quickly as they appeared.

In order to induce a hypnotic trance, Dr. Kashiwa decided to use his hypnotic couch coupled with the "swaying and falling technique". Dr. Kashiwa has had a very low couch especially built for him and installed in his office. This couch is about two and a half feet wide and six feet long and nine inches high. It is actually a fine foam rubber mattress fitted into a sturdy maplewood frame. When not in use, this hypnotic couch is raised and hooked in place against the office wall and thus takes up very little space. It is a simple matter to lower the hypnotic couch and put it in the center of the office and the use of this special couch has a great psychological effect on the subject as it indicates Dr. Kashiwa has used hypnosis in the past and has the proper equipment for this type of treatment.

Lindia was asked to remove her shoes and stand on the couch, near one end. Dr. Kashiwa told her to close her eyes when he counted to "three" and then he told her to "feel like a pole". He explained he meant she was to keep her hands tightly against her body and to hold her knees so straight it would be impossible for them to bend. He told her to imagine she was standing at the edge of a table with her back to the floor but not to worry about falling because he was ready to catch her. He touched her gently on her shoulder and found she was very responsive and her body began to sway slightly.

Dr. Kashiwa told the child that when he counted to "three" this time she was going to fall back into his arms. When her body was completely off balance, he caught her and gently lowered her onto the couch. Then he pressed his fingers against her closed eyes and said, "By my pressing here, your eyelids will become heavier and your eyeballs will roll upwards." Lindia began to breathe heavily and more slowly and her face had a rested appearance.

Dr. Kashiwa spoke to the little girl softly and told her the itching hives would disappear and she would rest easily and comfortably and if the hives ever returned while she was at home it would only be necessary for her to count from "one to ten" and the hives would go away. At that point, Dr. Kashiwa and the parents were amazed to notice the hives slowly fading away although they were very evident less than two minutes previously when the hypnotic session began. The girl was awakened at the count of "seven" and told she would feel well rested and refreshed and happy to have been so successfully hypnotized and pleased to know that she now had the power to control her hives and make them go away in the future.

The child's father called Dr. Kashiwa the next day and reported the hypnotic suggestions had been of some help but the girl still had hives and it seemed to be too much bother for her to count from "one to ten". The father was asked to return with her and two days later Dr. Kashiwa hypnotized the girl again using the same technique described above but this time he gave her the suggestion that she would be able to remove the hives by merely crossing her fingers. Also, he told her the harder she pressed her fingers together, the more control she would have over the hives and the faster they would go away.

The child's mother brought her back a week later and reported the hives had appeared less frequently and they had noticed when the child was aggravated the hives were present and by giving more attention and favors to the girl the hives appeared less frequently. On each visit thereafter an improvement was noted and the child was reminded during her hypnotic session that she was controling her hives and that she was doing a good job because they were appearing less frequently. On the sixth visit after the first hypnotic session it was reported that the hives had completely disappeared.

Induction technique used: Swaying and falling technique coupled with the hypnotic couch.

Hypnotic prescription given: You will have 'control' over your hives in the future. If the hives appear when you are at home you will find that by crossing your forefinger and middle finger the hives will go away. Also you will discover that the harder you press your fingers together the more control you will have over the hives and the faster they will go away.

Additional history: Lindia was brought to Dr. Kashiwa for periodic examinations during the following two years and there has been no reoccurance of the itching hives.

Unable to Swallow Pills

The five hypnotic sessions reported above makes this an exceptional case. Ordinarily one or at the most two hypnotic sessions suffice. By way of contrast we have the following case.

Name: Maria
Age: 12 years old in 1955
Complaint: Unable to swallow pills.

History: After examining 12 year old Maria in his office one afternoon, Dr. Kashiwa gave the girl's mother some very large pills for the girl to take three times a day. The mother said, "Oh, my daughter can not swallow pills at all. We have tried to make her swallow different size pills ever since she was a baby and we have found she can not swallow any pills, not even an aspirin and the pils you are handing me are much larger than any I have ever seen before so I know it will be impossible for her to take them."

Ordinarily, Dr. Kashiwa would have tried to prescribe the medication in some other form as it is very common to find some patients can not swallow pills or capsules. However, in this particular case it was difficult to find a prescription which would be equally effective. Therefore, Dr. Kashiwa told the mother he would hypnotize the girl so she would have no further difficulty in swallowing pills. Knowing his waiting room was filled with other patients, Dr. Kashiwa hesitated to take the time to un-hook his hypnotic couch and put it into the center of his examining room. He turned to the girl and said, "I am just going to take a minute to see how well you respond".

Dr. Kashiwa had the girl stand in front of him with her feet together. He said, "When I count 'three' you will close your eyes and imagine you are standing at the edge of a very high cliff." When she closed her eyes as instructed he said, "I am now going to stand behind you and when I count 'three' this time you will feel your body falling back and I will catch you." As the girl fell, he quickly pulled a nearby chair into position to receive her limp body. He noticed the heavy lethargic breathing which is often a good indication that the subject is responding to the hypnotic instructions.

He then said, "When I count 'three' this time you will continue to feel heavy and tired as you sit in the chair, but you will hold this paper cup of water in your right hand and this pill in your left hand. One, two, three." When the girl accepted the cup of water and pill, he continued. "When I count 'three' you will take the pill." After the girl drank the water and swallowed the pill with no difficulty, Dr. Kashiwa said, "Now you will have no difficulty in ever swallowing pills in the future because you have proved to yourself that you can do it." The girl smiled when she was awakened at the count of 'seven' and left with her mother who seemed unable to believe what she had just witnessed. Dr. Kashiwa smiled also as he noted on the girl's record that the hypnotic session had lasted less then two minutes.

Induction technique used: Falling backward technique.

Hypnotic prescription given: You will have no difficulty swallowing pills in the future because you have proved to yourself that you can do it.

Additional history: Maria's mother called a week later to ask if the girl should continue taking the pills since she seemed to be well. When questioned, she said that the girl swallowed the pills easily three times daily.

Warts

The appearance and disappearance of warts have puzzled many for centuries. We have authentic records of all sorts of "spells" and superstitious rigamarole which have caused warts to vanish and yet there are few physicians who feel they can prescribe any salve or ointment for this skin condition. The use of hyponosis for the removal of warts seems to be equally as effective as the rubbing of garlic on the troublesome growth and certainly less offensive.

Name: Akana
Age: 17 years old in 1954
Complaint: Warts.

History: Akana came to Dr. Kashiwa's office for a routine examination in order to receive permission to play football for his High School. In the course of the examination, Dr. Kashiwa noticed the boy had a great many warts all over his arms. When questioned, the boy said he had them for over five years.

Dr. Kashiwa told the boy he would remove the warts through the use of hypnosis and he began by telling the youth to sit well back in his chair, with his feet firmly on the floor and with his hands resting lightly in his lap. The doctor stood in front of the lad and told him to look deeply into his left eye and to allow his eyes to close when the doctor counted to "three". He said, "One, two, three, and now I want you to allow your eyes to close and your eyeballs will roll upwards and your head will feel very heavy and tired and it will begin to nod slightly." The response was perfect and, therefore, the doctor decided to give the subject a "test" in which he would feel no pain as he felt this would indicate a rather deep hypnotic state.

Dr. Kashiwa removed a sterilized hypodermic needle from his cabinet and said, "When I count to 'three' your right arm will feel numb." The hypodermic needle was then pushed into the upper arm and the doctor watched the boy's face to see if there was any reflex action to indicate the boy felt the needle or experienced any pain. The boy's face was calm and passive and he seemed to be completely relaxed and at ease.

This took place during the time when Dr. Kashiwa first began using hypnosis in his general medical practice and he was greatly concerned about getting his patients into the proper "depth" before giving them the necessary suggestions for their ailment or complaint. Therefore, he gave the boy these additional suggestions which were likely to put him into a somewhat deeper hypnotic state. He had the boy extend his right arm out in front of his body and he told him when he counted to "three" the arm would become very heavy and fall. When Dr. Kashiwa counted to "three", the boy's arm fell and hung limply at his side. Dr. Kashiwa then said, "Just as your arm fell, that is the way your mind is now going to fall into a very deep sleep." The boy's response to this suggestion was immediate and he had the appearance of being very sound asleep. Dr. Kashiwa continued, "The warts on your arms will melt away within the next two weeks and they will never return or bother you again." The boy was then awakened and dismissed.

Induction technique used: Eye-to-eye technique explained in great detail in Part Two of this book.

Hypnotic prescription given: "The warts on your arms will melt away within the next two weeks and they will never return or bother you again."

Additional History: One year later, the boy returned for another routine examination. Not until the physician was about to put the date of this examination on the boy's record did he see the notation that he had hypnotized the patient for the removal of warts. Thereupon, Dr. Kashiwa asked to see the boy's arms and he found them to be completely devoid of any warts. He asked the student what happened to the warts and he was told, "Oh, they just melted away two weeks after I saw you last year."

Warts are seldom considered to be much of a problem and I am not often asked to treat them. While traveling through Japan and visiting the military bases with a lecture and demonstration of Rapid Induction Techniques of Hypnosis I was asked to talk to the medical staff of The Itazuki Air Base Hospital. One of the doctors pointed to some warts on the hand of the Airman who was my escort that day and challenged me to do something about them.

Name: Marc
Age: 21 years old in 1963
Complaint: Warts

Induction technique used: Eye-to-eye technique.

Hypnotic prescription given: "The warts on your hand will melt away within the next few weeks."

Additional history: I received the following letter on January 31, 1964. I want to thank you for giving me such an interest in Hypnosis. Incidently, the wart on my thunb, that you hypnotized me for, in front of the Air Force Doctor last May, went away. I don't know when it went away but I just realized it was gone the other day.

Bed Wetting

The one single problem most frequently presented to me for treatment is bed wetting by small children. As I traveled around the world I am often invited for a "home cooked meal" and then find the host and hostess are worried about their child who has this problem. Some few years ago one of my best friends married a widow with two small children. The following week he called me to his house for a "home cooked meal" and once again I was presented with this very common problem.

Name: Bobby
Age: Eight years old in 1960
Complaint: Bed wetting

History: When the father and mother asked me to do something for the boy, I turned and asked him for his permission to use hypnosis. It was quickly granted and I arranged a large over-stuffed chair facing a blank wall and seated myself in it with my legs extended and my arms out-stretched. I then invited the boy to stand with his back against the wall. Since my chair was less than three feet from the wall, he was then standing between my legs and he then understood that I expected him to fall forward during the hypnotic session and I was prepared to catch him. This "back against the wall" technique is described in greater detail in Part Two of this book. After the boy responded to my hypnotic instructions and fell into my lap, I cradled him in my arms and said, "Now, Bobby, you know that three month old babies are not able to control themselves and so they wet their pants. However, when a boy is eight years old as you are, he has self-control and so you do not wet your pants, but you are able to control yourself until you are in the bathroom or restroom before you relieve yourself. Now that I have hypnotized you, I am going to give you more will-power and self-control so that in the future you will be able to control yourself at night while you are asleep the way you are now able to control yourself during the day-time when you are awake. Also, I want you to become stronger so that you will be able to run faster and play ball better and you will find that it will be easier for you to do your school work because you will pay very close attention to your teacher when you are in your schoolroom and you will find that you will have a better memory and therefore you will be able to do your homework with less effort."

I then stood the boy back up against the wall. This was easy to do since he had kept his body rigid during the entire time he was in my arms. I then ended the hypnotic session by saying, "Now, Bobby, wneh I count to 'seven' you will open your eyes and you will feel rested and refreshed and when you go to sleep tonight you will sleep well and tomorrow you will enjoy all your school activities and from now on you will find a little improvement in your ability to play ball and race with your friends and also from day to day you will find a little improvement in your school work."

Ordinarily, before beginning the "back-against-the-wall" technique I will look at the boy and tell him that I want to hypnotize him so that he wil not have to "study" in the future but instead will find it very easy to do his homework and other school assignments. As added motivation I may also promise to increase his ability to play baseball. This serves to remove some of the embarrassment the boy feels over the discussion of his problem of bed-wetting and it does help to establish rapport. However, I felt I knew Bobby very well and rapport had been established.

The next afternoon Bobby's mother telephoned me and reported that he had wet his bed the previous night as usual. I asked if he was near her at that time and she said he was in the same room. "Let me talk to Bobby", I said.

After Bobby said, "Hello" I said, "I want to ask you some questions."

He said, "All right."

"You were hypnotized last night. Is that correct?" I began.

"Yes", he replied.

"You know that you now have more will-power and self-control", I continued.

"Yes"

"Therefore, you will not wet your bed in the future", I stated firmly. "Do you understand?"

"Yes", he replied meekly.

"Good-by", I said ending the conversation since I felt impatient over having to discuss the matter with the boy after the hypnotic session of the previous evening.

When his mother called me the following morning she seemed elated and reported that she found the boy's bed dry and he seemed to be happier than usual.

Induction technique used: Back-against-the-wall technique.

Hypnotic prescription given: You will now have more will-power and self-control in the future. You will be able to control yourself at night when you are asleep as you are now able to control yourself during the day time when you are awake. If you must relieve yourself when you are asleep, you will wake up and go to the toilet and then return to your bed and go back to sleep.

Additional history: Since Bobby's mother and step-father are very dear friends of mine, I see him several times a year. They often remark to their friends how I hypnotized Bobby and stopped him from bed-wetting when he was eight years old. At this writing Bobby is fifteen years old and there has been no re-occurance since our brief telephone conversation the day after the hypnotic session.

While traveling in Japan in 1963 I met an optometrist with The United States Air Force who asked me to have dinner with his family so that I could meet one of his patients who had two children she wanted me to hypnotize. I wanted to demonstrate my rapid induction techniques to his doctor and his friends so I readily agreed. That evening the Mother asked me to hypnotize her eleven year old son for bed-wetting and her thirteen year old daughter who was not doing very well with her school work. I was asked to hypnotize the boy first. Using the back-against-the-wall technique I began by asking the boy to close his eyes when I counted to "three". This was one of the rare instances when the boy did not close his eyes as instructed. In al the rapid induction techniques given in this book there are one or more "check points" which the hypnotist can use to determine if the subject is responding or is resisting the hypnotic instructions. In the back-against-the-wall technique the only "check point" is to see if the boy closes his eyes promptly upon the utterance of "three" by the hypnotist. When the boy did not respond I asked myself the reason for this and decided it was because the boy was embarrassed and did not want his problem discussed or treated in front of so many people.

I stood up from the very large comfortable chair and announced that I would prefer talking to the boy on a "man to man" basis in privacy and our hostess invited us to make use of any of the rooms on the second floor of the house. This time the boy closed his eyes instantly when I said "three" and all indications were that he was deeply responsive to the hypnotic instructions. The hypnotic prescription for enuresis was given and eventually the boy's mother reported to the optometrist that the hypnotic treatment had been completely successful.

I was visiting Dr. Lester T. Kashiwa on the Island of Maui in The Hawaiian Islands in 1956 while we were collaborating in the preparation of our book, CASE HISTORIES IN HYPNOTHERAPY, when he called me to his office one afternoon. He wanted me to hypnotize a young girl as he had tried several techniques with no success. He asked me to just hypnotize the girl and then suggest that he would be able to hypnotize her in the future. This way, he explained, he would able to give her the hypnotic instructions in private as she had a personal problem.

Name: Angela
Age: 10 years old in 1956
Complaint: Enuresis

History: Once I was alone with the girl I wondered what induction technique to use. I knew the various techniques Dr. Kashiwa would have used so I decided to use a technique which I had not discussed with him. I had the girl sit in a chair in the middle of the room and I asked her to imagine she had a small hole in the top of her head. I explained that if she had such a hole it would come in very handy if she wanted to look at the ceiling without raising her head. I told her to close her eyes at the count of "three" and to just imagine she was looking up at the ceiling through the hole in the top of her head. When she closed her eyes, I watched carefully to see if she tried to roll her eyeballs upwards as I wanted her to do. Actually, she was unresponsive and I could not detect any movement of her eyeballs. I asked if she could see the ceiling through the hole in the top of her head and she opened her eyes and said, "I do not have a hole in the top of my head."

The error was mine in not having taken enough time to explain this technique properly so that it would be understood by a ten year old child. I knelt in front of the seated girl and told her I knew she did not actually have a hole in her head, but I wanted her to imagine she had a hole in her head. "Right here", I said, tapping her on the crown of her head.

"Do you mean you want me to play there is a hole in my head?" she asked.

"Yes," I agreed, "that is what I mean!"

This time when she closed her eyes, I asked her to "play" she was looking through the hole in her head and I could see her eyelids flutter and her head raise slightly as she gave every indication of trying to look through the imaginary hole in her head. I asked her to "play" she could see the ceiling and the ceiling light through the hole in her head and she agreed that she could.

I told her I wanted her to continue to "play" she was looking at the ceiling through the hole in her head but I wanted her to also listen to me very carefully since, when I counted "three" I wanted her to try to open her eyes and I told her she would find her eyes would be tightly stuck together and she would feel a little sleepy and tired but she would not mind at all because she would be able to hear every word I said and she would know everything that was taking place. I said, "One, two, three, and now keep right on looking at the ceiling through the hole in your head and just see how heavy your head feels and just see how heavy your eyelids feel and just try to open your eyes and see how tightly they are stuck together. That is fine, keep right on looking at the ceiling and no matter how much you try, you can not open your eyes but you don't care at all, do you?"

All this time, I was ready to tap her on the top of her head and remind her to keep looking through the imaginary hole if I saw her attention wander but that was not necessary since she was deliberately trying to keep her eyeballs rolled up and pull her eyelids open at the same time. This is, of course, impossible, and so the little girl found she could not open her eyes as I had promised. When I suggested she would feel her head grow heavy and tired I could see her immediate response to that suggestion as her head began to nod. I continued for a moment and saw her entire body sag with fatigue.

Several doctors and the child's mother were waiting to see what success I had so I decided to waken her and hypnotize her again to assure myself that she understood fully and would respond in the future. I told her I was going to have her open her eyes when I counted to "seven" and she would feel well rested and she would feel stronger in the future and have a better memory and be able to do her school work easier and she would be happy knowing she had been hypnotized. I told her the next time I asked her to close her eyes and "play" she was looking through the hole in her head I wanted her to go back asleep as she was at that moment so that she would again feel heavy and tired and rested. I asked her if she understood me and she nodded her head. I counted to "seven" and she opened her eyes and when I asked her how she felt, she replied, "I feel like I have been taking a nap."

I told her she had followed my instructions perfectly and I was very pleased with her and I would like her to try it again since I thought we would be able to do it much faster this time. She said, "All right," and responded very readily to all my suggestions.

I opened the examining room door and allowed the others to see the girl resting in the hypnotic state as I invited Dr. Kashiwa to enter. I told the girl she would be able to hear and understand everything Dr. Kashiwa was about to tell her and she would follow all of his suggestions which she knew he would be giving to her for her good and welfare and when he asked her to open her eyes she would follow his instructions and she would feel rested and happy for having been hypnotized.

Dr. Kashiwa asked me to hypnotize the girl's eleven year old brother who was waiting in the next office and he promised to join me as soon as he had finished giving some instructions to the girl. Since Dr. Kashiwa had not had a chance to use any of the induction techniques on the boy I felt safe in using my favorite back-against-the-wall technique as described earlier. The boy responded without delay. When Dr. Kashiwa entered the room I told the boy he would be able to hear Dr. Kashiwa and he would follow all the instructions Dr. Kashiwa was about to give him. Dr. Kashiwa then gave the boy the hypnotic prescription for bed-wetting and had the boy open his eyes at the count of "seven".

After the mother left with her two children, Dr. Kashiwa gave me the following information. He said this lady was not one of his regular patients. In fact, she lived quite far from his office and seldom visited the city of Wailuku. She heard from a friend about his having cured a boy of enuresis and so she made the special trip to see him although she felt there was little chance he could do anything for her two children. The mother said her family had a long history of bed-wetting and that both she and her husband had that problem almost until they were wed and she could recall her grandfather reporting that he had continued to wet his bed all of his life and so she felt it was perfectly natural for her two children to wet their beds since it was an hereditary problem in her family.

She explained that she had been putting diapers on the ten year old girl and the eleven year old boy every night before they went to bed. However, recently, they have been wetting the bed more often than usual. She even tried putting two sets of diapers on each child and yet would find the sheets and mattress completely soaked. Only because she hated the expense of buying so many new mattresses each year and the bother of putting the two diapers on each child did she feel compelled to ask Dr. Kashiwa to try to help the children, although, she concluded, she doubted very much if he would be able to hypnotize them or be able to get them to stop wetting the bed.

Dr. Kashiwa thanked me for taking the time to hypnotize the girl as it gave him a chance to speak to the mother alone. He told her that enuresis is never hereditary and very likely it was brought about by the children hearing their parents speak of their having had that habit and therefore, he insisted the mother stop putting the diapers on her children in the future and never to speak of them and the habit of bed-wetting or refer to their relapse, if they do occasionally wet the bed. The mother was not at all agreeable as she insisted without the diapers the children would be unable to sleep and also she thought the odor of the urine would bother the other members of the family. However, she finally did promise to follow his instructions and Dr. Kashiwa told me if she had been a regular patient he would have been tempted to hypnotize her to insure her following his orders.

Induction technique used: Hole-in-the-top-of-head technique

Hypnotic prescription given: "You will now have more will-power and self-control. In the future you will be able to control yourself at night, when you are asleep, as you are now able to control yourself during the daytime, when you are awake. If you must relieve yourself when you are asleep, you will wake up and go to the toilet and then return to your bed and go back to sleep."

Additional history: Several months later a woman from this distant village saw Dr. KaKshiwa and told him that both the boy and girl had stopped their bedwetting to the bewilderment of their parents.

Facial Tic

I have the utmost confidence when I speak to children regarding bed-wetting since I have had so many cases with complete success in the past. I felt completely helpless, however, when a lady brought her son to see me at The International House in Tokyo when I was just about to begin a lecture on Self-hypnosis for a group of Japanese physicians and dentists.

Name: Hozumi
Age: Five years old in 1964
Complaint: Facial grimaces or tic at regular intervals of every fifteen seconds.

History: The boy's mother is a physician and had received improper information regarding the time for my lectures on Rapid Induction Techniques of Hypnotherapy. At these all-day sessions I invite the physicians and dentists attending to bring a patient, if they wish, for me to treat in front of the class. This is the only way I accept patients and it is done without charge since I hypnotize the patients for demonstration purposes. Only those who have completed the course in Rapid Induction Techniques of Hypnotherapy are allowed to attend the course in Self-hypnosis. Therefore, I could not allow the mother to attend the lecture that evening and we do not have patients brought in for demonstrations at that lecture. However, I could not turn the poor lad away and yet I could not think of any reason for his behavior and I could think of no prescription applicable.

I asked the physicians in the room to help me, but they could not. The mother reported that she had had the boy examined by brain specialists and psychologists and psychiatrists and no one could find a reason for his facial grimaces and no one could help him.

I arranged an arm chair for the Back-against-the-wall induction technique and I gestured to the boy to come to me and stand between my legs. Mr. Takeo Omori, who is the interpreter for my lectures in Japan, came up to us and he explained to the lad that I would be speaking in English but Mr. Omori would translate my words into Japanese so the boy would understand me. I asked the boy to stand rigidly against the wall and he complied. I told him to close his eyes when I counted to "three" and he responded perfectly. When I told him he would try to bend over and that he would find he could not and would instead fall into my arms, he did exactly as instructed and we could see the change in his respiration. I held him in my arms and told him he would become stronger and healther and be able to play games better and run faster. As I gave these suggestions and Mr. Omori translated them for me we watched the boy and we could see that the facial grimaces were less intense and were spaced a bit longer apart. It was a pleasure for me to observe the boy a bit more comfortable and relaxed than before and I decided to give him the first part of the bed-wetting prescription. I told the boy he would have more will-power and more self-control in the future. I then concluded by telling him that he would sleep better and have a better appetite in the future. I promised him that there would be some degree of improvemnt in his condition and that the improvement would be progressive and get more and more as each day went by. Also, I told him that he would notice the improvement, no matter how slight it might be at first, and that he would be well pleased with the amount of improvement he would notice. I then lifted the boy's rigid body and stood him back up against the wall and instructed him to open his eyes at the count of "seven". After he opened his eyes and looked about him somewhat dazed, as almost all persons do when coming out of the hypnotic state, we saw that the facial grimaces were just about as they had been before I had the hypnotice session with him.

I told my students that Dr. Kashiwa and I feel it is often sufficient to use a prescription of General Beneficial Instructions when we do not have a specific prescription to give.

Induction technique used: Back-against-the-wall technique since this is my favorite for almost all children between the ages of five and twelve.

Hypnotic prescription given: You will have more will-power and more self-control in the future. You will sleep better and you will have a better appetite and you will become stronger and be able to run faster and enjoy playing games more. There will be some degree of improvement in your condition. The improvement will be progressive and will become greater and greater as each day goes by and you will notice the improvement, no matter how slight it may be at first and you will be well pleased with the amount of improvement you will notice.

Additional history: In March of 1966 I returned to Tokyo for another series of lectures. When the students were invited to bring forth their patients for demonstration purposes, I noticed that many of the physicians and dentists had brought their wife or one of their children for treatment. Sometimes I was asked to hypnotize a boy or girl who was nervous but often I was asked to hypnotize a child to do better in school. This is not much of a "complaint" but I accept the children anyway and suggest to the teen-agers that they will find it easy to speak to their school mates and become more popular by asking others regarding their experiences and opinions as all persons welcome the opportunity to talk about themselves. Near the end of one of the demonstration periods Mr. Omori told me that a physician had brought the seven year old boy in the front row to be hypnotized so that he would do better in school. I looked at the boy who smiled broadly at me and gayly swung his legs as they hung from the seat. Impatiently, I whispered to Mr. Omori that there was nothing the matter with the boy and it was foolish to expect a seven year old to be doing "well" in school. Mr. Omori beamed, however, and said, "This is different, I am so glad his mother brought him to our lecture today. This is the boy who had the facial grimaces and that you hypnotized in 1964."

It was therefore with great interest that I invited the youth to come forward and we noticed that he still has facial grimaces, but they were very slight and spaced several minutes apart. We talked to the mother later in the afternoon and she agreed that the improvement had been great and she feels confident that the grimaces will eventually disappear completely.

Nail Biting

Of all the problems and complaints brought to the attention of the hypnotherapists none seem more trivial than the request that the patient be hypnotized in order to help him stop the habit of biting his nails. However, a neighbor once came to me with a good reason for such treatment.

Name: Spencer
Age: 15 years old in 1950
Complaint: Nail biting

History: When Spencer came to see me one afternoon he asked me if I would hypnotize him to stop him from biting his nails. "It doesn't bother me," he explained, "but it does upset my Mother and so I would like you to help me as it will make her feel better." Spencer was about my size and so it seemed foolish to use any of the techniques applicable for children. I had every reason to expect him to be responsive and so without any preliminary remarks which today I would automatically give to any teen age boy, I asked him to sit in a firm chair and began with the eye-to-eye induction technique. There was no response and yet I knew the boy was friendly and trying to co-operate. Since I did not observe his head nodding or moving towards his chest, I could go no further with this technique and yet I hesitated to change to another technique for fear it would appear that I had failed, at least as far as that technique was concerned. I simply told him he would feel his head grow heavy and tired and I waited. After a few minutes he opened his eyes and said, "I don't think it is going to work right now and I better get back home as my Mother is waiting for me. Can we try again tomorrow?" I agreed and on the following day we had another session with no more success.

On the third day the boy came to my house and said, "I bet I can tell you why you have not been able to hypnotize me." I was frankly very much interested as he continued. "It is because you insisted I sit in a chair instead of lying down. I bet you can hypnotize me right away if I lie down on this couch." I allowed the boy to assume a comfortable position on the couch and he responded to the hypnotic suggestions immediately and it was possible to put him into a very deep hypnotic state. I then gave him the usual hypnotic prescription we use for all bad habits. I then told him he would be aware of the heavy tired feeling he had at that time and would be able to follow my hypnotic instructions in the future as easily while sitting or standing as he had on that occasion while lying on the couch. In that way I was able to condition him to respond regardless of his position.

Since then I have on several occasions asked children why they thought I was having difficulty in hypnotizing them and I found if I accepted their suggestions they always responded very quickly. Sometimes children have pre-conceived ideas regarding hypnosis which are very strong.

Induction technique used: Actually it was the eye-to-eye technique since that was the technique I had first tried and I wanted to present the idea to him that the technique was valid and effective when applied to him. The only difference was that he was lying on the couch instead of sitting in the chair. I arranged his hands with the palms upward and all verbal instructions were exactly the same as on the two previous occasions. This time, however, his head did move down towards his chest and his respiration showed a marked change.

Hypnotic prescription given: You will have more will-power and more self-control. You know that you can move your hands at will and you can move your feet and put them where you wish. In the future you will have much more will power and self-control and when you notice your hands going towards your mouth you will be able to direct them elsewhere. This is a habit which was acquired over a period of time. There will be some improvement in this habit during the next few days. However, the improvement will be progressive and that means as each day goes by the improvement will become greater and greater. You will notice the improvement, no mater how slight it may be at first and you will be well pleased with the amount of improvement you will notice. As you overcome this habit you will gain a great deal of personal satisfaction from this accomplishment.

Additional history: When I was in Japan in 1966 I visited this boy and his wife since we have remained good friends and have been in contact the past fifteen years. There has been no repetition of this habit on his part and a few years ago his sister asked me to hypnotize her for the same bad habit saying, "Everyone in our family knows you hypnotized Spencer to stop him from biting his finger nails and now I need the same treatment." This girl refused to file her nails or cut them until I visited her house a few weeks later since she was determined I would see how successful the hypnotic session with her had been.

Acne

One thing the physician must guard against when using hypnosis for therapeutic purposes is "third party intervention". We can not expect much response from the subject when, for example, a wife says, "I want you to hypnotize my husband and cause him to take better care of his clothing" or when a husband requests, "Please hypnotize my wife and tell her she will not spend so much money in the future." Childhood problems, such as enuresis, is almost always presented to the hypnotist as the result of "third party intervention" and we try to overcome the normal reaction and resistance in such a situation by speaking directly to the child and presenting additional motivation, entirely on a childish level. I might say to a young boy, "I want to hypnotize you so that you will be able to play baseball better and so that you will get good grades in school without having to study." One childhood problem which the child will present to the therapist, without any "third party intervention" is acne. Once the patient learns that hypnosis can be used for this skin condition, he is likely to be a most willing and responsive subject.

Name: William
Age: 15 years old in 1959
Complaint: Acne

History: I returned to the United States from Japan on board the S. S. President Cleveland. At the dinner table our first evening at sea, we introduced ourselves to our fellow passengers. The boy who sat next to me introduced himself as a High School student and I noticed that he had an extreme case of acne on his face and neck. When I introduced myself I mentioned having written a book regarding hypnotherapy and added that this form of treatment has been used successfully for childbirth and even for acne. As soon as the meal ended the student earnestly asked me to hypnotize him. I agreed to do so later as I wanted to be able to speak to him privately due to the personal nature of the prescription. After we saw the movie that evening, the boy turned to me and said, "You know, I wish I were dead."

"Why?" I demanded.

"When I look in the mirror and see how horrible I look I don't want my Mother and family back home to see me," he replied.

"We can take care of your acne right away," I assured him, "and your face will look fine by the time the ship arrives in San Francisco two weeks from now."

He was most responsive when I used the eye-to-eye technique and I gave him the following prescription. "The pimples on your face and neck are caused by waste matter from you body. We all eliminate some of our waste matter through our pores as we perspire. However, in your case the pores have become clogged and the waste material has backed-up behind the closed pores. You are at the adolescent period of your life and that means you have more waste material now then you had when you were a child and your body was developing and using a great part of your daily intake of food. Too much of this waste material has tried to get out by way of the pores and that caused your present skin condition. First of all, we will help your body get rid of a lot of waste material and then we will try to re-route the waste material so that in the future more of it will be eliminated through your bowels and less through the pores of your skin. Therefore, the first hypnotic suggestion I will give you at this time is that you are going to have a great flushing out of the waste material in your body. During the next twenty four hours you will have several bowel movements and they will be cleaning out your body, very much like a strong laxative. You are going to give a great deal of attention to your selection of food as you want to avoid, as much as possible, eating the type of food which might tend to clog your pores. Therefore, you will be careful to eat a little bit less of the fatty foods and the starchy foods and the foods with a great deal of sugar or chocolate. You will eat less pastry and less fried foods and less peanuts and drink less Coca Cola and other soft drinks. You understand that I am not suggesting that you avoid these foods completely. I am telling you that you will be taking a bit less of these foods while at the same time you will have a greater interest and desire to eat more meat and more of the fruits and vegetables and salads since you know these foods will give you more strength and energy.

You will also be most considerate of your skin which is now very delicate and must be treated gently so that it will be able to heal. You will be sure to wash your face and neck very carefully several times a day. Most importantly, you will carefully pat your face dry after rinsing it very well. Your memory will improve and you will find that you will have a greater interest in your school subjects and you will pay very close attention to your teachers and you will read your text books very carefully and you will find that you will have the ability ot recall what you have heard in class and what you have read and therefore it will not be necessary for you to do as much studying as you have done in the past."

The next afternoon this boy came up to me and said, "I don't know what you did to me least night, but I have never had such need to go to the toilet as I have had since you hypnotized me." By the end of the week the improvement was so great that others at the table mentioned how much better he looked and he said, "I guess it is because I have just stopped worrying about things."

Induction technique used: Eye-to-eye technique

Hypnotic prescription given: "The pimples are caused by waste material from your body. We all eliminate some of our waste matter through our pores as we prespire. However, in your case the pores have become clogged and the waste matter has backed-up behind the closed pores. We will help your body get rid of a lot of the waste matter and then we will try to re-route the waste matter so that in the future more of you will pass through your bowels and less through the pores of your skin. You will have a great flushing out of the waste matter which is now in your body. During the next twenty four hours you will have several bowel movements and they will be cleaning out your body, very much like a strong laxative. You are going to give a great deal of attention, in the future, to the selection of your food as you want to avoid, as much as possible, eating the type of food which might tend to clog your pores. Therefore, you will be careful to eat a little bit less of the fatty foods and the starchy foods and the foods with a great deal of sugar or chocolate. You will eat less pastry and less fried foods and less peanuts and drink less Coca Cola and other soft drinks. You understand that I am not suggesting that you avoid these foods completely, but I am telling you that you will be taking a bit less of these foods while at the same time you will have a greater interest and desire to eat more meat and more fruit and vegetables and salads since you know these foods will give you more strength and energy. You will also be more considerate of your skin which is now very delicate and must be treated gently so that it will be able to heal. You will be sure to wash your face and neck very carefully several times a day. Most importantly, you will carefully pat your face dry after rinsing it very well."

Additional History: I was able to observe a great improvement in the boy's condition during the two weeks of the voyage and I visited him several times during the following months. The skin condition was no longer any concern to him and he reported doing very well with his school activities.

Disobedience

Often when parents approach a physician complaining that a child is nervous or stutters or is disobedient, the physician is tempted to say to the parent, "This condition is no fault of the child. It is you who needs hypnosis since your over-concern and anxiety causes the child to behave as you report." On several occasions Dr. Kashiwa has been able to suggest to a Mother that she would feel more calm and relaxed and careful about allowing herself to become upset in the presence of her youngster and this hypnotic prescription benefited both of them.

A good friend came to me a few years ago and complained about a boy being disobedient. Although I wanted to correct the father's attitude, I agreed to speak to the boy as he had requested.

44

Name: Mike

Age: 12 years old in 1960

Complaint: Disobedience.

History: My friend had married a divorcee who had a 12 year old boy from her previous marriage. After the three of them lived together for several months my friend came to see me with the following report. "I just can't stand living with that boy in my house since he refuses to mind me and I don't know what to do. I think we will have to send him away to a boarding school as I am getting so upset over his refusing to obey me. For example, it was decided that he would have the chore of watering the front lawn every afternoon upon his coming home from school. He is supposed to do this between 4:00 P.M. and 5:00 P.M. I drive home at 5:30 P.M. and I find the water running and the garden hose stretched across the driveway. I then must get out of my car and turn off the water and roll up the hose and put it away and then I get back into my car and drive it into the garage. When I enter the house I find my son lying on the floor watching the television. I ask him if he was watering the lawn. When he says that he is I ask when he intended to turn off the water. He says, 'In a few minutes.' I then say, 'Never mind, I turned off the water and put the hose away, but tomorrow I would like you to turn off the water and put the hose away before I get home.' He says, 'Sure'. However, the next day it is the same story.

"The boy asked for a dog and I bought him one with the understanding that he would be responsible for the care and feeling of his pet. He was told that the dog can not ask for food as we might and so the dog should be fed before we eat. Each evening as we are in the midst of our supper I hear the poor dog out in the yard whining. I ask if the dog has been fed and the boy says, 'Oh, I forgot.' I then order the boy to feed the dog before he finishes his own meal. When the boy goes out to the yard he always returns saying, 'I can't find the dish for the dog food.' This happens because he forgot to bring in the dish the night before.

"Every time I ask him to do something, the boy says, 'Sure, in just a minute.' Half an hour later I remind him again and then an hour later I just go ahead and do whatever it was I had asked him to do. This is getting on my nerves and it worries me to find that he is not doing anything I ask. He sounds so nice and agreeable in front of his Mother and yet he never minds until he has been told a number of times."

When I saw the boy the following afternoon I said, "Mike, your new father is worried for fear that he is sot doing a good job of being a father to you." Mike said, "Oh, he is all right."

"Of course he is", I agreed. "You know that and I know that but he doesn't and it is getting him upset and worried and I honestly need your help for his sake."

"Sure", the boy said, "I'll do anything I can to help."

"Very well", I continued, "I want to hypnotize you and give you some instructions which I know will help your father."

The boy was very tall, but I remembered that he was just a twelve year old and I decided the back-against-the-wall technique would be best, at least as a beginning. Fortunately, the responce was very good. Since the boy was so large, I had him fall with his shoulders coming to rest against the outstreched palms of my hands held straight in front of my body and then I slowly pushed him back up against the wall. "Your father has had no experience in raising a family," I began, "and now he feels that a son your age should be trained to follow his instructions just like a service man is trained to follow the instructions he receives from his officers. When your new father asks you to do something and you do not respond right away he worries and feels that you do not know how to do as you are told. He does not feel he knows you well enough to punish you and yet he feels you are not behaving properly. This bothers him very much and is about to make him a nervous wreck. I am now going to give you some hypnotic instructions which will help to relieve his mind. In the future, when your father asks you to do something, you will feel compelled to respond instantly. You will stop whatever you are doing and hurry to comply as that is the sort of action which will help to reassure your father and cause him to stop feeling so guilty. When he asks you to water the lawn or feed the dog, you will do these things exactly as he instructs and you will do it in such a way that he will see that you are doing these things as he wishes. Very soon you will see an improvement in him and you will realize that you were the cause of helping him get well."

I also spoke briefly about the boy having a better memory and being stronger and able to take part in his school sports more effectively. When I asked him to open his eyes at the count of 'seven' he said, "You know, at first I did not think you were serious, but now I believe you and it will be easy for me to do the things you said, since it will he for his good."

Induction technique used: Back-against-the-wall technique.

Hypnotic prescription given: "Your father worries when you do not respond right away and do as you are told. He feels that a boy your age should be trained and know how to follow instructions and when you do not act as he feels you should, he worries and it makes him feel guilty in not having given you the proper training and instructions. The hypnotic instructions I will give you are designed to help relieve your father's mind. In the future, when your father asks you to do something, you will feel compelled to respond instantly. You will stop whatever you are doing and hurry to comply as that is the sort of action which will help to reasure him and cause him to stop feeling so guilty. You will do things exactly as he instructs you and as quickly

46

as possible. Very soon you will see an improvement in him and you will realize you were the cause of helping him get well."

Additional history: A few weeks later the father came to visit me and he reported, "I don't know what you said or did to that boy, but he is a changed person. I am so very happy to be near him. He does everything as he is told and I have bought him a hunting gun and we go out together and he is doing well in school and I am so proud of him." I have seen this father-son relationship develop over the years with understanding and mutual respect.

CHAPTER NINE

Prescriptions For Childbirth

Dr. Lester T. Kashiwa had a lady come to see him during her pregnancy with her third child. She complained of extreme nausea and vomiting. Her first two pregnancies had been treated by an obstetrician in Honolulu. She reported that she had been hospitalized for a period of four months during each of her two previous pregnancies. She had come to expect this to be the normal procedure and she told Dr. Kashiwa that the feeling of nausea was so extreme she could no longer bear it and asked him to make the necessary arrangements for her to be hospitalized for the remaining four months of her pregnancy.

Dr. Kashiwa told her he would like to use hypnosis and she responded readily. After just one hypnotic session her vomiting stopped completely and she had an absolutely painless childbirth. In fact, she had a steak dinner with her family one evening and then her husband drove her to the hospital and the child was delivered a few hours later.

Since that case in 1955, Dr. Kashiwa has used some hypnotic suggestions in every case of pregnancy as a routine course of procedure. He has found that one or two hypnotic sessions are usually enough. When Dr. KaKshiwa is able to treat the patient from the time when he informs her that she is pregnant to the time for the actual delivery of her baby, he will often give her one hypnotic prescription designed to prevent any occurrence of discomfort or nausea or any other ill feelings often associated with the early months of pregnancy and then another hypnotic prescription is administered just before the patient is about to enter the hospital for the delivery of the baby.

Name: Mrs. Harata
Age: 32 years old in 1955.
Complaint: Habitual aborter

History: When Mrs. Harata came to see Dr. Kashiwa she told him she had been informed that she was an habitual aborter. She had a history of seven miscarriages during the twelve years that she had been married and was then in her eight pregnancy. She said during her first pregnancy she vomited a great deal and had a miscarriage during the fifth month. Her second pregnancy ended with a miscarriage in the fourth month. She had been to many doctors who gave her various injections and medication but in each instance she vomited a great deal and always her pregnancy ended with a miscarriage.

Dr. Kashiwa induced hypnosis by the eye-to-eye technique and told Mrs. Harata she would feel some degree of improvement as far as the vomiting and nausea was concerned. He told her she would have a good appetite for all the food she ate and that she would have an interest and desire to eat the food which would be of the greatest benefit to her and the unborn child. He told her she would have an improvement in her posture and that she would look forward to the arrival of the baby.

Aside from the purely physical aspects of this situation, Dr. Kashiwa feels that some consideration should be given to the psychological forces that are likely to become operative at a time like this. He knows that the lady is apt to become fearful that her husband might lose interest in being with her once her body becomes mis-shapen and heavy with child. Therefore, under hypnosis he will tell the patient that she will notice how considerate and concerned her husband will become and she will notice an increase in his sexual desire. He tells her she will enjoy the entire period of pregnancy and look forward with anticipation to the arrival of her baby.

Immediately after the first hypnotic session this patient reported that all vomiting had stopped and she remained pregnant the full nine months. She called Dr. Kashiwa at 6:00 P.M. one evening just as he was about to leave his office. She said that she was unable to come to his office but felt he should see her right away. He arrived a few minutes later and once again using the eye-to-eye technique gave her the usual secondary hypnotic prescription relative to her being able to distinguish the difference between pressure and pain. He told her she would have the ability to follow the instructions given to her and that she would be able to relax when told to do so and be able to contract her muscles at the proper time. The baby arrived at 7:30 P.M. weighing six pounds and 8½ ounces. When she tells her friends about the delivery she insists that she does not know what a labor pain feels like since all she had experienced was a feeling of pressure.

Induction technique used: Eye-to-eye technique.

Hypnotic prescription given: At the first hypnotic session the prescription was as follows: "Mrs. Harata you will be pleased to feel you are going to have a child. During the coming months you will feel happy and comfortable. You will have a good appetite and enjoy eating all your food. The feeling of nausea which you have reported to me will improve to some degree and the improvement will be progressive and will increase on a day to day basis. As each day goes by you will notice an improvement in your condition and you will be very pleased.

You will be concious of your posture as you walk and sit and you will find it easy to adjust your body into a comfortable position. You will have a great interest in eating various types of food which will tend to be of the greatest value to you and your un-born child and your body will digest all this food very easily. You will notice how considerate and concerned over you your husband will become and also you will notice an increase in his sexual interest and desire."

At the final hypnotic session before the child was delivered, Dr. Kashiwa gave the patient the following prescription: "Now you will be able to tell the difference between pressure and pain. When you first feel some pressure you will recognize it and realize that you can withstand a great deal of pressure without much effort. During the first few contractions of your organ you will realize that you are actually feeling pressure. I will be giving you instructions as these contractions occur and you will be able to follow the instructions very easily. When you feel the baby's head passing through the birth canal and womb, you will relax with a tremendous feeling of satisfaction and relief."

Additional History: According to Dr. Kashiwa's records the mother brought her baby in for periodic examinations during the eighteen months following the birth and the baby has been healthy and developed in a completely normal manner.

After the first hypnotic session Dr. Kashiwa will invite the prospective mother to come to see him for periodic examinations and sometimes they will complain of very minor symptoms such as headaches or dizzy feelings. On these occasions he will agree to giving them another hypnotic session for these specific complaints.

Suggestions that the lady will have a good appetite and be able to digest all her food are designed to overcome the usual feeling of nausea which is so common in pregnancy.

Dr. Kashiwa feels that childbirth should in almost all cases be considered as a normal healthy process and completely painless. He tries to give some hypnotic suggestions to all of the cases of pregnancy that come to him and he finds in almost every case that the patients are responsive.

CHAPTER TEN

Prescriptions For Students

Small children are always interested in being able to do their school work well as they know this will please their parents. Older boys and girls will frequently feel awkward and self-concious when confronted by those of the opposite sex.

Name: Ward
Age: 17 years old in 1956
Complaint: Unable to speak to girls.

History: I was working out in a gym near my home in 1956 when one of the attendents came over and asked me to hypnotize him. I explained that I gave demonstrations in hypnosis to servicemen overseas and lectured on the subject to physicians and dentists but that I was not a hypnotherapist and did not accept patients.

"But my problem is psychological," the boy insisted and then added, "I would like you to help me so I could talk to girls. I had to buy two tickets to the Junior Prom, as did every boy in my class and I know the girl I would like to invite, but I can't talk to girls. I choke up and blush and get flustered and so I need your help."

Offering to give him the necessary suggestions in a minute or two, I ushered him into a small office near the gym floor and asked him to sit in a chair. After using the eye-to-eye technique I began with the "rigid arm" test since I felt it would help to impress the young man who was following a course of body-building. After putting his left arm into the air and asking him to try to bend the arm at the elbow, as explained in Part Two of this book, the boy exerted a great deal of effort and the arm did bend slightly. To anyone watching, the demonstration would have been very impressive. However, I later discovered the boy felt disappointed since he had been able to bend his arm a little and he thought that meant the "test" had failed.

"In the future, it will be as easy for you to speak to the girls in your class as it now is for you to speak to the boys in your class," I began. "You will ask the girls about *their* experiences and *their* plans and *their* opinions regarding books they have read and movies they have seen and you will find that once they feel you are interested in them, they will want to be with you. You will look at the girls as they talk to you and by showing them you are interested in what they have to say, they will become interested in you. When you become genuinely interested in them you will no longer be self-concious and you will enjoy talking to them and you will be completely at ease when you are near them."

"Now a word about your studies," I continued. "You will get better grades in school because you will become intensely interested in your school work. You will concentrate upon what your instructors say and you will concentrate upon what you read in your text books. Your memory will improve and you will have the ability to recall everything you hear in your classes and everything you read in your assignments and you will have the ability to use this information from day to day and especially you will be able to remember easily all this material when you have an examination."

"However," I concluded, "I want you to understand that there will only be some degree of improvement in all these matters at first. But the improvement will be progressive and so as each day goes by you will find it a bit easier to talk to the girls and also you will find a bit of improvement in your memory and your interest in your studies and your ability to concentrate on your school work. Soon you will notice the improvement will become greater and greater as each day goes by. However, you will notice the improvement, no matter how slight it may be at first, and you will be well pleased with the improvement you will notice."

The boy seemed rather dissatisfied when I asked him to open his eyes. He explained that the noises from the gym disturbed him and also he heard every word I said and was aware of everything that had happened and since he had been able to bend his arm, he doubted the effectivness of the session. I realized then that I had not had an ample interview before the hypnotic session to gain the proper degree of rapport between the boy and myslf and for him to understand that when one receives therapeutic hypnosis the patient is likely to hear everything said and to remember the instructions given. However, the prescriptions that were given I used hundreds of times, since I give them to almost all teenage subjects and therefore I felt they were likely to be effective in spite of the young man's doubts.

Five months later I returned from a trip to New York City and when I entered the gym the boy rushed over to me with the following challenge. "Do you think it was ethical for you to have hypnotized me?" he asked. "All the girls in my class say it was unfair since I am getting the best grades in the class. In fact, I lost my History book and so I was not able to review the chapters we had studied and yet I got an "A" in that subject as I did in all the rest."

I assured the young man it was perfectly proper for me to have hypnotized him since I merely made it possible for him to use the ability he possessed. Of course, I was delighted with the device he had used to inform me that he was communicating with all the girls in his class. Anxious for more information, I inquired, "Were you able to ASK the girl you had in mind to attend the Junior Prom?"

"Sure", he replied. "I can ask girls to do anything. By the way, I am now going 'steady' with the girl that I took to the Junior Prom."

Induction technique used: Eye-to-eye technique. Rigid arm technique was used as a "test" in this instance and not very effective, I later learned, because I told the boy his arm "would feel like a bar of steel" and the boy knew that he could bend a bar of steel. Since then I have changed the wording slightly and say, "You arm will feel like solid steel."

Hypnotic prescription given: In the future you will be able to speak to girls as easily as you can now speak to boys. You will ask the girls about their experiences and their plans and their opinions regarding books they have read and movies they have seen and when you become genuinely interested in them you will find that you will become less self-concious.

As far as your school studies are concerned you will find that you will have a greater interest in your studies and you will be paying more attention to what is said in your classes and to what you read in your text books. Also your memory will improve so that you will be able to recall the material which was presented to you at school and what you have read in your books. You will be able to use this information as you do your assignments from day to day and you will easily be able to recall all that you have learned when you are given examinations.

Additional history: Several years later I met Ward and learned that he was a senior in college. He invited me to visit him and some of his classmates. While vacationing in Mexico City he met a young lady who he married and he is now the father of two girls.

Overweight

When parents ask me to hypnotize a boy or girl who is overweight I hesitate since there are several negative factors which could easily be involved. First of all, the "third-party intervention" might be the cause of some resistance and the fact that the parents want the boy or girl to weigh less does not give the child a feeling of security or acceptance. Also, I am well aware that overweight can often be caused by a glandular disorder and therefore I prefer to have hypnotic prescriptions administered by the patient's personal physician rather than by a stranger.

Name: Harold
Age: 15 years old in 1960
Complaint: Overweight.

History: A school teacher asked me to visit her one evening as she wanted some help with a problem. When I arrived she told me that her son had a classmate who was fifteen years old and weighed 257 pounds. I said that sounded like a glandular condition but I was told that the boy had been examined by his personal physician a short time previously and was found to be in good health and he was told that his condition was due to his "eating too much". A classmate reported that when he and his friends visited the Hamburger Stand across the street from their school, the fat boy was able to gain the attention of those around him by demonstrating his ability to eat three times as much as any one in the group. I learned that his school work was only "average" and he could not participate in sports because of his physical condition.

The teacher was greatly interested in learning how hypnosis could be applied to helping students and so I agreed to having a hypnotic session with the heavy lad but I realized that I would have many factors to consider.

I insisted upon being alone with the boy and after he sat in a firm chair I had no difficulty causing him to respond when I used the eye-to-eye technique. To increase his self-confidence and self-respect I began as follows: "Now Harold, you are going to be a big man and most of the stars in Hollywood, such as John Wayne and Rock Hudson and Bob Mitchum are big men. When big men stand properly and walk properly they look handsome and are accepted everywhere. Therefore, from now on you will notice an improvement in your posture and you will notice that your body will feel lighter and you will be able to carry yourself well and stand with poise. When I count to 'three' you will rise from your chair and I will show you the proper way to stand."

As I said, "three", he stood and I continued. "I want you to imagine that your body is suspended from the ceiling and is attached to a hook right about here." I then tapped him on his chest. "Now when I count to 'three' you will raise your chest and stand very tall and you will feel your arms hang loosely at your sides and you will feel your pants hang loosely from your hips." When I counted to "three" this time I complimented him as he raised his chest and stood more erect. "That is fine," I went on, "from now on you will begin to notice an improvement in your posture as you stand and walk and you will begin to feel lighter and more stronger as you will find it easier to move about. You are much taller than the other boys your age and so it is natural for you to weigh a bit more than other boys your age. I want you to just lose a little bit at a time. In the future you will want to eat a little bit less of the fatty or fried foods and a little bit less of the pastries. You will eat a little bit less of the candies and peanuts and you will drink a little bit less of the Coca Cola and other soft drinks. Instead you will want to eat much more of the meats and vegatables and fruits.

56

You will drink a little less milk and take a little less butter with your meals. When you are given a choice between potatos and other vegatables, I want you to choose a little less of the potatos and a bit more of the other vegatables. I want you to find that you will be enjoying your food more, but once you finish eating whatever portion is served to you, you will lose your appetite and under no circumstance will you be able to eat a second portion."

"You will lose some weight" I said, "but it will be just a few pounds every week. Best of all, as soon as you do lose three or four pounds you will notice the difference and your clothing will feel very loose and you will feel so much stronger and full of energy and you will feel a great sense of accomplishment and you will be pleased to have your family and friends remark about the great improvement in your appearance. You will find that you will have a greater interest in your school studies and you will concentrate upon what is said in your classes and upon what you read in your text books. Your memory will improve and you will find that you can easily remember the things you heard and the things you read and you will be able to use this information from day to day and also it will help you greatly when you take examinations."

After he was asked to open his eyes he said, "When you hypnotized me my body felt heavier and heavier and I feel almost like I had been asleep because I do not remember very much of what you said." Perhaps the boy's obesity caused him more concern than we had imagined since "self-induced amnesia" is brought about when the patient is embarrassed by the suggestions given to him during the hypnotic session.

Induction technique used: Eye-to-eye technique

Hypnotic prescription given: You will stand and walk more properly in the future. You will accept the fact that you are going to be a large person and realize that many Hollywood Stars are large men. You will lose a few pounds a week in the future by being careful about your food and eating just a little less of the fatty and starchy foods. You will take a bit less sugar and a bit less candy and less peanuts and less of the soft drinks. You will eat more of the meats and vegatables and fruits and you will enjoy your food to a great extent, but you will lose your appetite as soon as you finish eating whatever portion of food has been served to you and under no circumstance will you be able to eat a second portion of anything. As soon as you notice you have lost a few pounds you will begin to feel much lighter and stronger and you will have more energy and you will feel a sense of accomplishment over your will-power and self-control and you will be pleased to have your family and friends remark about your improved appearance.

Additional history: Three months later I was asked to see the boy again. I was told that he lost ten ponds the first week after the hypnotic session and seven pounds a week for the next four weeks. He then lost five pounds a week for two weeks but from then on his weight remained constant. From 257 pounds he went down to 209 pounds but he could afford to lose much more. In the second hypnotic session I questioned the boy as to the extent of the examination his family physician had given him and found it was most superficial. I then arranged an appointment for the boy with an endocrinologist who gave him a series of injections over a period of several months. Within the year the boy lost another thirty five pounds and quit school to join the army.

Facial Birthmark

When a boy who is about 100 pounds overweight responds to hypnotic therapy the improvement is most apparent. However, in some instances hypnotic treatment is worthwhile even if there is no apparent change in the physical condition and the improvement is only psychological.

Name: Tom
Age: 18 years old in 1960
Complaint: Disfiguring birthmark over half of his face.

History: While visiting my friend, Bert Easely in Phoenix, Arizona I met one of his friends who was the President of the Arcadia High School P.T.A. and she asked me to come to her school with a program of hypnosis. The audience was very responsive and the entire student body rushed to the stage when I asked for volunteers. Of course, only the first few could be accommodated and the others were sent back. In demonstrations of this sort I allow the spectators from the audience to seat themselves on the stage and I start at one end of the row and move down towards the other without showing any preference. I do this as a matter of self-discipline for I then must use whatever technique and motivation is best suited for the individuals who present themselves to me, one at a time. However, in this instance I was greatly embarrassed to find myself standing next to this young man with a disfiguring birthmark over half his face. We had come to the part in my demonstration where I hypnotize a young man and have him remove his shirt and lie, bare-backed on a "bed-of-nails". This was hardly the boy I would have chosen to take part in my program. Nevertheless, I went ahead and concluded the program in the usual fashion. I went over to the boy as he was putting his shirt back on after the demonstration and I told him I would like to see if we could bring about some change or improvement as far as the mark on his face was concerned. He said, "I will appreciate it very much." Since the boy had responded so well to the "silent technique" in front of the audience a few minutes earlier, I felt it wise to use the same technique for we both knew he could respond to that technique. I knew the hypnotic prescription would have to be very general in nature. "Now, Tom," I began, "I am going to suggest that you will feel stronger and healthier and you will sleep better and you will have a greater interest in your school studies and you will concentrate upon what your teachers say in your classes and you will pay very close attention to what you are taught in school and to what you read in your text-books and you will find your memory will improve greatly. You will be able to recall all that you have heard and all that you have read and you will be able to use this information each day and also when you are given examinations."

"You will have a greater interest in the boys and girls in your classes," I continued. "You will ask them questions about their experiences and their activities and their plans and their opinions regarding books they have read and movies they have seen and you will find that the more you ask your friends about themselves the more they will want to be with you. Now I have had some experience in causing warts to go away and to cause scars from burns to go away and so we will suggest that there will be some slight improvement as far as the mark on your face is concerned. The redness will gradually blend into the other skin coloring and the size of the mark will become smaller. Of course, the improvement in your studies and memory and skin condition will all be very slight, at first, but it will be progressive and therefore as each day goes by there will be a bit more improvement. You will notice the improvement, no matter how slight it may be at first, and you will be well pleased with the amount of improvement you will notice."

Induction technique used: Silent technique as described in Part Two.

Hypnotic prescription given: I gave the usual hypnotic prescription that I give to all teen-agers for them to have a better interest in their studies and to concentrate more intently and to have a better memory and ability to recall all they have heard and read. Also, the usual prescription to increase the student's popularity by suggesting he will speak to others about themselves and their experiences. Finally, I said that the discloration would become less and the redness would gradually fade into the natural skin coloring.

Additional history: The program of hypnotic demonstrations at Arcadia High School had been so well received, I was asked to return two months later. When I arrived at the school I was told the Senior Class was having their traditional picnic that afternoon and had invited me to be the Guest of Honor. As I approached the picnic grounds, the first person who ran to greet me was Tom, the boy with the disfiguring birthmark. He was surrounded by half a dozen young girls who clung to him as he offered me a sandwich and drink. I looked intently at his face and could see no change or improvement. I asked him to speak to me, alone, for a moment and inquired if he had seen any change. "Oh, don't worry about that," he said in an off-handed manner. "It doesn't matter at all." He then returned to the girls who were impatiently waiting for him.

The Senior Class advisor came up to see me at that moment and he said, "You know, there has been a most remarkable change in that boy since you were here two months ago. He was always with-drawn and never took part in any of the school activities and had absolutely no friends. He came to school alone and left alone. However, he has changed completely and was just voted the "most popular boy" in the Senior Class and he is attenaing all the school dances and athletic events and his school work has improved greatly also.

Loss of Hair

Since the hypnotherapist is so fearful of "third party intervention" it would seem that it is always best for the subject to approach the hypnotist and ask to be hypnotized. This is not always the case.

Name: Robert
Age: 25 years old in 1961
Complaint: Premature loss of hair.

History: I was in New York City for a brief visit and pleased to run into a friend from Japan. I invited my friend to join my group for dinner since we had just come from a Cocktail party. My friend from Japan remarked that after I had left his country he read a magazine article about my being a hypnotist but he doubted I could hypnotize him. The cocktail party had put me in a joyful mood and so, jokingly, I said, "I will hypnotize you right here in this hotel lobby." Once I said that, I regretted it, since I saw that several persons had overheard my jest and one young man came forward. "You are a professional hypnotist," he said with a manner of firm accusation. When I admitted this he asked how he could get more information and I invited him to contact me later in the week.

When Robert learned I had written CASE HISTORIES IN HYPNO-THERAPY he asked to be allowed to buy a copy for he explained that he was a Psychology major at Columbia University and was greatly interested in hypnosis. I invited him to return after he had read the book and a week later he did.

"Can you hypnotize me?" Robert demanded. "Yes," I said, automatically, since I feel that all persons who can understand such simple instructions as stand up, sit down and close your eyes, can be hypnotized to some extent by one person or another.

"Let me tell you why I want to be hypnotized," Robert began. "You see, I have been hypnotizing my neighbors and friends for several years. I am successful about 50 per cent of the time. Also, I found those with the least intelligence were the ones most likely to be hypnotized. Recently the Psychology professor at Columbia University has been lecturing about hypnosis and he says that he can hypnotize about 80 per cent of the subjects and he has been attempting to hypnotize the various members of my class. My instructor maintains that the more intelligent a person is, the easier it is for him to follow the hypnotic instructions and become hypnotized. I am the only member of my class the professor has been unable to hypnotize and he says it is because I am unable to concentrate properly."

I tried to explain to Robert that having a high intelligence or a low intelligence is not an important matter as far as responding to hypnotic instructions are concerned. "After all," I said, "we can hypnotize three and four year old children as well as physicians, lawyers and college professors. What is important is for the hypnotist to be able to establish a feeling of 'rapport' with the patient and to give his instructions in such a manner that it is easily understandable and acceptable by the subject. I have met many college students who found it was much easier for them to hypnotize small children than adults. This is true because the person being hypnotized must have confidence in the hypnotist and be willing to put his trust in him. For that reason I suggest in my book that we choose for our 'first subject' an individual a bit younger than we are."

"Yes, yes," Robert said, "never mind the lecture. I want to be hypnotized."

I know many amateur hypnotists who feel they can not be hypnotized because their understanding of hypnosis is based upon the demonstrations they have seen presented by vaudeville and carnival entertainers. When hypnosis is presented in front of a group for entertainment it must be done in a false manner in order to give the false impression that the hypnotist is causing the subject to do something the subject does not want to do. The popular mis-conception of hypnosis is that the performer has a "power" or "control" over the subject.

When a "stage hypnotist" invites a committee of volunteers from the audience to come up to the stage to be hypnotized he finds those who respond are almost always exhibitionists who are willing to do almost anything, regardless how preposterous, if by so doing they can remain on the stage and thus satisfy their need to be "the centre of attention". Of course, these persons will often shrug off any responsibility for their absurd actions by insisting that they were compelled to act according to the instructions given by the hypnotist and frequently they will hide their embarrassment by saying they were unable to remember anything that took place during the performance. These performers will insist that the "volunteers" came forward only because they wanted to act foolish and then these performers will believe that only foolish persons can be hypnotized.

"All right," said Robert, "let us begin. According to your book I should sit in a firm chair with my feet flat on the floor and my palms upturned in my lap."

I could see that Robert had assumed the position for the eye-to-eye technique, but since he acted without instructions from me, I realized that *he*, not *I* was in command of the situation. I knew Robert had read my book and also had a knowledge of the subject based upon his own experiences and so felt that any technique dependent upon trickery or unusual positioning of his body, would be instantly recognized and become ineffective.

While he continued to insist that he wanted to be hypnotized, I knew he actually wanted me to try to hypnotize him since he wanted to convince himself that his theory regarding hypnosis was correct and therefore he could not be hypnotized.

Moving a bit away, to indicate I was not about to begin the hypnotic session, I said, "You know the correct position for the eye-to-eye technique and also you know that there must be some motivation before I can hypnotize you. I shall hypnotize you and suggest that you will be able to do better with your studies since you will have a greater interest in them and concentrate more upon what you hear in the lectures and what you read in your text books. Also, your memory will improve and your ability to recall what your have learned and what you have read."

"Fine," Robert said eagerly, "now hypnotize me."

"Also," I continued, "I will give you some suggestions which will serve to strengthen your body as well as your mind. You will have better muscular co-ordination and when you work-out in your gymnasium you will exert a great deal more effort and thus you will be taxing your muscles and they will respond by becoming stronger."

"That is good. Now hypnotize me," Robert insisted.

"And since you are interested in hypnosis," I went on, "I will suggest to you that you will be able to speak easily to others and you will be able to make your subjects feel you are genuinely interested in them. You will be able to think of the proper things to say and do so that your hypnotic sessions will have a greater likelihood of being successful."

"Yes, yes, anything at all," Robert said, ill-concealing his impatience.

I looked at Robert as he sat, alert in the chair, ready to resist any attempts I might make to hypnotize him and I knew I would have to continue in my search for the proper motivation, as far as this situation was concerned. I looked at his thinning hair and receding hairline and had an inspiration.

"Now Robert, I will do something else for you," I said as I moved toward him, "I will suggest that the sebaceous glands in your scalp will be stimulated and this increased secretion will cause an improvement in the condition of your hair and will result in a growth of new hair during the next few months."

The young man's attitude changed completely. His shoulders sagged. His hands slid off his lap and hung loosely at his sides. He looked up at me with abject wonderment as he meekly asked, "Will you do this for me?"

"Yes," I said firmly as I placed his limp hands back into his lap and pointed with my right forefinger to my right eye. "Look in this eye. When I count 'three' your eyes will close, your eyeballs will roll upwards and your head will feel heavy and tired." Robert's response was immediate as soon as he closed his eyes and I had to move quickly to support his body as it slumped and he almost fell out of the chair. I gave him the various hypnotic prescriptions as I had promised then had him open his eyes at the count of "seven".

Upon opening his eyes, he looked about the room for a few moments with a dazed expression and then made the following observation. "I know I was hypnotized. Oh, I could hear you, all right, but you seemed to be so very far away. I marveled that I could hear you since you seemed to be speaking so softly, but I noticed how clearly and distinctly each word was uttered. Most peculiar, I felt my body so heavy and tired I thought I would surely fall asleep if you stopped talking. However, I did not want you to stop talking. As you gave me the various beneficial suggestions I kept thinking how I wanted you to continue. I was a bit disappointed when you told me to open my eyes at the count of 'seven' and I wondered if I could keep them closed instead. However, I then felt I had no power to resist and so I opened my eyes as you commanded."

Induction technique used: Eye-to-eye technique.

Hypnotic prescriptions given: The usual prescriptions given to all students about an increased interest in their school studies and a better memory and ability to recall and better muscular co-ordination and added strength. The following prescription for an improved hair and scalp condition I have used on several occasions with success when speaking to very young men who seemed to be pre-maturely losing their hair: "The sebaceous glands in your scalp will be stimulated and this increased secretion will cause an improvement in the condition of your hair and scalp and will result in a growth of new hair during the next few months."

CHAPTER ELEVEN

Prescriptions For Psychological Problems

On several occasions my Father asked me to meet a friend with the understanding that I might be able to help the individual with hypnosis and, of course, I always agreed.

Name: Dr. Lennox
Age: 58 years old in 1946
Complaint: Lack of self-confidence.

History: Dr. Lennox introduced himself as a retired chiropractor who had used hypnosis to a very limited extent when as a younger man he had been an instructor at a Chiropractic College. He had an extensive library and after a short interview he handed me a book and gave me the assignment of reading the first five chapters so we would have a basis for discussion at our next session. He readily assumed the role as my teacher and I was pleased to be his student. This relationship was not conducive to hypnotherapy as the subject should feel some degree of respect towards the hypnotist and feel the hypnotist is giving him instructions for his behavior in the future.

Dr. Lennox explained that he had completed writing a manuscript dealing with a new concept regarding medical procedure and he felt he lacked the necessary self-confidence needed before he could properly present his revolutionary ideas to the people he wanted to contact. Dr. Lennox prescribed for himself a series of hypnotic sessions, twice a week for several months, and in return he offered to give me a personal course of instruction in the history and early uses of hypnosis for therapeutic purposes. As he outlined how we would exchange our services, I realized that I had a great interest in the information the elderly gentleman could give and also I knew he would derive some benefit from having the opportunity of assuming the role of teacher and my coming to listen and learn from him twice a week would help to increase his self-confidence.

At our first hypnotic session Dr. Lennox told me that it would not be very easy for me to hypnotize him since he had had some experience as a hypnotist and it is a generally accepted fact that it is most difficult for one hypnotist to influence another. However, he explained, he was prepared to give me fifteen or twenty lectures and in return he thought the fifteen or twenty sessions of hypnosis or relaxation might benefit him. This was not a very good start, but I had a great deal of respect for him and understood that he expected the therapy to be a long drawn out affair. I used the eye-to-eye technique for induction but once he closed his eyes I spoke at great length regarding his feeling heavy and tired and relaxed and repeated several times the general beneficial instructions for an improvement in his health and mental attitude and his relationship with others. Once I saw his head nod heavily and the distinct change in his respiration, I was satisfied.

When Dr. Lennox opened his eyes at the end of the session, he said, "I was not hypnotized at all. Of course, I did not expect you to be successful so I am not disappointed. I am looking forward to having you attempt hypnosis many, many times in the future and I feel we will both benefit."

I visited Dr. Lennox twice a week for several months and each time I could see he was relaxing a bit faster and had the outward appearance of going into a deep hypnotic state but always when I asked him to open his eyes at the end of the session, he would say that he did not feel we had been successful as yet, but certainly wanted me to cotinue trying.

Dr. Lennox lived near a railroad track and almost every night as I was giving him the usual suggestions to relax, I would hear an approaching train. Fearful that the noise of the train might upset the restful mood I was trying to create, I would suggest that he would not be disturbed by the noise of the train. After the train had passed I would ask him if it had disturbed him and he would say that it had not. Finally I got into the habit of telling him he would not hear the train and he would agree that he had not heard the train at all. At the conclusion of each hypnotic session Dr. Lennox would say, "We have not been successful as yet and I see no progress, but we will continue." On one occasion I said, "Well, at least you say you do not hear the train that passes here each evening and that is encouraging."

At the next session Dr. Lennox said he had something to tell me about himself that I did not know. He said he noticed I had been asking him about the noises of a passing train. The truth, he explained, was that he was actually deaf and had never heard the passing train. He also told me that he had to read my lips in order to understand what I was saying. "Now," he concluded, "I wanted to tell you this because you seemed so pleased when I told you that I could not hear the train."

That evening I gave Dr. Lennox the hypnotic suggestions as usual and then I held his hand in front of his body and told him his fingers would feel rigid. Speaking very softly I asked him to try to bend his first finger and he succeeded in bending it without any difficulty. Taking a few steps away from him, I asked him to try to bend all the fingers at the same time and once again he responded, bending all the fingers without effort. Having lowered my voice to a whisper and having moved away from him the entire length of the room, I said, "Dr. Lennox I am standing as far from you as I can get and I am speaking to you in a whisper. Tell me, can you hear what I am saying?"

As I had expected, Dr. Lennox said, "No, I cannot hear you."

I gave him the usual beneficial suggestions and asked him to open his eyes at the count of "seven". I then said, "Dr. Lennox, when I stood at the other side of this room and asked you in a whisper if you could hear me, what did you say?"

"I said, 'No'," came his reply.

"And," I inquired, "why did you say that?"

Quickly he answered, "Because I could not . . . ". Then he paused and looked very suprised and puzzled for at that moment he realized that he must have heard my question before he could answer it. I left him then, promising to return for the next session, as usual.

At our next session, I went into the eye-to-eye induction technique without the usual twenty to thirty minute preliminary discussion. As soon as I felt he had responded I questioned him regarding his deafness and he admitted that he was able to hear me distinctly when he was in the hypnotic state and yet, he insisted that he could not hear me at all at other times. This time I suggested that there would be some degree of improvement in his hearing and I suggested that he would be able to hear me as well after the hypnotic session as he could then hear me. I then counted to "seven" and had him open his eyes.

I asked him if he could hear me without looking at my lips and I held my hand up in front of my mouth. "Yes," he admitted, "I can hear you faintly. I realize now you have hypnotized me and I can tell the difference because I can hear you so much beter when I am hypnotized."

Induction technique used: Eye-to-eye technique.

Hypnotic prescription given: To instill self-confidence I told him that he would look directly at the persons to whom he would be speaking and he would be thinking of them and the questions they might ask and he would try to speak so that they would be able to understand him easily. By looking at his audience and thinking of his audience he would be less likely to think of himself or feel self-concious. I told him that he would feel that he had something to give to his audience and he would present the information in the simplest, most straight-forward manner, possible.

Additional history: The hypnotic sessions continued for a few more weeks. Dr. Lenonx responded very readily and when I told him he would not recall what was said or done during the sessions he accepted that suggestion as well. Finally, he agreed that he felt more confident, but insisted that he wanted to review his manuscript and make some revisions before submitting it to a publisher. He thanked me for my patience with him and I told him truthfully that I had learned much from my visits.

Deafness

One thing I had learned was that people who say they are deaf, often have difficulty in hearing, but are deaf only to some degree and are seldom completely devoid of the sense of hearing.

Name: Rudolph
Age: 37 years old in 1954
Complaint: Desire to sing better.

History: A dear friend in San Francisco telephoned me during one of my visits to that city and asked me to help him move out of one of the apartments in his building as he had rented it to a tenent who would be moving in shortly. When I arrived my friend apologized for having mentioned to the tenent that I was a hypnotist. The tenent said he had been trying to find a hypnotist who could help him and insisted that I see him. My friend asked me to see the singer, for he added, "I know you can hypnotize him in a minute or two."

When I knocked on his door, the tenent invited me in and introduced himself, saying, "I am an opera singer and I have just signed to sing with The San Francisco Opera Company." He then told me about his training in Europe and the various roles he had sung for various opera companies throughout the world. His resume of his operatic background took a long time and I grew impatient.

"Why do you want me to hypnotize you"? I asked.

"I would like to be able to sing better," Rudolph replied.

Disappointed over this routine request for self-improvement, I rose from my seat and indicated that I was about to begin. "Wait, wait," the singer demanded, "I have more to tell you. You see, I am deaf. I must wear shoes with very thin soles so I can feel the vibration of the music when I sing and I can not hear you if I do not look at your lips."

"That will make no difference. Come over here and sit down", I said as my feeling of impatience was mingled with a slight suspicion that Rudolph did not really want me to hypnotize him but rather was interested in proving to himself that he could not be hypnotized because of his affliction.

As he slowly took the chair I had indicated, Rudolph again explained that he was deaf and would not be able to hear me when he closed his eyes. I remained unmoved by this second recital of his hearing problem and began the eye-to-eye technique. This technique offers many "check-points" and in this instance, all of them were negative. His hands were firmly clenched in his lap. I had to shake them and insist that he relax them before I could turn them palms upward in his lap and even then he held them rigidly tense. When I asked him to look into my right eye he quickly turned his head and looked at the left side of the room. After he refused my third request to look into my eye, I grasped his head with both my hands and held him so he had no choice but to look at me. I told him to allow his eyes to close at the count of "three" but he did not do this, so I brought my two fore-fingers to his eyelids and closed his eyes, myself. When I withdrew my fingers he opened his eyes, so I closed them again.

As I slowly brought my right hand down past his face (this hypnotic pass causes a slight air current which the subject feels) I said, "Now your head will begin to feel very heavy and tired." I watched him intently and was suprised to watch his head very slowly begin to nod and descend towards his chest. Suddenly the head stopped moving and then it was raised defiantly. This rejection of my suggestion was most evident and eloquent. Whenever I see this upward raising of the head during the eye-to-eye technique I accept that as sufficient reason for me to terminate the eye-to-eye technique at that instant and I always move into the "dry lips technique" since it takes such a short time and it does give me several more chances for success.

"Although your head does feel heavy and tired, you will find that you have the ability to hold it in an upright position", I continued. "When I count to 'three' your lips will become dry and parched. Your mouth will feel thirsty and uncomfortable and you will have a great desire to swallow." I watched the singer carefully and saw no response.

"When I count to 'three' this time," I continued, "I want you to open your mouth and take a deep breath and swallow the air and you will feel as though you had a sip of water." Again there was no response as I said, "Three" and he did not open his mouth or swallow the breath of air."

I knew there was no hope but I continued anyway with the third portion of this induction technique. "When I count to 'three' this time," I said, "you will run your tongue over your lips and your lips will feel better and your mouth will feel better and your throat will feel more comfortable." As before he failed to follow my instructions and I felt sure I understood the reason for his disobedience. I then spoke at some length, giving him a few hypnotic prescriptions as to his being able to sleep better and feel stronger and sing better in his various operatic roles. I concluded by saying, "When I count to 'seven' I want you to open your eyes. You will feel well rested and refershed with a general sense of well-being." I then began to count from 'one' to 'seven' but I counted very, very softly so that my voice was scarcely above a whisper. When I said, "seven", the singer opened his eyes instantly and quickly explained, "The reason I did not do the things you asked me to do is that I could not hear what you were saying when my eyes were closed. Like I explained to you, I am deaf and I have to read your lips to understand you and so I don't see how you can expect to hypnotize me when my eyes are closed."

"What makes you think I asked you to do anything when your eyes were closed?" I asked.

Rudolph lost some of his self-assurance and looked very puzzled as he questioned, "Didn't you ask me to do anything?"

"Of course not!" I lied. "After all, you told me that you were deaf and so why should I waste my time talking to a person who could not hear me? You did not hear me talking to you, did you?"

"Yyyyyes, I thought I did," he said, completely off guard.

"Then let's have no more of this nonsense," I commanded. Jumping from my chair, I threw my hands hypnotically at his face and shouted at the top of my voice, "SLEEP!" This is the "shock" technique described in Part Two of this book and something I use very seldom but it is most effective in emergiencies and special instances like this.

Rudolph responded to this "shock" technique by slumping in his chair and his breathing was noticeably lethargic in the manner which so easily distinguishes the person who is in the hypnotic state.

The hypnotic prescription this time was more detailed as I told him he would notice an improvement in his breath control and his acting ability and his memory and also an improvement in his ability to hear. Upon opening his eyes the singer insisted that he could hear me much better than before and also he felt that he could breathe much easier than before and he had a general sense of improvement.

I returned to my friend in the apartment below and half an hour later we were invited to have some sandwiches and coffee which the singer had prepared. While we ate, the singer pointed dramatically to a half-smoked pack of cigarettes which laid on the table, and said, "You see that pack of cigarettes. I have not had a cigarette since the hypnotic session and I will not smoke any more!"

My friend was pleased and asked if I had suggested that he stop smoking. "No," the singer replied. "The hypnotist told me my singing would improve. I know that I will sing better if I stop smoking and so I have decided to stop smoking and I know my singing will improve."

Induction technique used: Shock technique was used successfully after the eye-to-ey technique and the dry-lips technique were resisted by the subject.

Hypnotic prescription given: There will be an improvement in your breath control and your acting ability. You will notice an improvement in your memory and your ability to recall what you have learned in the past. You will feel more at ease with better poise and self-control as you move about the stage. The interesting thing here is that the general suggestions that the singer have the ability to sing better in the future were translated into the specific action that he stop smoking as that was something he knew would contribute greatly to his ability to sing better.

Fear of Dentists

On another occasion my Father brought to our house, Bill, one of his fellow workers at The Norton Air Force Base in San Bernardino, California.

Name: Bill
Age: 30 years old in 1947
Complaint: Fear of dentists.

History: Bill told me he was about to have some dental work done on his teeth. This work was past due, but he had such a fear of dentists it amounted to a phobia. He demonstrated this by showing me that it was only necessary for him to say the word, "Dentist" and his hands and forehead were instantly covered with perspiration and his entire body shook with nervousness. Bill told me that there was several hundred dollars worth of work that had to be done on his teeth and The Veteran's Administration would pay the entire cost, but only if it was done immediately.

He had finally seen the dentist who told him it would take two weeks to complete the dental work. Bill asked me to hypnotize him and remove his fear of dentists so he would not be so nervous during the coming two weeks.

I hypnotized Bill and told him he would look forward to having the dental work done at this time as it would prevent the situation from getting worse and he would be pleased to realize it would cost him nothing and his health would improve as the result of this work being done. I told he would have confidence in the dentist who would be able to treat him in such a manner that he would be comfortable and at ease at all times. At the conclusion of the brief hypnotic session, Bill thanked me and said, "I feel much better now. Look, I can think of going to the dentist and my hands are not covered with perspiration."

Induction technique used: Eye-to-eye technique.

Hypnotic prescription given: "You will look forward to having the dental work done. You will realize that this is the best possible time for it to be done as it will prevent the situation from becoming worse and in this way your health will improve because of your taking this action at this time. You will have confidence in the dentist and you will find that he will be able to treat you in such a manner that you will be comfortable and at ease at all times." This last sentence is designed to remove the possibility of the subject feeling any pain or discomfort.

Additional History: I saw Bill one week after the hypnotic session. He said that he was on his way home from the dentist after the final visit. "It was like this," he explained. "the dentist said that since I was such a good patient and did not feel any pain, it was possible to complete the work in just half the usual time." Bill then ended the brief visit saying, "You know, once I got to the dentist's office and he started to drill on my teeth and I found it did not hurt me, I realized that my previous fear of going to the dentist was all in my head and I know that I never needed your hypnosis at all."

Fear of Throat Cancer

Some fears are less founded on fact than the fear of visiting the dentist and fortunately such foolish fears respond readily to hypnotic suggestions.

Name: Pedro
Age: 45 years old in 1954
Complaint: Fear of throat cancer.

History: Pedro was a Filipino worker in the pineapple fields on the Island of Maui in the Hawaiian Islands. Pedro came to Dr. Kashiwa as a very sick man. Pedro reported that after reading the newspaper reports concerning the suspicion that throat cancer was caused by excessive smoking, he realized that he had been smoking excessively all his life and he began to fear that he might have throat cancer, himself. After examining himself very carefully in his mirror for several mornings, he began to notice a pain in his throat and he experienced great difficulty in swallowing. He went to five different medical doctors, who each examined him carefully and reported that they could find no trace of throat cancer or any illness whatsoever.

However, his condition grew steadily worse and he lost thirty pounds within a period of two months and, finally, he found it impossible to swallow solid food and he adopted a liquid diet while continuing his search for someone who could help him. Dr. Kashiwa examined the man and found nothing of a physical nature wrong with him and so he prescribed a placebo. The man returned and reported that there had been no improvement in his condition but he greatly appreciated the fact that Dr. Kashiwa had been willing to give him some medication and thus indicate his willingness to treat the ailment.

This was during the period when Dr. Kashiwa began using hypnosis in his general medical practice and often thought of it as a "last resort". He spoke to Pedro as follows: "I can see now that medicine will not help you but I do know one powerful treatment which will benefit you greatly. You must let me use hypnosis on you right now."

The patient agreed readily and Dr. Kashiwa used the eye-to-eye technique to induce hypnosis. The subject responded completely and actually fell out of the chair. Dr. Kashiwa raised the man's body back into the chair and could think of nothing better than giving the man a true statement of facts as the prescription. He told Pedro there was no cancer in his throat and no reason for him to have any pain or difficulty in swallowing. He concluded by telling the man he would have a good appetite and enjoy his food and feel a great improvement in his general condition. When the hypnotic session, which lasted no more than two minutes, was terminated and the patient opened his eyes, he walked over to the doctor, smiled and shook his hand warmly saying, "Dctor, that was good. I have no pain now." This was one of Dr. Kashiwa's first experiences with hypnosis and he wanted to examine the man again and thus complete his record as to the results of this brief session. He asked the man to return a week later.

When the patient returned he reported that he felt completely cured and was now eating everything and had no pain or any difficulty in swallowing. However, he insisted that Dr. Kashiwa hypnotize him again because, he explained, he did not want to take any chances that the severe pain might ever return. This the hypnotherapist did because he knew it would relieve Pedro's worries and put his mind at ease.

Induction technique used: Eye-to-eye technique.

Hypnotic prescription given: A simple statement of facts. The final portion consisted of the usual general beneficial instructions incorporated in almost all hypnotic prescriptions.

Additional History: For a number of years Dr. Kashiwa has been meeting Pedro on the streets of Wailuku and on each occasion Pedro stops to thank the doctor warmly for "having cured him."

Fear of Cancer

Pedro's fear of cancer is sometimes shared by professional people and sometimes with tangible evidence to support such fears.

Name: Dr. Walter Grow
Age: 59 years old in 1957
Complaint: Fear of cancer.

History: A very dear friend asked me to his house in San Bernardino one afternoon. He introduced me to an elderly gentleman who he said was his neighbor and wanted very much to be hypnotized. My friend was an amateur hypnotist and he insisted he was interested in seeing me hypnotize someone I had never met before. When I agreed, the elderly gentleman offered to pay me my fee in advance and when I told him I did not accept a fee, he seemed very disappointed. I started with the eye-to-eye technique and after he closed his eyes when I said, "three", I waited for his head to begin to nod. I know that some subjects respond more slowly than others and so I sometimes add a few beneficial instructions while waiting for a response. In this instance I said, "your mind will become clearer and sharper and your organs will function more properly." Instantly the man jumped up from the chair, opened his eyes and said, "I can see that this is not going to work."

He then explained the situation as follows: "My name is Dr. Grow. I have an office across the street. I have known your friend for several years. Six months ago I had an operation for the removal of my prostate gland and as I am a physician I have been changing the bandage regularily since the operation. I find the incision is not healing as the bandage is always full of blood. I have been to see surgeons and they always tell me not to worry. However, I am worried. A professor at the medical college suggested hypnosis might be a solution but he could not recommend anyone. I have read all the books I could find on the subject as I have much time. I have not re-opened my practice since the operation as I can not be sure the operation has been successful as long as the bleeding continues. Some of my colleagues scoff at hypnosis and others say I am too old to be a good subject. I know a hypnotist in Beverly Hills who is very expensive but I thought today I would try to find out what hypnosis is like and if there is such a thing or if I am just wasting my time considering it. When you said my organ would function more properly I had to jump up because you see, I know my organ will never function again."

I said, "Thank you for the explanation, now when can I see you again?"

"Are you willing to try to hypnotize me again?" he asked. "Your friend said you always hypnotize your subjects during the first visit and since you do not accept a fee, how can I impose upon your time?"

"Yes," I agreed, "I often induce hypnosis to some degree during the first session. However, I am interested in seeing you again and perhaps in the privacy of your office and when we both have much more time, it will be easier for me to hypnotize you."

Dr. Grow was profuse with his thanks and agreed to see me the following afternoon. On my way home I reviewed the un-successful session in my mind and I could think of several errors I had made. I should have found out more about the patient's background and I should have sought a valid motivation. On the other hand, I realized that several unfortunate aspects were not really my fault. Dr. Grow was a professional man and naturally lost some confidence in me when I refused to accept a fee. That could not be helped. When I said, "organs of your body will function more properly" I was thinking of the internal organs of the body. He mis-understood me as he was thinking so strongly of his sex organ. As I considered the explanation he gave I came to the conclusion that he did not want to be hypnotized as much as he wanted to be informed and re-assured that hypnosis was a legitimate form of therapy and not a device used by charlatans to take money away from ignorant superstitious fools. Yes, I decided, if Dr. Grow wants more information about hypnosis, I can certainly arrange for him to see that it does exist as an effective tool used by honest physicians and dentists in their daily practice.

The next afternoon I called the High School boy who lived across the street from me and I said, "Ernie, I would like you to allow me to hypnotize you in front of a doctor. You will be doing him a favor as he is ill and needs some hypnotherapy but is not sure it actually exists." When we arrived at Dr. Grow's office I said, "I have decided to have you watch me hypnotize this boy.

I realized my assumption had been correct when Dr. Grow invited us into his examining room and said, "This is what I want more than anything in the world," I had hypnotized Ernie many times and knew he would be responsive to all my instructions. I said, "Dr. Grow please sit next to Ernie and take his pulse."

As he counted the boy's pulse, I said, "Now Ernie when I count 'three' your pulse will beat faster." The physician seemed suprised as he became aware of the change. "Now," I continued, "when I count 'three' your pulse will become much slower than normal." Once again the elderly gentleman nodded his head as the pulse rate changed. Ernie's respiration was very heavy and noticable and Dr. Grow looked at the boy with awe as he said to me, "This boy is hypnotized."

"Yes," I agreed, "that is correct. Now please take his blood pressure." I then demonstrated how I could suggest to the boy that his blood pressure would go up and then down and his body responded to my instructions. That ended the visit and the doctor thanked us again and again as he hurried us out.

A few weeks thereafter Dr. Grow resumed his general medical practice and I learned from my friend that he attributed his recovery to hypnosis. He came to visit me often and on one occasion said, "I feel that I owe my life to the hypnotic demonstration you and Ernie presented for me in my office that day. As soon as you left I got into my car and drove straight to see the hypnotherapist in Beverly Hills. The wonderful thing is that it all worked even faster than he said it would."

After much questioning, he gave me the rest of the story. He told the hypnotherapist in Beverly Hills, California the entire history of his case. He was asked to sit in a comfortable chair and allow himself to become drowsy. The prescription given him was that he would go back to his home in San Bernardino and then since he was a physician, he would think of the proper thing to do for his problem. However, as soon as he returned to his automobile in the parking lot, he had a sudden inspiration. Up to that time he had been trying to stop the bleeding by taking various types of coagulants. Immediately following the hypnotic session he decided the bleeding might be due to a condition of capillary fatigue. He then took massive doses of the vitamin which relieves this condition and very soon thereafter the bleeding stopped.

Induction technique used: It did not appear to be a rapid-induction technique and therefore it is not likely to be found described in this book.

Hypnotic prescription given: You will go home and then you will think of the proper course of action you should take.

Additional history: My father and I continued to see Dr. Grow as a close family friend. He always seemed very active and in good spirits.

Desire To Commit Suicide

The following case history is one I have often recounted as it illustrates the value of knowing several different induction techniques and in knowing how to prepare a hypnotic prescription for a problem the therapist has never dealt with before. This is also a good example of what I refer to in this book as the "brush-off" technique.

Name: Bob
Age: 23 years old in 1950
Complaint: Desire to commit suicide.

History: I was attending an informal gathering at the home of Mr. Elmer T. Howard who had once traveled with me as my business manager. We sat on the patio of his home in Altadena, California and he spoke of some of our experiences. As it grew late and the twilight of evening approached we were invited back into the house for coffee. As we crossed the lawn one of the guests stepped up to me and said, "Hearing Mr. Howard speak of your ability as a hypnotist made me wonder if you might be able to help me. This afternoon I was on the verge of committing suicide and I honestly think I will go through with it, tomorrow."

I stopped walking and he continued his story. "My girl friend left me," he explained, "and I find that I cannot go on living without her. I was swimming at the beach this afternoon and I saw her with another fellow and I was so miserable and depressed when I realized I had lost her forever, I began thinking how easy it would be for me to go into the water and swim out as far as I could, knowing I would not have the ability to turn around and swim back to shore. I have been thinking of that all evening and I am now determined that tomorrow afternoon I will go out to the beach and end my miserable existance."

My thoughts were that here we did not have a simple problem like nail biting or thumb sucking. Since I believe the most effective manner of treating a problem is to use the "brush-off" technique, I felt compelled to force myself to act in that fashion for I knew that if I failed with this one hypnotic session I might never have another chance. Therefore, I acted very casual and said, "I can help you with some hypnotic suggestions in just a few minutes." I pulled around one of the canvas backed lawn chairs and asked him to sit down. Twilight had passed and it was rapidly growing dark. I felt it was too dark to ask him to look into my eye and even the eye-to-finger technque seemed to call for more light than we had. I decided the technique I use when hypnotizing people in total darkness would work and also it might have some of the elements of the "shock" technique since I clapped my right palm across his eyes and said, "Close your eyes and your head will begin to feel heavy and tired." I knew he was responding as I felt his head begin to nod and his forehead brushed against the palm I held gently in front of his face.

Now I said, "When I count 'three' your head will begin to fall down towards your chest and your head and body will become very heavy and tired and relaxed." He responded quickly and then I began to search my mind for a prescription. As I thought of the basic rules for all prescriptions I said the following sentences.

First of all, this girl you are so very much concerned over was not the first girl friend you ever had. Berhaps you liked her better than all the girls you knew in the past but now you will be looking forward to meeting a girl that you will like even better than this girl. Until you had met this girl, you did not know such a fine person existed and that is the same way you will feel about your next girl friend."

"You had a great many happy and wonderful experiences with this girl friend and so in the future, everytime you see her or hear her name mentioned you will think of all the very happy experiences you shared together and you will find that the mere thought of her will make you very happy."

"Furthermore," I continued, "knowing that you are going to meet a lot of new girl friends who will be interesting and exciting will make you anxious to attend many parties and social functions where you will be likely to make new friends and have new experiences. When I count to 'seven' you will open your eyes feeling wide awake and well rested and refreshed. You will have the feeling as though you took a pleasant nap but you will remember everything I said and tonight you will sleep well and awaken tomorrow with an eagerness to see your old friends and, at the same time, you will be looking forward to making some new acquaintances." I then counted to "seven" and he opened his eyes.

The young man thanked me repeatedly during the remainder of the evening and a week later I met him on the street and he said, "Say, I can't thank you enough for what you did for me that night at Mr. Howard's house. I saw my former girl friend a few days later and I waved at her and she waved back at me and I felt good all day."

Induction technique used: Hypnotizing-in-the-dark technique as described in part Two of this book.

Hypnotic prescription given: The next girl friend you will have will be more wonderful than the girl you are now so concerned about. Until you meet your next girl friend you will not be able to imagine anyone as fine as she will be. However, since you are going to meet some new girl friends who will be interesting and exciting, it will be necessary for you to go to many parties and social functions where you will be likely to make new friends and have new experiences. You have had many happy and wonderful experiences with this girl friend and so in the future, everytime you see her or hear her name mentioned you will think of all the very happy experiences you shared together and these thoughts will make you very happy.

Additional History: Here we have one of the rare instances where a person I have helped has continued to express his gratitude by writing to me and inviting me to his home whenever I visit the city where he now lives. This friendship is in it's seventeenth year and we see he has recovered very well since I hypnotized him in 1950.

Anxiety Complex

The hynotherapist need not feel any case is hopeless since he can always resort to the General Beneficial Prescription and promise the patient some degree of improvement. Sometimes a little improvement is enough.

Name: Mr. Lee
Age: 42 years old in 1963
Complaint: Anxiety complex.

History: Following the successful series of lectures I presented in Tokyo in 1963. I agreed to give a few lectures in Hong Kong before returning to the United States. My business manager arranged for some newspaper publicity and Mr. Lee came to my hotel, saying he had read about me in the paper. Mr. Lee explained that he had been living in San Francisco the past few years and had returned to Hong Kong a few months previously to dispose of some of his property and financial interests. One day as he was riding on the Ferry Boat between Victoria and Kowloon he suddenly had a mysterious attack and fell to the floor. He was taken off the boat in a stretcher and brought to a hospital. The medical people could find no reason for his attack and he was put under the care of the leading psychiatrist for the British Armed Forces in Hong Kong. This doctor diagnosed his case as an Anxiety Complex and assigned a male nurse to accompany Mr. Lee at all times. Mr. Lee found that he could walk about the city when accompanied by the male nurse, but he could not ride in an automobile or bus or street car or boat or any form of transportation. The doctor had tried psycho-analysis but had to admit it would take a long time before it could result in a cure and Mr. Lee was worried for withing a few weeks he would have to return to the United States or lose his immigration status. The psychiatrist had suggested hypnosis and that was why he came to see me.

Mr. Lee asked me if I thought I could hypnotize him and I said I could. However, I said I needed a little time to give his problem some consideration. After two days I could think of no reason for his problem or any specific prescription I could give him. I came to Mr. Lee's luxurious apartment as I had agreed and I told him I did not know the reason for the anxiety condition or complex but I was sure it, was caused by some problem he had and hypnosis might relieve his worries and thus bring about an improvement in his condition.

"But I have no problem," said Mr. Lee.

"I do not know what the problem is," I admitted, "but I feel sure it was a problem which caused your condition. Perhaps it was a business matter."

"I have no business problems," Mr. Lee said. "I sold all my property and disposed of my various business interests and so I have a great deal of money and nothing to worry about. No problems."

"Well, it might be a problem of love," I continued.

"I have no problems of love," Mr. Lee said firmly. "In fact, I have two young ladies here in Hong Kong who want to marry me. They have both been helpful to me in the years before I went to San Francisco and I wrote and promised them that when I returned to Hong Kong this time I would choose one of them to return to the United States with me as my wife. They both want to marry me, however I have not decided who to chose. I know one loves me more than I love her, but the other is more attractive and I find her more desirable. Since I have been ill they have both been very patient and under-standing. I told them I am under the care of a psychiatrist and in my mental state I am unable to get married at this time and they have agreed to wait until I recover from this illness."

I wanted to explore this subject further so I asked, "Was it necessary for you to return to Hong Kong to find a wife? Were you unable to find any girls in San Francisco?"

"Oh there are so many wonderful beautiful girls in San Francisco," said Mr. Lee and he beamed as he recalled them to his mind. "However, I have a moral obligation to marry one of these two girls in Hong Kong as they were my friends during the years before I made my wealth and they waited for me to return from San Francisco so I will have to keep my promise and choose one of them after I get well."

I then asked Mr. Lee to sit in a firm chair as I began the eye-to-eye technique. Mr. Lee was un-responsive. It almost seemed like he did not want to get well. The check-points had all been negative and I could not see any indication that he was responding, but I was determined to give him the following prescription. "You have been very ill," I began, "and I want you to realize that it will take a long time for you to feel that you are completely cured. You will tell these two young ladies here in Hong Kong that you are too ill to get married at this time and you will know in your heart that this is indeed the truth."

At this point I could see a change in Mr. Lee's respiration and his entire body seemed to become heavy and for the first time his head started to nod and move down towards his chest.

"There is going to be some slight degree of improvement in your condition but the improvement will be very slight at first and then it will become progressively greater and greater as the days go by.

You will be able to go down stairs and walk around a bit outside without the male nurse. Then you will find that you can buy passage on an airplane to San Francisco and you will be able to return to San Francisco on an airplane, but this will only be the result of a little bit of improvement of your anxiety complex. And even though you will be able to take an airplane back to San Francisco, you will still feel that you are not well and that there will still remain much more improvement needed before you will have fully recovered from this illness. Now, you will notice the improvement in your condition, no matter how slight it may be at first, and you will be well pleased with the amount of improvement you notice since you will realize that eventually you will make a complete recovery."

At the count of 'seven' Mr. Lee was instructed to open his eyes and this was the only positive check-point of the session. He opened his eyes slowly and looked about him, somewhat in a daze and he seemed very puzzled. "Do you think I was hypnotized?" he asked. "I could hear every word you said and I did not feel different at all. Do you think I can actually go out alone and buy a ticket to San Francisco and take an airplane there? It would be wonderful as it means so much to me to be able to return this month. I feel I could go out with you right now, but after all, that is not the same as going out along. I don't know if I was hynotized. I guess I will have to wait and see if there is some improvement in my condition."

I told Mr. Lee that I was sure he had been hypnotized and that there would be a slight improvement. When he asked me to send him my bill, I explained that I did not accept a free. He asked if I would allow him to enroll in my course in hypnotherapy and I agreed.

Induction technique used: Eye-to-eye technique.

Hypnotic prescription given: I felt that he did have a "problem" and that by remaining "sick" with only a slight improvement he would be able to escape from the situation where he had to choose one of the ladies in Hong Kong to be his bride. The prescription was the usual beneficial suggestions included in all hypnotic prescriptions but stress was upon the improvement being very slight and gradual.

Additional History: Mr. Lee sent us his enrollment fee for my course the following Sunday, but he failed to attend. He also sent a gift to my hotel. The day after my course I saw the male nurse who had been Mr. Lee's companian. He recognized me and shook my hand. I asked him how Mr. Lee was feeling and he replied, "Didn't you know? The day after you came to visit him at his apartment he went out alone and he bought an airplane ticket to San Francisco. I offered to go with him to the airport but he said it would only cause him to feel worse. However, he sent all his belongings and I saw him drive away in a taxi so I guess he is much improved and is surely back in The United States by now."

Anxiety Complex

Some patients have a more valid reason for their anxiety.

Name: Edward
Age: 22 years old in 1964.
Complaint: Anxiety complex.

History: As I left a small gathering one evening a young man asked me my occupation. He said my conversation caused him to think I might be a psychologist. He asked if he could see me and tell me his problem and I agreed. Edward said he was a student at U.C.L.A. and had tried to get treatment from the Psychiatric Clinic at U.C.L.A. but they turned him down.

"You see, it is like this," he began. "I have an anxiety complex and I am a homosexual. I would like to have my anxiety complex cured but I do not want to stop my homosexual activities. At U.C.L.A. they said they would accept me as a patient only if I was willing to have them treat my homosexuality and I refused."

I told Edward I would be willing to help his anxiety complex and he then began telling me about all the things that worried him. Finally he complained that he had a severe headache and that seemed like a good chance to stop his seemingly endless recitation and begin the hypnotic session. I was pleased to find Edward most responsive to the eye-to-eye technique. He slipped from the chair down to the floor when I told him his head would begin to move down towards his chest. It seemed easier to allow him to rest on the carpet as I gave him the hypnotic prescription. I told him his head would feel clear and comfortable and he smiled to indicate that he felt an immediate improvement. I decided to give him an understanding of my personal philosophy which does not allow one to be worried or concerned. I told Edward my philosophy is that "all things happen for the best." Therefore, if I were to miss a train, I believe that I will be happier because I rode on the later train and that I would gain because I arrived at the later hour. I included many other general beneficial instructions that I give to all students; such as his having a greater interest in his school studies and having a better memory and then I realized that I could give him the hypnotic prescription which I have found effective in treating homosexuality and it would not disturb or upset him at all.

"You will have more will-power and self-control", I began. "You will feel that you can smoke if you wish to smoke and you can stop smoking if you wish to stop smoking. You can drink or not drink as you wish. Also, I want you to feel that you have the ability to enjoy sexual experiences with girls or boys, as you wish. The fact that you may have limited your activities in the past does not prevent you from enjoying to the fullest extent any other form of sexual activity. You will recognize your sexual capabilities and your ability to channel them in any direction you desire."

I concluded with the usual suggestions that the improvement in his anxiety complex would be gradual and progressive and he would be pleased with the amount of improvement he would notice.

When Edward opened his eyes at the count of 'seven' he said, "I think the reason I have never had any sexual experiences with girls is because I do not know any girls. I do not dislike them, as I know some homosexuals do. It is just that I don't know how to meet them."

I told Edward I would be giving a talk to a group of young psychology students later that week. He was interested but could not attend since his car needed repairs. I suggested that he could ride with me and then he worried about where we would meet and what time and insisted upon knowing the address and telephone number. As he continued, I realized how very ill he was with worry and anxiety over every detail. I promised to meet him the following Friday evening at 7:30 P.M.

On my way to meet him the following Friday, I was unavoidably delayed. I could not telephone to him as he was waiting on a street corner. I drove as fast as the traffic would permit and I thought to myself, this is surely the one person I would not want to keep waiting for an appointment. I arrived at the designated street corner forty five minutes late, full of remorse and apologies. However, Edward stopped my outburst of explanations saying, "Never mind, I did not worry. I knew you would be here so I did not notice the time."

After I finished my talk to the group that evening coffee was served and the members visited with each other. Edward came up to me and said, "I met a girl who lives in my neighborhood and she offered to drive me home. Do you mind if I go with her?"

Induction technique used: Eye-to-eye technique.

Hypnotic prescription given: A brief explanation of my personal philosophy was given as it keeps me from needless worrying. Otherwise the general instructions as to some degree of improvement, gradual and progressive and he would be pleased with the improvement which he would notice.

The brief hypnotic prescription for homosexuality was that he have more will-power and self-control and recognize his ability to enjoy sexual experiences with boys or girls, as he choose.

Additional history: I met Edward at a gathering about one year later. He seemed in very good spirits and happy to see me. He came over to me and said, "The hypnosis you gave me did not work. I could not accept that philosophy of yours that 'everything happens for the best'. I have just decided that the worse possibility that can happen will be the outcome of all situations and therefore there is no need for me to worry. I know that I can never alter or improve matters and so I have stopped worrying completely." I admitted that my personal philosophy could not be accepted by everyone. I asked him if he had any girl friends. "Yes," he replied, "I found that once I stopped worrying about it, girls began to ask me for dates and to parties and such.

Acne

Hypnotherapy is something I seldom suggest. I prefer to have the patient seek my help as this is often a good indication that he wants his condition altered or improved. A condition of acne, however, is sometimes an exception to this rule since few people know that hypnosis can be be used for this skin condition and also, this problem is often so apparent.

Name: Sgt. Brown
Age: 23 years old in 1964
Complaint: Condition of acne on his back.

History: While touring the U.S. Armed Forces military installations in Japan with a program of hypnotic demonstrations I offered to give some hypnotherapy to a sergeant in the Air Force. This was during a performance at an N.C.O. Club. I invited those in the audience who wanted to be hypnotized to take part in the demonstrations. Several responded and were seated on the stage. For the sake of variety, I invite each participant to come forward and I use a different induction technique in each instance as I illustrate rigidity, removal of pain, etc., etc. I conclude the program by hypnotizing a young man using the "silent technique" and I then suggest to him he is walking to a swimming pool and anxious to go swimming. I then tell him to remove his jacket and shirt and finally I tell him to remove his undershirt. He is then placed on a "bed of nails" and is able to rest very comfortably in that position. On this occasion I found Sgt. Brown responded in the usual manner as I had him remove his jacket and shirt. However, when I whispered to him to quickly remove his undershirt, his arms remained at his sides and he shook his head slowly from side to side.

I have never had a subject indicate unwillingness to follow my instructions at this point before, but my many years of experience as a professional hypnotist caused me to recognize that any further insistence on my part would result in the young man opening his eyes and thus terminate this part of the performance. I was certain all in the audience would know that a thin undershirt could afford him little protection from the sharp spikes in the "bed of nails." Therefore, I allowed him to keep his undershirt on as I continued with my presentation. I had him fall backwards and lie on the stage. The "bed of nails" was then shown to the audience and he was placed on it. A young lady from the audience then stepped upon his chest. After the serviceman was lifted off this "bed of nails" and asked to open his eyes at the count of "seven" I felt the demonstration had been successfully completed and I then felt it was safe for me to lift his undershirt. It was my intention to show his bare back to the audience so they could see the indentations the spikes had made in his flesh.

However, when I raised the undershirt, I saw his back was covered with a mass of boils and sores. I quickly dropped the undershirt, thanked him for his participation and then asked him to come back and see me later.

When Sgt. Brown came to my dressing room I told him I realized when I saw his bareback why he did not want to remove his undershirt. "Yes," he said, "I have had this condition of acne for some time and my wife is very disturbed over the fact that the Air Force is so slow about treating it."

"I have seen many cases of acne," I told him, "and I would not refer to the skin condition on your back as acne."

"Well, my wife made me go to the base hospital last week and the medic there said it was acne and he arranged for me to have an appointment with a skin specialist next month," he explained.

"All right," I agreed, "if the medic at the hospital says you have acne, I will not argue. I do have a hypnotic prescription which I have found to be very effective in treating acne and if you wish, I can take a minute and give you that prescription at this time."

The sergeant said, "That will be fine and I know my wife will appreciate it very much as she is now most upset over the fact that I can not rest at all on my back and at night, if I turn over on to my back when I am sleeping, the pain is so great I scream and that wakes her up. She tried calomine lotion and talcum powder but nothing helps and it gets worse and worse and when I finally agreed to go to the hospital they said I would have to return in several weeks and she is now very impatient."

When I asked his age and he said, "I am twenty three" I had to insist that I could hardly blame his condition of acne on his "adolescence". Once again I told him that it did not appear to be a condition of acne.

"Well, if it is not acne," he challenged, "what is it?"

"I would guess that your skin condition is psycho-somatic in origin," I replied. "When did you first notice this condition?"

"One year ago, when I arrived in Denver, Colorado," was his answer.

"Were you under some mental strain at that time?" I asked.

"Oh yes," he replied. "I had been stationed in England for over a year and I had been seeing this girl often. One day her father went to the commanding officer of the base and reported that his daughter was pregnant and insisted that I be compelled to marry her or else he would turn the matter over to the local authorities. My commanding officer knew I was assisting the chaplian and so the two of them called me in for questioning. When I saw how concened they were and embarrassed as they asked me if I was the guilty person, I could not bring myself to admit it. Therefore, I looked them squarely in the eye and swore I had never been intimate with the girl. The commanding officer said he could not believe the father's accusation and saw no reason for me to be subjected to a civil arrest and trial since he could easily have me transferred back to the States. I was flown to Denver that evening and my military record was sent later.

"Once I was safely back in the U.S., I found that I had no zest in living. I suddenly found that I had no interest in going anywhere or doing anything and after one week I realized that I did not want to continue living if I could not be with that girl. I went to the Red Cross and asked if they could help to bring her to the United State: and they offered to loan me the money for her transportation and to arrange for her passport and such. I went to the service club and I wrote an eight page letter to this girl saying I did not know why I refused to admit my guilt, but when the charges were expressed by the commanding officer in front of the chaplian, I found myself able to deny everything. However, I wrote that I wanted to marry her and I asked her to join me. As soon as I mailed the letter I realized that it would be impossible for me to wait several days for her reply. I telephoned to her that evening and I told her I loved her and did not want to live without her and I asked her to marry me and she agreed. I told her the Red Cross would send her an airplane ticket and she promised to use it the moment it arrived.

"We were married as soon as she got to Denver and I have never been happier. In fact, she is now expecting our second child. Yes, the skin condition developed during the first week I was in Denver. However, we are now happily married. Why doesn't it go away?"

"I don't know," I admitted. "Can you think of anything that is causing you a mental strain at this time?"

"Yes," he replied readily, "I feel terrible whenever I think of the way I lied to my commanding officer and base chaplain. I know they trusted me and had faith in me and I allowed them to send me out of England when it might have caused them to get into much trouble. This is on my conscience and I can't forgive myself."

"I will now hypnotize you," I said. "Stand up against the wall and look into my eye. When I count 'three' your eyes will close, your eyeballs will roll upward and your head will feel heavy and tired." When he responded, I began giving him these instructions. "I prefer to believe that all things happen for the best. I want you to understand that because of this unfortunate incident your marriage has more meaning and depth and is more firmly established. You know that you asked this girl to marry you, not because of any threats or coercion but only because you loved her and wanted to live with her. She knows that you asked her to marry you, not because she was pregnant with your child but because you wanted to spend the rest of your life with her. Your children will now have the benefit of growing up in a home where there is much love and mutual understanding.

"You have not hurt your former commanding officer or base chaplian," I continued. "Because you allowed them to do this favor for you, they had a feeling of satisfaction and accomplishment and I am sure they were pleased to feel that they had been of service to you. They did have faith and trust in you and you can live in the future in such a manner that this faith and trust will be justified. As you and your wife raise your family you will always feel grateful to these two gentlemen who made your brief separation possible and in this way, your love and devotion was tested and found to be stronger than you had suspected. There will be some improvement in the skin condition on your back. The improvement will be gradual and progressive but you will notice the improvement and you will be well pleased with the amount of improvement which you will notice."

After I asked him to open his eyes he said, "I feel that I was just hynotized deeper than I was hypnotized during the performance." I was impressed when he mentioned his inability to lie on his back when he was in bed at night. I knew a few minutes previously he had been resting on his back without complaint for several minutes on the stage and also he had been on the "bed-of-nails".

Induction technique used: Since he had been hypnotized earlier that evening in front of the audience, it was a simple matter to use the eye-to-eye technigue with him standing up against a wall instead of sitting in a chair.

Hypnotic prescription given: "Because of the unfortunate incident your marriage is now on a firmer basis with greater depth and more meaning. You will be able to conduct your life in the future in such a manner that it will justify the faith and trust your former commanding officer and base chaplain had in you." Ending, of course, with the general beneficial suggestions of a gradual, progressive improvement.

Additional history: Several weeks later I received this short note from Sgt. Brown. "My wife asked me to send you this note of thanks. I just went to the hospital and cancelled my appointment to see the skin specialist since my back is so much better."

Mental Retarded Girl

I am often asked the difference between a neurotic and a psychopath. I explain that a neurotic person knows he is troubled and wishes to be helped. A psychopath is not aware that he is defective and often will refuse treatment if any is offered to him. I have found mentally retarded children respond to hypnosis when treated according to their mental and not their chronological age. After giving my course in Rapid Induction Techniques of Hypnotherapy in Japan several years ago I was asked to hypnotize the mentally retarded daughter of one of one of my students.

Name: Fumiko
Age: 16 years old in 1964
Complaint: Mentally retarded.

History: I was asked to meet the sixteen year old girl who was mentally retarded with the understanding that I might be able to bring about some degree of improvement after I had hypnotized her. The following afternoon, Mr. Omori, my interpreter, and I went to the Doctor's house and met his wife and several children. We were left alone as they went to fetch Fumiko and they returned, without her, a few minutes later with the explanation that Fumiko had refused to meet me unless I was willing to agree that her Mother and Father could be present during the hypnotic session. I could see no harm in having the parents observe the treatment, but I had not met the patient and under no circumstance could allow her to feel that she was to be able to dictate to me. Before I could expect to hypnotize her she must be made to feel that I was "in command" of the entire situation and that she was about to accept all the conditions and instructions which I would be giving to her. I told the girl's parents I wanted the girl brought to me so that I could meet her. I also explained to them why it would be necessary for me to decide, after I met her, if the parents would be allowed to remain or if they would have to leave the room during the hypnotic session.

The Doctor and his wife were gone for a longer period of time and in the interval, seven or eight small children entered the room and they quietly seated themselves about on the floor with eager faces and it was obvious that they anticipated viewing the performance. The parents of the girl returned to inform me that Fumiko had finally agreed to meet me and would be down presently. We had a very long wait and my blood pressure mounted.

"Who are these children?" I demanded, pointing to the assembled youngsters. "They are Fumiko's younger brothers and sisters", I was told.

I could no longer allow myself to resent the presence of these uninvited guests since they were indeed in their own home. I told their parents I could see they were very well mannered and likely to behave properly, but I felt it best for the patient's sake that the small children be asked to play elsewhere and so they were dismissed and silently left the room though obviously disappointed at having to miss the proceedings.

Shortly thereafter Fumiko entered the room accompanied by her 14 year old sister. Mr. Omori and I were introduced to the two girls but Fumiko ignored us completely as she sat alone on the divan and aimlessly toyed with a small scarf. Her mother handed the scarf to me, explaining that Fumiko had knitted it herself. I examined the scarf very carefully commented upon it being so well constructed as I turned it about several times, all the while trying to observe my young patient who sat on the divan and gave us no heed. She seemed unaware of our presence and determined to avoid looking in our direction.

Fumiko's younger sister seemed to be extremely alert and capable. She smiled and answered all the questions I had Mr. Omori translate to her. I knew it would be extremely easy to hypnotize her as soon as we presented as "motivation" my promise that by hypnosis I could improve her memory and thus make it easier for her to do well with her school studies with less effort on her part.

It was apparent that Fumiko had no intention of submitting to hypnosis willingly and I doubted that I would have any success otherwise. I thought of the "indirect method of hypnotic induction" used by several professional stage hynotists. This seemed like a wise course to take as I would be helping the 14 year old girl and at the same time showing Fumiko that hypnosis was painless and nothing to fear and also she would be made forcefully and dramatically aware of my ability to hypnotize others.

I told the Doctor and his wife I would hypnotize the younger girl and Fumiko would thus have an opportunity to see what I intended to do and she could observe the entire procedure and question her sister, if she choose. They were asked to leave the room and they did. I knew I would have to use the same induction technique on both girls and therefore decided to clear a small bench and I invited the eager schoolgirl to sit at one end of the bench with her feet firmly placed on the floor and she was aware that the full length of the bench was behind her and ready to support her body as she fell backwards. This "low bench or bed technique" is one of the most effective I know and when performed properly uses the law of gravity as a powerful ally.

Mr. Omori translated as I began to give the first few sentences in this induction technique and was not at all suprised to find the girl completely responsive in every way. All the "check-points" were favorable and the girl's respiration soon indicated she was hypnotized. I gave her a short prescription regarding her memory and her physical strength and well-being. I used the "rigid arm test" and frequently looked in the direction of Fumiko to see if she was becoming impressed. However, Fumiko seemed well occupied with her scarf and the arm rest on the divan where she sat and ignored us completely although we were only a meter's length away.

After I asked the young girl to open her eyes, she did so, looking about the room, somewhat dazed, as though awakening from a nap. Mr. Omori questioned her and she informed him that she could hear everything and was fully aware of everything but knew she had been hypnotized and did feel greatly refreshed. Fumiko was asked to sit on the low bench as her sister had done and she complied with a great show of indifference. When Fumiko was told her body would become heavy and fall backwards, she responded readily and for a moment I thought I detected a change in her respiration. When I began the "rigid arm technique" I could see that she was not following our instructions and she did not close her fist tightly as I requested and finally, commanded. At no time could I feel certain that she was putting forth any effort to close her fingers or push her fist away from her body so I did not ask her to make an attempt at bending her arm. I did inform her that it would feel very rigid and un-yielding. She was raised to a sitting position and told her head would become increasingly heavy and tired. It did nod slightly and her breathing became heavier for an instant. Nothing remained for me except to give her some general beneficial suggestions that her health and strength would improve and she would find a greater degree of pleasure and enjoyment from her knitting and other activities. When asked to open her eyes at the count of 'seven' she did so, readily and seemed greatly relieved.

The Doctor and his wife questioned the two girls and they both reported that they had been hypnotized and felt well and strong. Fumiko hurried from the room and returned quickly with a picture she had drawn and she asked her mother to present it to me as her gift. We went outside to be photographed and Fumiko asked permission to be included in the photos. She stood beside us, smiled as we shook hands and waved her hand in a childish gesture as we departed.

I told the Doctor and his wife that I felt his daughter was not mentally retarded but mentally defective and they said that this was something they had suspected.

Induction technique used: The low bench or bed technique was used as the induction technique for both the girls but the "indirect method of induction" wherein one person is influenced by watching as another person is hypnotized, was perhaps an important contributing factor.

Hypnotic prescription given: Only the standard general beneficial suggestions for a progressive improvement.

Additional history: The fact that Fumiko no longer ignored our presence and asked to be photographed with us and stood with her arm about my waist and smiled as she waved to us, seemed to indicate some degree of improvement, at least as far as her attitude towards us was concerned. The next day her father brought us a gift and he reported that Fumiko had seemed elated the rest of the day as she went about the house, singing and in an unusually happy mood. She had slept well and seemed friendly towards everyone.

CHAPTER TWELVE

Prescriptions For Overcoming Bad Habits

When a man smokes cigarettes because he wants to smoke, that is fine. When a man smokes cigarettes because he feels that he MUST smoke, that is unfortunate. When a man feels himself to be a "slave to nicotine" and comes to the therapist and asks for assistance in breaking a bad habit, it is comforting to know that with an increased sense of will-power and self-control the individual can govern his actions and alter his pattern of behaviour.

Desire To Stop Smoking

Name: Bill Haney
Age: 52 years old in 1956
Complaint: Desire to stop smoking.

History: I was visiting my friend, Bill Haney, of Great Falls, Montana and as I was about to leave, Bill said, "Just one more question. How long would it take for you to hypnotize me in order to get me to stop smoking?"

We had spent several hours that evening discussing my experiences with hypnosis and I had explained my preference for the "brush-off technique." Therefore, I felt obligated to use that technique and yet I wondered if it would be effective when used on someone to whom it had just been explained.

"Oh, I can stop you from smoking in less than one minute," I said, airily.

"In that case, why don't you give me the treatment right now?" my friend demanded.

"Sit in this straight backed chair," I began, "look into the pupil of my right eye and listen to my voice. When I count 'three' I want you to allow your eyes to close, your eyeballs will roll upwards and your head will feel heavy and tired."

As I counted "three" he responded and his head nodded slightly. The "brush-off technique" does not allow for any "tests" and so there was nothing more for me to do but give the suggestions regarding the habit of smoking. A common sense presentation of facts was indicated since I knew my friend would prefer to feel he had stopped smoking because of his own good judgement and not because he had been forced to stop. I spoke as follows: "I am going to suggest that you will have more will-power and more self-control in the future. You will stop smoking until you feel the NEED to smoke. You know you must have water after a certain number of days for without water you will die. Also, you need food, after a certain number of days, for otherwise you will die. I want you to wait until you feel that you must smoke or die."

"Of course, that is silly, "I continued, "because smoking is actually an irritation and so the longer you go without smoking the less likely you will want a cigarette. I know you can go for an hour or two without smoking as you have done that in the past. One hour from now you will have less interest and less desire to smoke than you have right now. Two hours from now, you will have even less interest or desire to smoke. Thus as each hour goes by you will have less interest and less desire to smoke."

I asked Bill to open his eyes after I gave him the customary beneficial suggestions. Several months later I heard from mutual friends that Bill had been telling many people about his extreme pleasure over the results of our brief hypnotic session. I wrote Bill Haney and asked him to send me a testimonial. He wrote to me on his stationery as Circulation manager of The Great Falls Tribune.

Dear Mr. Furst:

Today is May 22nd. Since the latter part of September, 1956, I have not had the urge to smoke. The hypnotic suggestions you gave to me at that time firmly implanted in my mind the lack of necessity for smoking. Previous to this time I had been buying and smoking over one carton of cigarettes a week. Often I opened my third pack of cigarettes in one day. I have smoked since I was eleven years old. I am now 52 years old. Under these circumstances, I think it is marvelous what you have done for me and I want to thank you sincerely.

Induction technique used: Eye-to-eye technique presented in the "brush-off" manner, mainly because that had been discussed and I had insisted that a short hypnotic session was often the most effective.

Hypnotic prescription given: "You will have more will power and self-control in the future. You will be able to smoke, if you wish to smoke and you will be able to not smoke, if you wish not to smoke. You will realize that smoking is a form of irritation and that the longer you go without a cigarette the less need you will have to smoke. One hour from now you will have less interest in smoking than you feel at this time. Two hours from now you will have less interest in smoking than you will have one hour from now. Thus as each hour goes by you will have less interest, less desire and less need to smoke."

92

Insomnia

Is it wise to argue with patients and tell them they are foolish to be worried or concerned? Often this will only waste time and destroy any feeling of rapport that might exist between the therapist and his client. It is often wiser to listen to the complaint, mentally decide upon the prescription to be administered and the induction technique to be used and without discussion agree to accept the request for hypnotherapy. Once the patient has responded to hypnosis he is receptive and willing to agree that he need no longer worry about his situation which is going to improve in the future.

Name: Mrs. Ito
Age: 51 years old in 1956
Complaint: Insomnia. The patient said, "I have a bad habit of dreaming."

History: Dr. Kashiwa asked me to hypnotize his patient who had an unfortunate high blood pressure and complained about being unable to sleep at night. When I met the woman who was of Hawaiian ancestry, married to a Japanese, she explained her problem, saying, "You see, actually, I have a bad habit of dreaming. I have dreams all night and these dreams keep me awake. I would like you to hypnotize me so I will stop having dreams."

Rather than try to explain to her everyone has dreams every night and actually she must be asleep before she could dream at all, I decided it would be wiser to agree to her request. She was a large, heavy-set person and extremely overweight. I had her sit in a chair for the eye-to-eye induction and when I moved her hands that rested in her lap, I was disappointed to feel her arms tense and she moved them back into their original position. Dr. Kashiwa, standing behind the patient, saw this negative check-point and he sadly moved his head from side to side.

"Look into this eye", I said as I pointed to my right eye, "when I count to 'three' your eyes will close, your eyeballs will roll upwards and your head will feel heavy and tired." She followed these instructions perfectly and I discounted the first negative check-point after I saw her head begin to nod and drop towards her bosom.

Her hands seemed to be in an awkward position so I decided to raise them slightly and allow them to drop to her sides. I knew this would make her body feel heavy and tired and I expected this would assist me in inducing hypnosis. As soon as I began to lift her hands, she quickly raised them into the air. This amounted to another negative check-point as she was not accepting my unspoken instructions but instead was maintaining control over the position of her hands. Dr. Kashiwa shrugged his shoulders to register his frustration since he had tried to hypnotize this patient earlier that day and had failed.

Here was a situation where the orthodox hypnotic "test" could be used as an induction technique. I knew it was somewhat risky to attempt a "test" so early but I decided that a firm, positive statement indicating my confident self-assurance would have more than a fifty per cent chance of being accepted. I realized that if the "test" was successful it would be most impressive to observe and I was conscious of Dr. Kashiwa's interest. Speaking a bit more loudly, I said, "When I count to 'three' you will go deeper asleep. Your entire body will feel heavy and tired with the exception of your arms and hands. They will become so light they will feel like something is pulling them up towards the ceiling and you will be unable to bring them down. One, two, three." We both watched, fascinated as she struggled in vain to lower her arms. After it was apparent she was unable to bring her hands down, I suggested she no longer cared about the position of her hands and actually they felt rested and comfortable in the air. At this point we could see a distinct change in her respiration which became more rapid and labored.

"When you go to bed at night and wish to sleep, you will lie on your back, turn your hands palm upwards and then your body will feel as heavy and as tired as it feels now. Then it will begin to grow heavier and heavier. You will not have as many dreams in the future as you have had in the past. When you do have a dream in the future, you will find that as soon as you awaken you will completely forget the dream. The fact that you have any dreams at all will seem most un-important to you. When you awaken each morning you will feel rested and refreshed regardless of how many hours sleep you might have had," I said, as I combined our usual prescription for insomnia with the patient's request that she no longer be troubled by so many dreams.

Dr. Kashiwa came up to me and said, "Don't forget her high blood pressure." I offered to lower her blood pressure instantly and I asked him to prepare to take a reading of her blood pressure. When Dr. Kashiwa indicated he was ready, I touched the woman on her shoulder and said, "When I count to 'three' your hands will drop limply into your lap and your entire body will relax and your blood pressure will go down. One, two, three."

Dr. Kashiwa noted on the lady's chart that her blood pressure was 186 and he said to me, "That is very good because this morning her blood pressure was over 200. Now see if you can bring it down to 180 as that is where I would like it to be."

I told the patient she was going to take three very deep breaths and each time she exhaled she would feel her body relax and her blood pressure would continue to drop. The blood pressure reading was then 180 and Dr. Kashiwa insisted upon waiting several minutes and then checking the reading again. It was still 180.

After being told to open her eyes, this patient slowly looked about the room and then said, "You know, I was trying very hard to keep you from hypnotizing me. When you told me I would not be able to lower my hands, I did not believe you and I tried very hard but I found my hands were stuck up there in the air and I could not bring them down." I am always suprised when a subject tells me after a hypnotic session that he was trying very hard to resist my instructions. I know this is caused by a popular misconception that the hypnotist is able to overcome the subject's will-power and in that way is able to "control him". If I am alone with a person who has requested hypnotherapy and I see the check-points are predominately negative, I will take a moment and explain that the individual seeking my help must give me his full co-operation and consciously try to follow all my instructions.

Induction technique used: Eye-to-eye technique. The arms being up in the air and the patient finding that she could not lower her arms made this "test" act as an induction technique.

Hypnotic prescription given: "When you go to bed at night and wish to sleep, you will lie on your back, turn your hands palm upwards and then your body will feel heavier and heavier and heavier." Since the patient reported she had a "bad habit of dreaming" she was given a modified version of the hypnotic prescription used for all bad habits. This was as follows: "You will not have as many dreams in the future as you have had in the past. The fact that you have dreams will seem most un-important to you." Since I know it is normal for us all to have dreams and then forget them soon after awakening, I was able to "make a contribution" to this woman's problem by saying, "When you do have a dream in the future, you will find that as soon as you awaken you will completely forget the dream."

Additional History: The receptionist reported that this patient left the office in very high spirits and was actually singing. She called for an appointment the next day and said she had the first night of sound sleep without any dreams, for as long as she could remember and she wanted her blood pressure checked since she felt so much better. The next day the blood pressure registered 186. During the two years following this hypnotic session she was examined three times and on each occasion the blood pressure was found to be at 186. However, Dr. Kashiwa found her weight dropped during this period and she reported feeling much stronger and more rested.

Bad Habit

When using hypnosis for the removal of bad habits, the suggestions should be given in a most casual manner and care must be taken that too much importance be not given to the bad habits to be overcome. The hypnotist must tell the subject that the bad habit will no longer seem important.

Name: Thomas
Age: 23 years old in 1947
Complaint: Desire to overcome an unmentioned bad habit.

History: While attending a party in Hollywood, California I was asked to demonstrate hypnosis. Several days later the person who gave the party contacted me and said that a reporter from one of the metropolitan newspapers wanted to see me. I could not refuse the interview but I did not want any publicity as a hypnotist. When I met the reporter I discovered that he wanted to be hypnotized. I was so relieved, I quickly agreed.

The young journalist asked if I could hypnotize him in order to break him of a bad habit even if I did not know the nature of the habit. I told him I could. Using the eye-to-eye technique I had his head fall against his chest and then his head and chest fell forwards until his shoulders rested on his knees. I then said, "When I count to 'three' you will raise your head and body, with my help, but you will feel as heavy and as tired as you feel now." I then counted to 'three' and put my hand under his brow, but did not make any attempt towards lifting his body and in this way I could see if he was going to wait "for my help" as I had indicated or if he was going to raise his head and body without my help. If he raises his body without my assistance, I consider this to be a negative check-point as far as his being in a responsive hypnotic state is concerned. In this instance, the young man allowed me to raise his body from the bent-over position and I was confident that he would be responsive to my instructions regarding his bad habit.

"You know you have a bad habit which you wish to discontinue", I began. "It is not always possible to completely stop a pattern of behavior which has been established over a number of years. Therefore, I suggest you will find yourself giving in to this habit less and less. This habit will become very unimportant to you and you will very soon realize that you are not so much addicted to this habit as you have been in the past and you will be well pleased and satisfied with the improvement. You will not think of this habit as often in the future as you have been and you will be contented to know that you have been hypnotized and that you now have more will-power and self-control and the ability to slowly overcome the habit."

After giving a few of the general beneficial suggestions as to his having some degree of improvement which would be progressive and that he would notice the improvement and be satisfied with the amount of improvement, I asked him to open his eyes when I counted to 'seven'. He opened his eyes slowly and we consider this to be a final corroborative "check-point" since we know those who have not been hypnotized open their eyes readily and those who have been hypnotized open their eyes more slowly and seem to be trying to orient themself. He grinned and said, "You know, I could hear every word you said, but I sure feel fine and I am pleased that you did hypnotize me. I don't mind telling you that the bad habit I wanted to overcome was masturbation. It seems so very unimportant to me now and so I feel that it will no longer be a problem."

Induction technique used: Eye-to-eye technique.

Hypnotic Prescription given: "You will find yourself giving in to his habit less and less. This habit will become very unimportant to you and you will soon realize that you are not so much addicted to his habit as you have been in the past. You will now have more will-power and self-control and the ability to slowly overcome the habit."

Stuttering

I received a great deal of speech therapy as a child and had the habit of stuttering until I was fourteen years old. Therefore I am extremely sympathetic towards those who have a similar speech problem.

Name: Ernie
Age: 10 years old in 1948
Complaint: Stuttering.

History: I was visiting my parents. A small boy knocked at the door and he seemed to be very nervous and upset when I answered his rapping. He tried to speak but had much difficulty since he stuttered very badly. With a great amount of effort, the boy was finally able to inform me that his mother wanted me to see one of the old books which had belonged to her father. He thrust the volume at me and started to run back to his house across the street.

"Wait", I shouted. "I want to say 'thanks' and ask when you want the book returned."

The youth tried to make some reply but all he could manage was a sputter while his face turned red with embarrassment and frustration. I wanted to help the young boy but I was also aware that I had overslept and friends were due to arrive at that moment to take me with them. I asked him to come inside and sit in a chair and close his eyes when I counted to "three". I explained very quickly that he could speak well if he took the time to speak slowly and carefully. I told him that I once had the same problem but that when I learned to speak with a rhythm I discovered that it was no longer necessary for me to stutter. I promised that his speech would slowly improve and soon he would be able to talk without any difficulty. I asked him to open his eyes when I counted to "seven" and I dismissed the youth, ending a session which lasted little more than one minute.

Five years later I again met the boy and found that he had absolutely no trouble with his speech. He told my Father he was so grateful to me for having "cured" him. All those years I had felt guilty over not having taken more time in treating the lad's problem. I now know the adviseability of keeping the hypnotic session as brief as possible. It takes a great effort for me to control myself and resist the urge to repeat the hypnotic prescription.

However, we have learned that the problem must be treated in the off-handed manner which in Part Two of this book we call "the brush-off technique."

I recall with amusement the response I received a few years ago when I hypnotized at a party a young man who stuttered. This fellow was about nineteen years old and when I asked him to open his eyes after the extremely brief hypnotic session he was greatly disappointed and concerned over the fact that he had heard everything. Apparently he had some pre-conceived ideas about hypnosis which had not been realized.

"I don't believe I was hypnotized", he insisted. "Nothing has happened to me! I could hear everything that you said and I felt completely awake. I don't feel different in any way.. but.. how come.. I am not stuttering?"

Induction technique used: Eye-to-eye technique along with "the brush-off" technique.

Hypnotic Prescription given: "You know that you can speak properly when you are speaking out loud to yourself if you are alone in a room. Actually, you can speak perfectly, if you speak very slowly and carefully. You only stutter when you are nervous or excited and try to speak too rapidly. In the future you will have more self-control and you will speak a bit more slowly and carefully and you will find that you will be speaking more properly. You do not stutter when you are singing. That is because when you are singing, you are speaking with a rhythm. Well, for the next few days you can practice speaking with a rhythm. You can tap your finger on the table and say, 'One, two, three, four, I will speak more carefully and more slowly.' You say each word as you tap your finger and you will be speaking properly. I remember tapping my finger in my pocket when I first learned how to speak with a rhythm. After a few days of speaking in this manner you will soon forget that you once had a speech defect and you will find yourself speaking as well as any of your friends. There will be a gradual improvement in your ability to speak slowly and carefully and you will notice the improvement and you will be well pleased."

Aditional history: This neighbor has remained a close friend since 1948 and has had no difficulty with his speech since the one brief hypnotic session.

Overweight

A condition of overweight can be due to the habit of over-eating and it can be treated, like any other bad habit, with the "brush-off" technique.

Name: Mr. Crow
Age: 51 years old in 1967.
Complaint: Overweight.

History: I was about to attend a meeting of the Torii Oasis Shrine Club of Japan at The Sanno Hotel in Tokyo when I was approached by Mr. Crow who explained that he was a pilot and was about forty five pounds overweight. I agreed to hypnotize him before the luncheon and insisted that one short hypnotic session would be ample. I tried to find a firm chair as I intended using the eye-to-eye technique and finally had to accept an ornate dining room chair. He was a very large man weighing about 240 pounds and he seemed to respond properly when I asked him to close his eyes when I counted to "three". The "brush-off" techniques does not allow for any "tests" and so when his head began to move towards his chest I recited this prescription: "In the future you will have more will-power and more self-control. You will be able to eat the food which you know will give you more strength and energy and you will eat a little bit less of the food which you know contains starch or carbohydrates. You will take a little bit less of the food which contains fats and more of the protein foods like fish and meat. You will enjoy all the food that you will eat but as soon as you start to eat you will lose your appetite. That means you will be unable to complete eating any portion of food that is served to you. As soon as you begin to eat you will feel full and completely satisfied. You will feel that you have had too much to eat and will be unable to eat "second portions" or any "snacks" between meals. As soon as you lose a pound or two you will notice how much your clothes will feel loose and you will have more energy and interest in walking and taking part in sports.

"You will lose just a pound or two each week as this improvement in your weight is going to be slow and progressive. Therefore, you will continue to lose a pound or two of weight each week and you will notice the improvement and you will be well pleased with this gradual improvement which will make you feel healthier and stronger and more alert."

Mr. Crow opened his eyes as I instructed and he slowly looked about him and then asked, "Do you think it worked?"

"Oh yes," I assured him. "You were certainly hypnotized and I gave you a very good hypnotic prescription."

"I could hear every word you said", he informed me, "and I do not feel any different and don't think I was a very good subject. Do you think I should make an appointment to see you again and have you try once more?"

The luncheon was about to begin. In spite of his apparent dissatisfaction I felt that he had certainly been responsive with all the usual "check-points" favorable and so I walked with him to the dining table and once again insisted that he need not worry as he had indeed been hypnotized and we could better evaluate the session after we saw the results.

Mr. Crow was so completely disappointed, however, that he proceeded to voice his dis-satisfaction by telling all those at the table that

I had tried to hypnotize him and I had failed. He spoke to each person present, saying, "Have you ever been hypnotized? I have never been hypnotized. Dr. Furst tried to hypnotize me but he was not able to do it."

After the luncheon he requested another hypnotice session but I refused and told him to be patient and await the outcome of my therapy. He left me with this remark, "I know the names of some other hypnotists in this city so I will get in touch with them and see if they can hypnotize me."

One week later, Mr. Crow called me and insisted that it was most important for him to see me that morning.

"I guess it worked," he admitted. "Just look at me. I lost five pounds this past week and best of all, I feel so full and completely satisfied and I have no interest in eating. My wife has noticed the change. She might make me a cup of soup for supper and I eat some of it and then when she asks me what else I would like, I tell her that I have had enough to eat."

Induction technique used: Eye-to-eye technique with a "brush-off" manner.

Hypnotic prescription given: "You will have more will-power and more self-control. You will have the ability to eat the food you want to eat and you will have the ability to not eat the food you do not want to eat. In the future you will eat a little bit more of the protein foods such as fish and meat as these foods give you needed strength and energy. You will eat a little bit less of the starches and carbohydrates as these foods create the fat in your body. You will enjoy all the food you eat but as soon as you start to eat you will lose your appetite. That means you will be unable to complete eating any portion of food that is served to you. As soon as you lose a pound or two you will notice the improvement in your appearance and feeling of well-being and you will have more energy and interest in walking and taking part in sports. Also, you will have a feeling of accomplishment."

Additional history: Three weeks after the first hypnotic session Mr. Crow complained that he had lost five pounds on both the first and second week but only two pounds during the third week. I told him that it made no difference if he lost five pounds or as little as one pound each week. The important thing was for him to realize that he was losing some weight each week. He then complained that he felt so weak and tired and had a muscular ache in his shoulder. I agreed to hypnotize him to improve this condition. At the end of the fourth week he reported a loss of only two more pounds. This time he asked for hypnosis to improve his memory and his ability as a salesman. Once more, I had to agree. At the end of the fifth week he and his wife reported that he had lost an additional five pounds and that he was eating about one third of his usual intake of food and had begun to learn to Ski. Also, he reported an improvement in his alertness and his flying ability.

However, he came to see me each week and reported a loss of two to five pounds and always had a new reason for another hypnotic session. At the end of seven weeks he had lost about 27 or 28 pounds and I left Japan. I am aware that a patient can become addicted to hypnosis and request additional hypnotic sessions, however, this is the first case I have treated and a situation developed where I found myself hypnotizing the same person on many occasions.

Desire To Stop Drinking

Of all bad habits, excessive drinking is perhaps the most unlikely to respond to hypnotherapy. Very often this problem is brought to the therapist's attention as the result of "third party intervention". This is the unfortunate situation where one party says to the hypnotist, "I would like you to hypnotize that person and cause that person to stop drinking." Of course, this is not likely to result in the feeling of rapport which is so necessary before hypnosis can be induced. However, when the individual comes to the hypnotist and requests hypnotherapy for himself, I am pleased to report the results have been completely satisfactory.

Age: 32 years old in 1958.
Name: Bill S.
Complaint: Desire to stop drinking.

History: Late one evening my good friend, Bill, telephoned to tell me that he had been arrested on a charge of drunk driving. I suggested that he engage a lawyer and he agreed, asking me to recommend someone. I called Alan Selznick, a college classmate who was successful in arranging for my friend to receive a suspended sentence and be placed on probation. I was ready to congratulate Bill on his good fortune when he told me how unhappy he was over the outcome of his trial. "I agreed to stop drinking in public places while I am on probation and I don't see how I can abide by this promise . . . unless you hypnotize me and cause me to stop drinking," he explained.

This close friend had seen me hypnotize several patients and was very much aware of my ability. I knew he would be completely responsive and it took less than a minute for me to induce hypnosis by the eye-to-eye technique and give him the following prescription. "You will have more will-power and more self-control in the future. You can eat what you wish and not eat anything you choose. You can smoke or not, as you choose. You can drink, in the future, if you wish and you can abstain from drinking alcoholic beverages, in the future, if you wish."

Bill seemed perplexed as well as disappointed with my prescription. "I thought you were going to make all liquer taste bad or else tell me that it would be impossible for me to ever swallow any liquer again. Do you think this short suggestion will be enough?"

"It all depends upon your own wishes", I told him. "Do you want to stop drinking?"

"I never want to drink again," he insisted. "But I just thought of something. I have been going to Cocktail Lounges and Bars in order to meet girls. Now, what will I do?"

"These are many places you can meet girls other than Cocktail Lounges and Bars. For example, you can meet many girls in church."

Bill accepted this idea readily, saying, "I promised my Mother, when I left Ohio, I would attend church here in California."

I saw Bill a few weeks later and he told me that he had found it was so very easy to go without drinking and therefore he realized that when he asked for my help he had been mistaken since he had considered himself to be an alcoholic. "However", he concluded, "I now realize that I had been doing all that drinking as the result of a 'habit' and not as the result of a 'disease'. I went to Church as you suggested and met a fine girl and we are going to get married. If anyone offered me a drink right now, I would find it impossible to visualize my accepting. In fact, I would sooner put a handful of dirt in my mouth than take a swallow of beer."

Induction technique used: Eye-to-eye technique.

Hypnotic prescription given: "You will have more will-power and self-control in the future. You will be able to drink or not drink, as you wish."

Additional history: My mother and I attended Bill's wedding and I visit him and his wife whenever I am in the small city where they live. One night Bill came home after a meeting of the Volunteer Fire Department and said, "When I was offered a glass of beer this evening, I accepted and then came home. I wanted to determine if it was possible for me to drink one glass of beer and stop and it was. Of course, the rest of the fellows are still drinking and I guess they will continue drinking for some time. I am so happy to realize that I can take a glass, if I wish."

Here is an entirely different situation although the patient voiced a similar desire to stop drinking.

After a performance at the N.C. O. Club at The Itazuke Air Base in Japan in 1963 I was asked by one of the club members if I could help someone to stop drinking. "Yes," I answered, "I can help a person to stop drinking, if that person wants to stop drinking."

"My friend wants to stop drinking", I was told, but I soon learned that this was another instance of "third party intervention". When I was introduced to the Sergeant who asked for my help, he was antagonistic and insisted that "I try to hypnotize him then and there." I offered to help him if he came to see me the following morning and left. He did come to see me and challenged me, saying, "You did not expect to see me this morning, did you?"

Name: Sgt. Jones.

Age: 38 years old in 1963.

Complaint: Desire to stop drinking.

History: "I don't know if I need hypnosis or not," Sgt. Jones began. "You see, I do not have a problem. Some people drink because they have a problem and that is why they join Alcoholics Anonymous. However, I do not have any problem. I just drink because I do not know what to do with my time. I have a very important classified job and so I do not drink when I am working. But when I finish my work on a Friday afternoon, I do not know what to do with myself and so I go to the N.C.O. club and I start to drink. I drink all night and after the club closes I go into town and I drink for a few more hours until my friends carry me back to the base. When I wake up on Saturday I have a hang-over and there is really nothing to do for a hang-over except have a few drinks and so I go back to the N.C.O. club and drink all day Saturday and all Saturday evening and when I get back on Sunday morning I am so drunk I stay in bed all day Sunday and get to work on Monday with a hang-over and do my work from Monday to Friday without any drinking, but on Friday afternoon, I go back to the N.C.O. club and drink the entire week-end."

I accepted his statement without comment for I knew it would be difficult to establish a feeling of rapport and without this mutual feeling of trust, I could not expect to hypnotize him. Since he indicated that he needed something to occupy his time, I began to mentally consider various possible activities. My first thought was Bowling and then I instantly dismissed that sport for I remembered that often beer and other liquers are served to the bowlers. I decided photography might take him out-of-doors and cause him to travel to the various scenic spots. I decided to suggest to him he would devote his weekends to photographing various places in Japan. Now, for the motivation. I turned to Sgt. Jones and said," Do you have a camera?"

"Oh, yes I have a movie camera and a 35 mm camera I bought at the PX". He assured me. "How long have you been in Japan?' I questioned. "Two years". "Have you taken any pictures in Japan?"

"No I haven't had a chance to take any pictures yet."

Realizing that he needed a motivation, a reason to take pictures, I felt it might be wise to suggest that he would be taking these pictures to send to his family.

"Have you any children" I asked.

"Yes, five girls. Five, seven, nine, eleven and thirteen years old."

"Alright, this is what I will suggest to you, you will go out on weekends, you will take pictures of the many scenic places in Japan, and you will send these pictures to your family. Then your children can take these snapshots to school to show to their teacher and their classmates. Where is your family?"

"Two blocks from here." He said.

"Come here and sit down in this chair." I said as I began the eye-to-eye technique. He offered no resistance, all the check-points were favorable and his respiration changed instantly.

"I want you to know that you are providing your family with the finest educational facilities available in the world by having them here with you overseas. Their school is equipped with the latest educational aids and the finest teachers available in the United States. Your family is receiving the greatest medical protection available in the world because they are your dependents here in Japan. I saw a story in the Stars and Stripes a few days ago about a three year old girl who fell from a second story window and hurt her head. When she was examined, by the doctors on Okinawa, they discovered that she needed brain surgery. Within one hour, the small girl and her father, who was a Sergeant in the Air Force, and her mother were taken to the Kadena Air Base and flown to the Walter Reed General Hospital in Washington D.C. The doctor who performed brain surgery on this girl was the same doctor who would be called upon to perform brain surgery on the President of the United States if it were necessary.

"I want you to know that you are making a great contribution to your family's welfare by 'being there'.

"You will have more will power and more self control in the future. You will be able to spend more time with your family. You will take them on weekend trips, picnics and outings. You will feel stronger and healthier, with a great sense of accomplishment in the future."

Sgt. Jones opened his eyes very slowly. He looked about the room and then said "Yes, I know I was hypnotized, I could feel the difference. I am going to take my family to different cities near here every weekend and I will take pictures of the Japanese shrines and temples and resorts.

"Oh, one thing more" he concluded, "I am going to stop drinking."

Induction Technique used: Eye-to-eye technique.

Hypnotic prescription given: "You will have more will-power and self-control in the future." The other material was designed to give this serviceman some self-respect which he needed so badly.

Additional history: Sergeant Woolsey, manager of the Itazuke Air Base NCO Club, told me a few months later that Sgt. Jones had stopped visiting that club.

CHAPTER THIRTEEN

Prescriptions Used In Emergencies

I first met Dr. Lester T. Kashiwa when I visited the Island of Maui in 1954. He questioned me regarding the various induction techniques I used and repeatedly asked me if I knew of any possible dangers or ill-effects which might result from the use of hypnosis for therapeutic purposes. I told him that I knew of nothing which could be harmful or injurious to the patient. The hypnotic subject is at all times fully awake and is keenly aware of all that is taking place about him and is following the instructions only because he is fully convinced that the hypnotist is sincerely concerned about him and is trying to assist him to become healthier and happier. Therefore, the person in real jeopardy is the hypnotist who might attempt to use hypnosis in a wrongful manner. He would be taking the serious risk of having the patient reject him instantly and later expose him to society.

When I returned to Maui in 1956 to prepare the material for our book, "Case Histories In Hypnotherapy", Dr. Kashiwa and I had more than twenty sessions during which time he recounted to me several hundred of his cases in which he has used hypnosis and we discussed at great length the different techniques which were likely to prove most effective in various instances. Often Dr. Kashiwa would remark, "I used hypnosis in that case because it was so much easier than giving a more conventional anesthesia but actually it was not important for me to have used hypnosis at that time."

Dr. Kashiwa insisted that we should not think of hypnosis as a "cure all" but only as an effective method for giving proper instructions and sometimes it serves to expedite the natural healing processes of the body. We feel that since the greatest value of hypnosis as an anesthesia is the complete absence of the post-operative nausea and other undesireable complaints, it is often enough to prepare the patient for the operation with encouraging hypnotic suggestions and conclude the hypnotic session with a few sentences designed to overcome any of the usual unfortunate after effects of the intended operation. The best use of hypnosis as the anesthesia for an operation is during an emergency, where for one reason or another, the inhalant or other forms of local or general anesthesia can not be given.

Dr. Kashiwa concluded one of his dictating sessions with this remark, "You know, I can only think of one instance where the patient's life was saved by the use of hypnosis. It was when the man fell into the barrel of hot tar."

Burns From Hot Tar

Name: Lee Kato
Age: 29 years old in 1955
Complaint: Burns resulting from his head, face, neck and arms being covered with molten tar.

History: One Sunday afternoon, Dr. Kashiwa was called back to The Maui General Hospital to treat a man who had fallen off his home-made ladder into a barrel of hot tar. It took about fifteen minutes for Dr. Kashiwa to reach the hospital and when he arrived he found the man standing in the center of the receiving room as the upper part of his body and most of his clothing was covered with the sticky black tar.

Instantly, Dr. Kashiwa saw that the patient was in great pain from the burns and as a re-action from his accident, was in great danger of dying from shock. The "shock technique" is often discussed by students of hypnosis but can never be practiced. The physician put down his handbag. Put his two arms out-stretched in front of his body and leaped towards the man as he shouted at the top of his voice, "Sleep".

All in the room were suprised to see the man slump to the cement floor. Dr. Kashiwa knelt and spoke into the man's clean ear, "When I count to 'three' you will go way down. I will remove your pain and you will feel nothing." The ward boys were sent for a container of gasoline and at the doctor's instructions they used it to remove the tar from the patient's head, face, neck and arms. As the tar was removed, the skin peeled off with it. Once the tar was completely removed, Dr. Kashiwa's concern was the considerable possibility of infection since the tar and also the gasoline as a cleansing agent was not likely to be completely sterile and free from germs. He asked that raw alcohol be brought to him and he thought, this extreme method for cleaning the exposed raw flesh will certainly be most painful and impossible for any person to withstand. He regretted the necessity which compelled him to take this form of preventive action. He expected the injured man to scream and perhaps pass into unconsciousness. However, throughout the cleaning process, instead of writhing with painful agony, the prone man lay very still, breathing heavily and completely indifferent to the raw alcohol which was applied generously to his body.

Pleased that it had been possible to clean the injured tissues so quickly and efficiently, Dr. Kashiwa gave the man lengthy suggestions as to his recovery and for the removal of any possible after-effects. The man was then transferred to one of the hospital rooms where he slept well that night and remained for only three days. The man insisted that he was at ease and had no pain or discomfort. Best of all, he had no vomiting or loss of appetitie. The burned parts of his body healed perfectly and there were no scars.

Induction technique used: Shock technique.

Hypnotic prescription given: "When I count to 'three' you will go way down and I will remove all your pain and you will feel nothing." The post-hypnotic instructions dwelt upon his having a good appetite and sleeping well and resting properly in any position in which he was placed.

Menstral Cramps

Name: Mary Lynn
Age: 20 years old in 1955
Complaint: Menstrual cramps.

History: Dr. Kashiwa had this interesting experience once when a young lady came to see him because of her migraine headaches. While making a preliminary physical examination, Dr. Kashiwa noticed the patient seemed to be very pale and he decided to have a blood count taken. He idly reached for one of her fingers and pricked it with the surgical instrument designed for that purpose. When the young lady saw the drop of blood appear on her finger tip she fell to the floor and began to have what almost amounted to an epileptic seizure.

Dr. Kashiwa asked her what was the trouble and she said she was having some menstrual cramps. He asked her if she was having her menses and she said, "No, it has just passed." The doctor then asked her why she thought she was having menstrual pains and she explained that the symptoms were the same.

Dr. Kashiwa knelt to the floor where the patient was writhing in what was obviously great pain and said, "By the use of hypnosis, I can cause your pain to melt away. I want you to look at my eye and very quickly we will relieve this condition."

At that point the patient vomited, covering the front of his white jacket and his trousers and his shoe. He knew this was caused by her great pain. However, partly in anger over being soiled in that manner and partly due to his recognizing that she was on the verge of shock, he threw his two hands at her face, hypnotically and shouted, "Sleep". She stretched her body out at that command and seemed to go into a very deep trance.

When he had first knelt beside the young lady he felt her pulse and it was very weak. Once her respiration rate increased he noticed that her pulse was also stronger. Seeing that she was relaxed and at ease, he slowly changed his jacket as his nurse came in and cleaned up the floor.

Dr. Kashiwa asked her many questions regarding her experience with menstrual pains. He soon realized that she had been having an abnormal amount of pain and discomfort each month. He gave her several instructions to insure a normal flow without any further difficulty. He also mentioned that she would find some degree of improvement in her general condition and that she would sleep well and feel healthier and stronger in every way.

After the young lady was awakened and helped to her chair by the doctor and his nurse, she explained that she had been told by her mother that Dr. Kashiwa could remove the pain of headaches by hypnosis and that was why she had decided to visit him. She had not mentioned having had such severe menstrual cramps because she had been under the impression that all women suffered from the same type of seizures as she had just been experiencing on his examining room floor.

Induction technique used: Shock technique.

Hypnotic prescription given: "You now realize that this was not a real case of menstrual cramps as you are not having your menses at this time. These pains you experienced were caused only by the sight of the small drop of blood. You will understand in the future that your passing of blood during your menstruation period is a natural and normal function and it will give you no further bother or discomfort. In the future you will be able to sleep well at night and you will get more rest during the day. You will notice an improvement in your appetite and as you eat the proper food you will notice an improvement in your health and you will feel stronger in every way."

Additional history: Dr. Kashiwa saw this patient on the street about three months later and when he questioned her about her health she reported that she had had no further headaches or menstual pains. Dr. Kashiwa wanted to compare her blood count with the laboratory report he had from her first and only visit but realized it might be detrimental to invite her to return for further examination.

Sometimes the situation might be classified as an emergency and yet the "shock technique" would not be appropriate.

Dilation and Curettage Operation

Name: Mrs. Evans
Age: 31 years old in 1955
Complaint: Emergency dilation and curettage operation.

History: Dr. Kashiwa was called to the hospital late one evening. He found his patient bleeding profusely and her hemoglobin was 90 grams. An emergency dilation and curettage operation was indicated but the surgical anesthesiologist refused to administer the anesthetic because the patient had just eaten a very heavy supper. There was the danger of vomiting and he was advised to wait about six hours until the food

108

was out of the stomach and then it would be safe to give the patient an anesthetic.

The idea of going back home and returning in the small hours of the morning was unpleasant and certainly an immediate operation would be best for the patient. Dr. Kashiwa decided to use hypnosis as the sole anesthesia but he felt it would be wise to inform the patient that he was going to combine a little hypnosis with a spinal anesthetic as he knew she had some past experience in receiving spinal anesthetics. Since she was a large woman, weighing 180 pounds and 5 feet 10 inches in height, he decided to wait until she had climbed upon the hospital cart before he began to induce hypnosis.

The induction technique used when the patient is on the hospital cart is very similar to the eye-to-eye technique but since the patient is sitting with her legs outstretched on the cart, it is necessary for the hypnotist to support her body with his right arm as he points towards his left eye with his left forefinger. The patient's hands are turned upwards and are placed well back on her lap, near her body and she is told that "her head and her body will feel heavy and tired". When she fell back as instructed, he put one arm up in the air and told her she could not move or lower it. With her hand straight up, she was wheeled through the corridors and into the operating room.

The patient was placed in the proper position to receive a spinal anesthetic. He washed her back with a small amount of tap water since he knew he had no intention to insert the needle into her body. He explained to Mrs. Evans that since she was hypnotized it was possible for him to give her the spinal anesthetic and she would not be able to feel the needle.

This lady was then turned over and put in the usual lithotomy position and scrubbed and was told that she would feel completely numb. Dr. Kashiwa explained that she was not to feel numb everywhere, just in the portion of her body where he would be operating. He pressed a needle lightly against her arm and she said, "Ouch". He quickly pressed this same needle in the area where he was going to operate and she said nothing and apparently felt no pain.

Dr. Kashiwa said, "I am now satisfied that the anesthetic is working perfectly." He went through the entire procedure of dilating which is usually the most painful part of the operation. There was no change in the patient's facial expression. It took him about fifteen minutes to perform the scraping and then she was transferred back to the hospital cart and returned to her room.

Since the lady was so large it would have been necessary to call several attendants to assist in moving her from the cart to her bed. Realizing that she was fully awake, though hypnotized, Dr. Kashiwa told her that the effect of the spinal anesthetic would disappear when she dropped her arm at his command. When the arm dropped, the patient began to move her legs and so she was asked to open her eyes at the count of 'seven' and then she jumped, unassisted into her bed, saying, "This spinal ansesthetic is wonderful. The last time I had one, it was different."

Ordinarily, the after effects of an operation like this one is that the patient has pain in her back and can not move her legs easily and often has difficulty urinating. In this instance the recovery was rapid with no after effects.

Induction technique used: Hospital cart technique. This technique is often used by Dr. Kashiwa for childbirth and operations.

Hypnotic prescription given: "You are going to receive a spinal anesthtic under hypnosis and therefore the anesthetic will be easier to control and also I will be able to give you the spinal without your feeling the needle. Your back has been washed and you have received the anesthetic painlessly so it will make part of your body numb. Not all your body, just the part where I am going to operate. You can feel the needle if I touch your arm but you feel numb between your legs."

Hypnosis should be suggested by the attending physician. When it is offered to a patient by a stranger, it is not likely to be as acceptable.

Fractured Jaw

Name: Joeseph
Age: 13 years old in 1956.
Complaint: Fractured jaw.

History: One night, while Dr. Kashiwa was dictating his case histories to me, he received an emergency call. I went with him to his office as he examined a thirteen year old boy who was brought in with a compound fracture of his lower jaw. I stood by, feeling so useless, as Dr. Kashiwa began to prepare the huge X-ray machine in his office. Hesitantly, I asked if I should hypnotize the lad and Dr. Kashiwa said, "That is a good idea".

However, when I asked the lad if he wanted to be hypnotized, he shook his head from side to side. I stepped back as Dr. Kashiwa passed by and said, "Don't be a fool. Dr. Furst gets $25 to hypnotize a patient on the Mainland and here you can get it for nothing as he will do it as a favor for me."

I waited a moment and then said to the boy, "How about it?" This time he nodded his head in agreement.

The "swaying technique" seemed to be the easiest to use as I did not want to move the boy and yet I wanted to take a minimum amount of time. I did not feel that the feeling of "rapport" was strong enough to insure my being successful with "the silent technique." I told the boy to stand with his feet together and his hands at his side and to look at my left forefinger which I held about two feet in front of his face. I asked him to close his eyes at the count of 'three' and he followed my instructions. I then told him that he would not sway or fall until I was standing behind him and I would tap him on his shoulders so that he would realize when I was directly behind him.

I placed myself behind him and then tapped him on his shoulders, telling him I was now ready to catch him. I told him I would count to 'three' again and this time he would feel like he was standing on the deck of a small boat that was being gently rocked by the waves. I told him the movement of the boat would be very gentle and he would feel his body swaying a little bit forward and a little bit backward. His body did sway as I had promised and then I told him the swaying would become greater and greater until he fell against my body. The swaying did increase but when it appeared that he might fall backwards, he moved his right foot back a bit and was thus able to regain his balance.

One great value to this induction technique is that it can be tried over and over without losing it's effectiveness. Therefore, I insisted he put his feet together as before and this time I insisted his legs would become firm and stiff and impossible to bend or move. This time he swayed promptly and fell back against me after he lost his balance. His breathing changed then so I proceeded to tell him he would feel calm and confident that the doctor would be able to treat him properly and that he would recover from this accident quickly. I then gave him the usual prescription I give to all students; suggesting that they have a greater interest in their studies, the ability to concentrate upon what they hear in their classes and what they read in their textbooks and that their memory will improve so that they will be able to easily recall what they have heard and what they have read. Thus I was able to tell the boy that his school work would improve because he would find it easier to do his lessons in the future.

By that time, Dr. Kashiwa was ready to take the X-ray pictures so I assisted the boy on to the X-ray table and continued to talk to him and assure him that he could remain very still and calm. When Dr. Kashiwa developed the films he told me that they indicated it would be possible to bandage up the boy's head for that evening and a dentist would be able to wire the boy's teeth together in the morning. Dr. Kashiwa then asked me to assist him as he wanted to make a fluoroscopy of the boy's jaw. This would have normally been painful, but I continued to speak to the boy and he followed all the instructions without hesitation. When Dr. Kashiwa was ready to put the temporary bandage on the boy, I awakened him with the final assurance that he would be comfortable when his teeth were being wired together by the dentist.

Induction technique used: Swaying technique.

Hypnotic prescription given: "You will feel most calm and you will be confident that the attending physician will be able to care for you properly and you will make a speedy recovery from this accident. Also, you will have a greater interest in your school studies and you will be able to concentrate properly upon what you read in your text books and upon what your teachers say in your classes. Also, your memory will improve so you will find it easier to recall what you have heard and what you have read and you will be able to use this information when you must apply it to your assignments and when you are asked questions in your tests and examinations."

Additional history: The following evening, the boy's mother called Dr. Kashiwa to say that she had seen a light burning in her son's room after she had gone to bed. She opened his door slightly, thinking perhaps he was in pain as an after-effect of his accident. However, she was amazed to find him sitting at his desk with his books open and busily doing his homework. I met the dentist who attended the boy and he reported that as he wired the teeth together he stopped several times and asked the boy if he was hurting him. Finally the boy remarked, "There is no use in your asking me if I feel any pain. I was hypnotized last night and I feel no pain at all in my jaw, so go ahead with your work."

Sometimes the patient requests hypnosis as a form of emergency treatment while the physician considers the operation to be routine.

Fear of Operation

Name: Mrs. Williams
Age: 29 years old in 1961
Complaint: Fear of operation.

History: Mr. Julius M. Klein is with the Los Angeles County Human Relations Commission. He has been a valued friend for many years and I am always pleased when called upon to help him with his official duties or other interests. He asked me to meet one of his fellow workers, a Mr. Williams, who told me his wife was about to have an operation and needed my help as she was so greatly upset and fearful.

I met Mrs. Williams a few days later and was informed that she was going to enter a hospital that afternoon to prepare for a Hemorrhoid operation. I confess that I felt disappointed when I learned the nature of the forthcoming operation as it sounded so trivial.

There were several interested spectators so I decided the eye-to-eye technique would give me the greatest opportunity to evaluate the patient if she did not respond readily. Fortunately, all the "check-points" were favorable and she quickly appeared to be hypnotized as her head fell upon her breast and her breathing became noticeably heavier and more rapid.

The hypnotic session was brief, not because I felt the "brush off technique" adviseable, but simply because I could think of little more than this short prescription. "I want you to look forward to this operation", I began. "I want you to realize that this is the best time that you can possibly have this operation performed. It is wise for you to have this condition corrected before it becomes serious. It is now something that can be treated readily and easily and your body will respond properly and will recover very quickly."

When Mrs. Williams opened her eyes as I counted 'seven' she smiled and then thanked me warmly. "I feel so much better now," she explained, "but you will never realize how much I dreaded the thought of having that operation. This is something I have never told my husband or my physicians. However, I have a great fear of cancer. Both my father and my mother died of cancer and I have been aware that they were not told the truth when it was first discovered that they had cancer. In each case they were told that they were being taken to the hospital for a minor operation and they never recovered. Therefore, I have been thinking that I might have cancer."

When I realized the need Mrs. Williams had for re-assurance, I was happy that I had agreed to meet her and as I thought back, the simple prescription was adequate but I felt a compulsion to expand and amplify it once I learned the true and genuine nature of Mrs. Williams' problem. "Yes," I began, "as I said before, this is the best time for you to have this operation. If the doctor finds that you have a cancer, it is best for him to know this as soon as possible. Today, it is possible to treat and cure cancer, if it is found early enough. On the other hand, if you do not have cancer, as I feel certain, it is best for this operation be performed and you can then be assured that your body is once more healthy and strong and you will be able to properly perform your duties in the future as a wife and mother."

Induction technique used: Eye-to-eye technique.

Hypnotic prescription given: You will look forward with anticipation to this operation and you will realize that this is the best time that you can possibly have it performed. Your condition can now be corrected easily and your body will respond properly and you will recover very quickly.

Additional history: I met Mr. Williams several weeks later and reported that his wife was in the best of spirits as he drove her to the hospital. "In fact, she sang all the way and jumped out of the car when we arrived," he said adding that she had made a rapid recovery from the operation.

Extraction of Infected Tooth

Sometimes the therapist is apprehensive before an operation because he is aware of some unfortunate after-effect which might occur.

Name: Sgt. Smith
Age: 38 years old in 1967
Complaint: Infected tooth.

History: In November of 1967 I was invited to present my course in Rapid Induction Techniques of Hypnotherapy at the U.S. Army 249th General Hospital in Tokyo. The nine hour course was divided into three three-hour sessions and given to a small group of physicians and dentists who met with me once a week. After the second session, Dr.

George Sardina formerly of Los Angeles, California, expressed his disappointment over the fact that he had not been given the opportunity to practice any of the induction techniques that had been described. Before returning to my hotel, I insisted that he practice the eye-to-eye technique in my presence and we were both pleased to find that he was able to induce hypnosis with this method.

The following morning he was summoned by Dr. Henry Kluka, another student in that group, for consultation. Sgt. Smith had been flown to Tokyo from Vietnam in order for him to have an infected tooth removed. Dr. Kluka learned from Sgt. Smith's medical record that he had previously suffered a mild coronary thrombosis and therefore had received several doses of an anti-coagulant. Dr. Kluka told Dr. Sardina that he hesitated to extract the infected tooth as he might not be able to stop the blood flow if any bleeding occurred and there was a possibility the patient might bleed to death. Hypnosis was considered since the previous evening I had reported that when a dental surgeon severs a vein or artery he can cause the bleeding to stop by hypnotizing the patient and saying, "When I count to 'three' the bleeding will stop."

The situation was explained to Sgt. Smith who readily gave his consent to the use of hypnosis and he responded promptly when Dr. Sardina applied the eye-to-eye technique for the second time in his life. The tooth was removed easily and without any bloodshed.

Induction technique used: Eye-to-eye technique.

Hypnotic prescription given: "You will relax and the left side of your face will go to sleep and you will feel comfortable and rested."

There are rare instances where normal anesthetics can not be used. Such an emergency was reported in the Seattle, Washington Post-Intelligencer of May 27, 1958.

Perforated Stomach

Name: William Young
Age: 51 years old in 1958

Complaint: An ulcer had perforated his stomach. Peritonitis had set in. He was bleeding internally and the hole in the ulcerated stomach had to be sewn up quickly or the patient would bleed to death.

History: William Young, a pit recorder of the Jones and Laughlin Steel Corp., was brought to the Aliquippa Hospital near Pittsburgh, Pennsylvania on April 28, 1958. Clutching his bloated stomach he was obviously in great pain as sweat poured from his ashen face. When the nurses lay the man on the examining table he began to choke and gag and his face turned blue. An upper respiratory infection made breathing impossible unless he sat up. Besides the arrested tubercular condition and upper respiratory infection he was weakened by gall bladder and kidney ailments.

The surgeon and attending anesthesiologist found that his lungs could not take the traditional inhalant type of anesthetic and a spinal injection might knock out some of his respiratory muscles and he would cease to breathe altogether. After Mrs. Young gave her consent to the use of hypnosis, 40 cc's of novocain was injected in the sitting patient's abdomen. Hypnosis was induced quickly and the vertical incision was made.

It was discovered that the perforation was on the anterior wall of the stomach so the surgeon had to flip out the stomach, stitch up the hole and replace it in the abdominal cavity. Often under deep anesthetic a patient will breathe so deeply he will push the stomach wall, making it difficult to hold the contents of the open abdominal cavity in place. In this instance, the anesthesiologist asked the patient to breathe shallowly to facilitate the closing of the abdominal cavity. He was then allowed to resume deep breathing after the surgeon had the retention stitches in place.

Induction technique used: The patient was asked to stare at the overhead lights in order to produce eye strain. After he was told to close his eyes he was told that he would feel like he was sitting in a soft easy chair.

Hypnotic prescription given: "You will feel like you are floating away around the world on a soft, billowy cloud. Floating, floating, floating. You can hear us talking and can follow our instructions but you will keep your eyes closed and feel very relaxed."

Additional history: The surgical team shaved twenty minutes off the usual operating time for similar operations since they were able to proceed so easily with the patient controlling his breathing. Forty minutes after the first incision the seated patient was wheeled out of the operating room. He was completely relaxed while holding his body constantly in the desired position. He reported that he heard everything spoken and felt the sensation of knots being tied in his stomach but absolutely no pain.

Substitute For Morphine

Dr. Owaki asked me to come out to his hospital in Tokyo and hypnotize a patient from Taiwan who was in the terminal stages of cancer of the liver. The patient understood English and had many friends in America.

Name: William Chan
Age: 69 years old in 1963
Complaint: Cancer of the liver.

History: Dr. Owaki informed me that the patient had been receiving large doses of morphine several times a day and continued to complain regarding his pain. I entered the patient's room with Dr. Owaki and Dr. Ishizuka. I saw that it would be most difficult for the man to look into my eye from his prone position in the center of the large bed so

I extended my right forefinger and held it directly in front of his face as I commanded him to look at it.

"When I count 'three' you will close your eyes," I began.

"No, I will not close my eyes," he stated firmly.

Of course I was suprised by this unexpected refusal. However, the "brush off" technique seemed wiser than trying to find out the reason for his reply and perhaps have him agree to follow my instructions when a greater degree of rapport was established.

"You may keep your eyes open," I agreed, "but you will listen to my voice and you will keep your eyes on my finger."

"When I count 'three'," I continued, "your head and your body will feel heavy and tired and then with each breath your chest will become heavier and heavier. One, two three."

Instantly his body seemed to sink deeper in his mattress and his feeble gasping for air indicated that he was aware of the heavy feeling I had promised. I then deliberately extended my right forefinger and middle finger and slowly drew down his eyelids while his stare remained fixed. I then gave him the prescription we use for those who wish to go to sleep easily.

When he opened his eyes as instructed, he smiled and asked me to visit him when he was back in his home. He remained in Dr. Owaki's hospital for several additional weeks and never again complained of pain or discomfort.

Induction technique used: I had intended using the "eye-to-finger" technique but modified it slightly by allowing him to keep his eyes open and then caused induction by stating firmly and simply that his body would feel heavy and tired and become heavier with each breath he took. Closing his eyes so deliberately was somewhat of a shock and gave him an added feeling of helplessness.

Hypnotic prescription given: "In the future, when you wish to rest or sleep you will close your eyes and lie on your back with your palms upward and then you will feel your head and your body grow heavier and heavier and heavier."

Additional History: Before the hypnotic session the patient had complained constantly to his family and physician regarding his pain and asked for information concerning the exact time when they expected him to die. After the one session he indicated that he was looking forward to his recovery and return to his house and he assured his wife and children that he was comfortable.

Dr. Owaki had prepared Mr. Chan and his family for our meeting and the conditions were ideal. In contrast, I might say that in the following case, the conditions seemed to be the most unfortunate if no impossible. from a hypnotist's point of view.

Removal of Pain

Name: Rick Decker

Age: 19 years old in 1967

Complaint: Severe pain which was not removed by regular injections of morphine.

History: I had been visiting my friend, Allen Lundberg, in Pasadena, California. It was past eleven and as my friend cautioned me to drive carefully, young Rick Decker came in the front door and expressed his pleasure at seeing me. He was renting a bedroom in the house at that time and had heard his friend speak of my books and lectures. He had been wanting to meet me, he explained, since he needed my help with a personal problem.

"Can you use hypnosis to help me read"? he implored. "When I was fifteen years old I entered Junior High School but my teacher told me that I could not read and so I dropped out of school and got a job in a garage. Now that I am engaged to get married I think it would be better for me to learn how to read and perhaps help my children with their studies when they come home from school".

This was certainly a new problem for me to consider. I did not know if he did have a "psychological block" as he insisted or if there were other reasons for his professed inability to read. When a person asks me to help him stop smoking I feel it is enough to induce hypnosis as quickly as possible and deliver the appropriate prescription. However, in this case I felt it would be wiser to find out more about the young man and his background and explore the possible causes for his complaint before I would be able to prepare an effective prescription. I therefore, promised to return the following Tuesday with the understanding that I would be able to devote several hours to consideration of his problem.

I arrived promptly for this appointment and my friend informed me that Rick had been in an auto accident two days previously and was now at The Los Angeles General Hospital. When I visited him the next morning he was obviously in great pain since he had suffered a fractured skull, a broken knee cap, a fractured pelvis and a fractured ankle.

"I am in great pain!" he shouted in reply to my foolish question as to his condition. "I want you to talk to the doctors here and I want you to tell them to give me more morphine. They give me some morphine shots every four hours but it is not enough. I still have a lot of pain and they can't seem to understand that I need more morphine."

At this point I was filled with regret over my decision to postpone the hypnotic session he had requested at our first meeting. If, on that occasion, I had induced hypnosis and offered to have further consultations it would have been very simple for me to instruct him to relax and rest and I would have felt confident as to his responce. However, there had been no attempt to induce hypnosis at our first encounter and his present situation was not suitable for any of the induction techniques I prefer to use at the initial hypnotic session. He was in a ward with twenty others. Many of his room mates had arms and legs in traction and several television sets were tuned in to various channels. Hospital attendants moved from bed to bed and there were other distractions such as announcements coming from the public address system and the arrival and departure of friends and relatives visiting the other patients of that ward.

Although I expected to achieve very little, I felt compelled to make an attempt at hypnosis as I wanted him to realize my sincere concern over his unfortunate situation. I was standing at the foot of his bed and so I could hardly ask him to look into my eye or at my extended forefinger. I did remove my eyeglasses and I asked him to look at the tip of a pencil I withdrew from my pocket. It is necessary to have the patient focus his attention somewhere before hypnosis can be induced.

"When I count to 'three' you will allow your eyes to close and your eyeballs will roll upwards and you head and body will feel heavy and tired," I said. As I counted I saw an immediate change in his respiration and his head slowly dropped to his chest which then began to rise and fall in the labored manner so often appearing in the early stages of hypnosis.

"You are concious of this heavy feeling in your head and body and in the future when you wish to rest, you will close your eyes and then your head and body will feel heavy and tired as it does now and you will feel relaxed and more comfortable," I stated as that was the only prescription which I felt appropriate for his condition.

When he opened his eyes in response to my request I told him I would return the next day and I left.

"You may think I am crazy," were the first words he spoke when I returned, "but as soon as you left here yesterday my pain disappeared and I have been comfortable ever since. When the nurse offers to give me morphine I tell her to forget it and everyone is so surprised."

Induction technique used: Eye-to-pencil technique which is so similar to the eye-to-finger technique.

Hypnotic prescription given: "In the future when you wish to rest you will close your eyes and turn your palms upwards and then your head and your body will feel as heavy and as tired as you feel right now."

Additional history: I visited Rick several times each week thereafter and when his leg was put into a plaster-of-paris cast I handed him a newspaper article and asked him to read it aloud to me.

"I can't read this," he protested, "there are too many big words."

"Do the best you can," I insisted, "I want to see how well you can read."

He read the first few words easily and then halted abruptly saying, "I can't read the next word, it is too hard."

"Can you sound it out?" I asked and he then pronounced the word, syllable by syllable. Some words he had to repeat two or three times before recognizing them. However, he did succeed in reading the entire article without any help or prompting from me.

"Now we have learned something," I said. "You can read. You can not read very well, but you can read. All you need is practice. The only way you can learn to swim well is by going into the water and practicing and the only way you can learn to read well is by practicing."

I then handed him another newspaper article and instructed him to practice reading the article several times so that he would be able to read it to me when I returned the next day. He read the assignment without much difficulty, explaining that he had spent many hours sounding out the longer words, syllable by syllable.

I visited him once upon his discharge from the hospital and he showed me a magazine he had purchased from the neighborhood drug store and he read several paragraphs to me. He told me that his fiancee helped him practice reading each evening.

Loss of memory is unfortunate but when an accused murderer can not recall his actions on the night of the crime and his attorney insists that this information is imperative for his defense, this presents a situation which can be described as an emergency.

Loss of Memory

Name: Paul LeClair Conrey
Age: 28 years old in 1958.
Complaint: Loss of memory due to being drunk on the night of the crime.

History: Paul Conrey was arrested in San Diego, California and was accused of having beaten to death a Mrs. Maria Martin on the night of October 1, 1958. He answered the description of a man last seen with the victim and the police reported that tire marks found at the scene of the crime matched the tires on Conrey's car.

The defense attorney, Harold D. Cornell, pleaded with Conrey, asking him to reveal his movements that evening in order for an alibi to be established or at least for his actions to be explained and perhaps justified. The only reply he received was that Conrey could remember nothing and since this gave him absolutely no defense against the overwhelming circumstantial evidence it seemed inevitable that a death sentence for first degree murder would be the outcome. In desperation, the attorney asked my friend, Richard N. Mikesell to hypnotize his client in order to jog his memory.

Mikesell tied a short length of string to Conrey's right forefinger. A red marble was attached to the string and this formed a pendulum which the hypnotist explained would swing from right to left if the answer to his question were "yes" and the marble would swing forward and back if the answer were "no".

Conrey seemed dubious when this form of hypnotic questioning was explained to him in his cell in the San Diego County Jail. He closed his eyes as a slight hypnotic state was induced and the first question put to his was, "Did you kill Maria Martin?"

The pendulum moved from side to side. Paul Conrey opened his eyes, pulled the string from his finger and hurled the marble into a corner of his cell, shouting, "I'll be damned if I will let a marble decide if I am going to be found guilty of committing a murder!"

It was decided that automatic writing would allow Conrey to answer questions with freedom of expression and opportunity for clarity with all pertinent details that might be recalled. A petition was then filed with Superior Court Judge John A. Hewicker asking for permission to conduct the hypnotic questioning and it was denied.

The matter was then brought to the Fourth District Court of Appeal and Judge Hewicker's decision was sustained. The petition which begged to be allowed to conduct this hypnotic experiment early in December of 1958 was finaly brought before the California Supreme Court in May of 1959 and the unprecedented order gave permission for the defendent to be questioned under hypnosis. The high court said that the results would not be admitted as trial evidence but could be used by the defense in preparing it's case.

Once this authorization was granted the hypnotist and attorney returned to Conrey's cell. After Mikesell had induced a slight hypnotic trance, Conrey was asked various questions by his lawyer and he wrote out the answers, slowly and at great length. This hypnotic session lasted two and a half hours.

As a result of this session, the following story evolved. Paul Corney said that he had been fired from his job as a warehouseman on the morning of October 1, 1958. He was told to return that afternoon for his paycheck. He went to a bar and drank several beers. He cashed the paycheck in a liquor store and purchased a pint of gin. He went to the coffee shop where Maria Martin worked and asked her to go for a ride in his car, offering her one hundred dollars to compensate for the loss she would receive in her salary as a consequence of going home at that time.

He drove with Maria Martin to a place near Mt. Hope Cemetary and she then challenged him to show her the one hundred dollars he had promised. He placed the five twenty dollar bills on the dashboard and she then left the automobile with the explanation that she had to relieve herself. Conrey said that he then finished drinking the pint of gin and closed his eyes while waiting for her to return. He opened his eyes a bit later to find the twenty dollar bills on the dashboard but the woman was gone. He therefore started the motor and with much difficulty was able to maneuver the car around and drove back to his home in Clairemont.

After much consideration Conrey came to the conclusion that after drinking the last of his pint of gin he dozed off for a minute or two and mistakenly supposed that he had slept for a longer period of time and actually he drove away without realizing that Maria Martin was squatting behind his automobile.

This was essentially the defense offered to the jury by Conrey's attorney and he was found guilty of involuntary manslaughter and given a sentence of from one to three years in jail.

Induction technique used: A slow induction technique with the understanding that he would be able to hear all questions and write out his answers.

Hypnotic prescription used: You will be able to answer all the questions that will be put to you at this time.

Additional history: Since we know that a person who is hypnotized will very often give incorrect information we can understand why some people doubted this story. We do know that a person who is hypnotized will say the things that he thinks the hypnotist wants him to say. His primary desire is to please the hypnotist if he can do so without harm to himself.

CHAPTER FOURTEEN

Prescriptions For the Aged

Difficulty in sleeping is a common complaint amongst the aged. When a husband tells me his wife has insomnia, I am apprehensive since this might be a situation of "third-party intervention". When the patient asks for help, I have found this is more often a sincere request.

Insomnia

Name: Dr. Suzuki
Age: 60 years old in 1964.
Complaint: Insomnia.

History: Following my lecture at The International House in Tokyo, in July 1964, Dr. Suzuki reported that he had been taking sleeping pills every night for the past ten years.

Induction technique used: Armchair technique.

Hypnotic prescription given: "When you go to bed at night, you will lie on your back, you will turn your hands palm upwards and your head and your body will feel heavy and tired. And then your head and your body will get heavier and heavier and heavier. The medical people who have been doing research in this matter, have discovered that if you go to bed at night and keep your eyes closed and do not sleep at all, you will receive eighty per cent of the value that you would have received had you been sleeping." This second sentence is designed to remove some of the "fear-of-failure" regarding sleep. There are so many people who do not sleep at night for no reason other than this fear that they might not get a full night's rest.

Additional history: A few months later, Dr. Suzuki handed me a note saying· Thank you for your hypnosis. I am sleeping well every night without any pills.

When Mr. Cruz came to me in Manila and asked me to hypnotize his wife in order to cure her of insomnia, I am pleased that I insisted

123

the husband understand something regarding the induction of hypnosis and our concept of "check-points".

Insomnia

Name: Mrs. Cruz.
Age: 57 years old in 1964.
Complaint: Insomnia

History: I was in Manila in 1964 to give my course in "Rapid Induction Techniques of Hypnotherapy". My manager called me one morning to tell me that a man wanted to have private instruction. He had agreed to pay double fee and would like to see me that day in my hotel room. When Mr. Cruz arrived, he was very businesslike and said "Never mind wasting your time teaching me hypnosis. I want you to hypnotize my wife. Your manager tells me that you will not accept patients but that each person who enrolls in your course is entitled to bring a patient for you to hypnotize as part of your class demonstration. Therefore, I would like you to consider that I have enrolled in your course and I want you to accept my wife as our 'class demonstrator'.

"My wife has had insomnia for over twenty years. We are very wealthy. I have taken her to hospitals in London, Paris, Berlin and Rochester, New York. The doctors have examined her and treated her but she is still unable to sleep nights. Now I feel what good is our money if my wife cannot enjoy a good night's rest. I am a very active man, we own several factories. I am busy from the minute I wake up till I come home at night. When I go to bed, I fall asleep instantly. When I am awakened by the alarm at 7:00 my wife says, 'I did not sleep a wink last night'.

"I say that I will make my breakfast and go to work and I ask her to remain in bed in hopes that she might be able to get some sleep after I am gone. I know I am happy to be so busy with my various interests and activities. At night my wife complains that she is so tired because she had been unable to sleep. I want you to hypnotize her."

I told Mr. Cruz I would accept his proposition but, I would like to tell him something regarding the induction techniques that are taught in my course. I knew this would give him a better understanding of my situation when I tried to treat his wife. I suspected that this was indeed a true example of "third-party-intervention".

I briefly discussed our theories regarding the induction of hypnosis; demonstrated the "eye-to-eye" technique and Mr. Cruz responded nicely. At the conclusion of the hypnotic session, he agreed that he had been able to hear me at all times but had also felt his head grow heavier and fall against his chest, and his arms had felt rigid and unyielding as I had promised. I explained the various "check-points" of this induction technique to him and he promised to bring his wife to meet me the following morning.

Mrs. Cruz came to my room in the Filipinas Hotel. She indicated by her manner that she had little faith in hypnotists and hypnosis.

I arranged a firm chair in the center of the room so that she would be facing her husband during the hypnotic session. Therefore, it was apparent to him that she looked away from my face when I pointed to my right eye and said "Look in this eye".

Mr. Cruz saw that his wife did not close her eyes when I asked her to do so and he noticed that she opened her eyes after I had closed them myself. As each "check-point" was negative in this instance, I looked at Mr. Cruz and he nodded to indicate his awareness. After using the "dry-lips" technique, there was a slight change in Mrs. Cruz's respiration. I gave her the usual prescription for insomnia.

Mrs. Cruz opened her eyes readily when I counted to "seven" and stood to indicate she had had enough of our foolishness. Mr. Cruz shook my hand warmly as followed his wife out the door.

Mr. Cruz called the next morning and asked me to eat lunch with him. "When I got home last night," he began, "I decided to determine how much effect your hypnosis would have on my wife. Therefore, when we went to bed I propped myself up and began to read a financial repoi t from my company. My wife complained that she would not be able to sleep while the light was on and I agreed that it was unfortunate that I had to read that report but I promised her the light would be turned off in a short while. I urged her to lie on her back and turn her palms upwards as you had instructed. She did this and instantly went to sleep.

"I made a note of the time since I wanted to give you an exact report. I decided to remain awake and tell you exactly how long she had slept. When I finished the financial report I started to read a magazine. When I finished reading the maganize I started to read a novel. I watched my wife constantly and noticed that she did not change the position of her body and her breathing remained deep and rhythmical. After five hours I fell asleep while in a sitting position. I awakened at six o'clock this morning, stiff and uncomfortable due to my awkward position. My wife was still sleeping in the same position.

"I got out of bed, turned off the alarm clock which had had no chance to sound since it was earlier than my usual waking time and I took a warm bath. It was after seven and my wife still slept. I went down to the kitchen, prepared my breakfast and then decided it would be best to wake her and tell her I was leaving for my office.

"When I awakened her at seven thirty she opened her eyes, looked around and seeing I was fully clothed said, "I see you are about to go to work. Well, I did not sleep one wink last night."

"As usual, I insisted she remain in bed to get a little rest and now I want you to know how happy I am. I realize that she does enjoy talking about her condition of insomnia. Now that I know she can sleep my conscience is clear and relieved."

Induction technique used: Dry lips technique.

Hypnotic prescription given: When you go to bed, you will lie on your back and close your eyes with your palms turned upwards. Then your head and your body will become heavier and heavier and heavier. With each breath you will notice yourself getting heavier and heavier.

Sometimes it is best to not inform a patient if there is a slight deviation in their blood pressure readings.

High Blood Pressure

Name: Mrs. Murakami
Age: 53 years old in 1955
Complaint: High blood pressure.

History: Mrs. Murakami seemed to have gone through her menopause with little difficulty except her blood pressure was too high. Dr. Kashiwa had a brief hypnotic session with her during one of her regular visits to his office and he told her that her blood pressure would return to normal and that it would trouble her no longer and she would have no reason to be concerned about it in the future.

She did not return to his office and so when he saw her on the street several months later, he stopped her and she told him how well and fit she had been. One year later she applied for a new Life Insurance Policy and she returned to Dr. Kashiwa's office for the medical examination. He found her to be in splendid health and he told her this, adding that her blood pressure was still a little high, but nothing serious.

Mrs. Murakami asked to know what the reading was and he told her it was 130/80. She demanded to know the normal figure for her age. Dr. Kashiwa told her that her blood pressure should be 120/70 and the difference was slight and certainly nothing to worry about. However, he could see she was upset so he invited her to return the following week and he promised to check her blood pressure again.

When she returned the following week, she complained that she had been dizzy with headaches and restlessness and palpitations. Dr. Kashiwa decided to use the "brush off technique". He told her that he wanted to have another hypnotic session with her but since he was very busy, she would have to wait. After half an hour he called her into his office and he began by saying, "I will have you come in now, although I have just one minute to spare, I know we will not need any more time."

Dr. Kashiwa found her to be most responsive and within a few seconds she appeared to be in a deep hypnotic state. He told her simply that her blood pressure would return to normal and this would clear

126

up her condition of dizzyness. When he asked her to open her eyes after this extremely short session she was very happy and thanked him and said that she could feel instantly that she had been "cured". He than took her blood pressure reading and found it to be 120/70.

Induction technique used: Eye-to-eye technique with the "brush-off technique" approach.

Hypnotic prescription given: "Your blood pressure will drop down to normal and this will clear up your condition of dizzyness.

Additional history: During the past twelve years Dr. Kashiwa has been seeing this lady in the neighborhood stores and on the street and she reports that she is well with no return of the headaches, dizzyness and other unpleasentness which Dr. Kashiwa felt was not due to her blood pressure that was just a bit higher than normal but was due entirely to his unfortunate statement that her blood pressure was a bit too high.

In contrast to this application of the "brush-off technique" we have the case of one of Dr. Kashiwa's earliest hypnotic patients.

Overwork and High Blood Pressure

Name: Mr. Saito
Age: 52 years old in 1954
Complaint: High blood pressure.

When Mr. Saito first came to Dr. Kashiwa in December of 1954 he was on the verge of a nervous breakdown. Other doctors had given him various types of sedation but in spite of all medication his blood pressure was 210/110 and he complained of being restless, unable to sleep at night, no appetite, a chocked up feeling in his throat, palpitation, with a general feeling of weakness and often breaking out in a cold sweat. Mr. Saito became so ill he was forced to stay at home, away from all his business activities and that was when he asked Dr. Washiwa to try hypnosis since apparently, all other forms of treatment had failed.

Dr Kashiwa tried using the "eye-to-eye technique" on Mr. Saito but found he was not responsive and it did not appear possible to put him into a hypnotic trance of any depth. Dr. Kashiwa felt that he had failed to hypnotize him since he never responded to any "tests". However, after several sessions, which were so disappointing from Dr. Kashiwa's standpoint, Mr. Saito reported a most remarkable improvement. The blood pressure finally fell back to normal and Mr. Saito returned to his various business activities, but followed Dr. Kashiwa's advice and adopted a slower, less strenuous routine.

Induction technique used: Eye-to-eye technique.

Hypnotic prescription given: There will be some improvement in your condition. You will be able to sleep better and you will rest easier and your will find your blood pressure will gradually go down and you will feel healthier and stronger as each day goes by. The improvement will be slow and gradual, but you will notice the improvement and be well pleased to realize that you are recovering from this illness.

Additional history: I arrived in Wailuku, Hawaii in 1956 to gather together the material for our book, CASE HISTORIES IN HYPNOTHE-RAPY. Dr. Kashiwa asked me if I felt there were some persons who could not be hypnotized. I insisted that all persons who can under-stand simple instructions can be hypnotized. Dr. Kashiwa then told me he was anxious for me to meet Mr. Saito for several reasons. He wanted me to hear from the patient the wonderful results from the hypnosis and also he wanted me to see if I could hypnotize Mr. Saito and put him into a hypnotic trance of some depth.

I found Mr. Saito very unresponsive to several of the induction tech-niques. However, eventually he did go into a fairly deep trance and almost fell out of his chair. When I asked Mr. Saito to open his eyes he told us that he realized then what it felt like to be deeply hypnotized and he could feel the difference between the trance I had induced and the light stage of hypnosis under which Dr. Kashiwa had given him the general beneficial suggestions.

"However," he concluded, "I do want you to know that the sugges-tions Dr. Kashiwa gave to me practically saved my life and relieved all of my symptoms and lowered my blood pressure even though he gave those suggestions to me while I was in a very light stage of hypnosis".

In Tokyo I once found it very difficult to hypnotize a person who had high blood pressure.

High Blood Pressure

Name: Mr. Tanaka
Age: 47 years old in 1963
Complaint: High blood pressure.

History: Mr. Takeo Omori, president of the Tokyo Hypnotism and Psychological Association, came to see me at the Dai-ichi Hotel when I returned to Japan from Korea in February of 1963. He asked me to present a series of three lectures for his group at The International House in Tokyo the following month and I agreed. After the first lec-ture, Mr. Omori told me some of the physicians in his association were anxious to see me demonstrate my techniques on one of their patients and I readily agreed to have them bring someone to the second lecture for me to hypnotize for demonstration purposes.

Mr. Omori brought Mr. Tanaka, a business associate, to be the patient at the second lecture. I saw Mr. Shibata, editor-in-chief of the Tokyo and Osaka Mainichi Daily News, in the audience and he had with him one of the staff photographers from his newspaper. Since I was interested in having the demonstration photographed I decided to use as the induction technique the "'silent technique" as this is perhaps the most dramatic and photogenic of all the induction techniques. When I touched Mr. Tanaka's temples and exerted a slight pressure backwards, he swayed, then stumbled back and regained his balance. After several attempts I realized that Mr. Tanaka was too old for this or any other falling technique and I had to ask him to sit in a firm chair as I resorted to the more orthodox "eye-to-eye technique". I was relieved to find Mr. Tanaka responded promptly to this technique which was, of course, better suited for him.

One of the physicians in the room took Mr. Tanaka's blood pressure and reported it to be 224/120. I then told Mr. Tanaka he would relax and feel more comfortable and find it easier to breathe and then his blood pressure was found to be 180/120. The photographer took a picture at that time and Mr. Shibata wrote an article about the demonstration and it appeared in The Mainichi Daily News on March 16, 1963. **Induction technique used:** Eye-to-eye technique after the silent technique proved to be inappropriate.

Hypnotic prescription given: You will relax and feel more comfortable and find it easier to breathe. With each breath you will notice some degree of improvement in your condition. The improvement will be slow and gradual, but you will notice the improvement and be pleased to find that you will be recovering from your illness.

Additional history: The Tokyo Hypnotism and Psychological Association has arranged for Mr. Tanaka to have his blood pressure recorded each month and for a period of five years it has remained 180/120.

Arthritis

Name: Charles W. Preston
Age: 63 years old in 1946
Complaint: Arthritis

History: Mr. Preston is a retired school principal and a close personal friend. He had seen several of my hypnotic demonstrations and one day he asked me to hypnotize him to relieve the arthritic pains in his shoulder. I promised to hypnotize him the following week. I felt that I needed some time to learn more about arthritis and determine the proper prescription.

I went to see Dr. Lennox in San Bernardino, California. He was a retired physician who had used hypnosis to a limited extent in his own practice. Dr. Lennox explained that arthritis is a condition caused by a calcium deposit between the bones and this calcium can cause an irritation when the affected arms or legs are moved. Rather than discuss the pain or try to remove the calcium deposit I was told that it would be best for me to suggest to my friend that a slight amount of lubrication would be secreted every time he moved his arm. This lubrication would cover the calcium deposit and tend to reduce any pain or discomfort.

A few days later I saw Mr. Preston at a small party. He asked me to hypnotize him then and there as the pain in this shoulder was so great, he was unable to enjoy the party. It hardly seemed like the proper time or place but I had no choice but to agree. I knew that I had had some success in using hypnosis for therapeutic purposes at very noisy parties in the past partly because under such circumstances the patient realizes he will have to concentrate intently in order to hear the suggestions given to him and frequently I have felt that helped account for the satisfactory response.

I sat on the arm of an occasional chair and my friend faced me as he sat in an overstuffed chair. "Please close your eyes and listen to the sound of my voice," I began. Just then one of the guests came up and asked me to dance. I turned and told her that I would join her in a minute but out of the corner of my eye I could see Mr. Preston and he had opened his eyes and winked at the person who was sitting next to me.

I realize now that the brief interruption caused my friend to become very self-conscious as he sat with his eyes closed in the midst of our friends and he tried to cover his embarrassment by playfully winking and thus showing the onlookers that the hypnotic session was "all in fun". However, at the moment my only reaction was to feel that my friend was taking advantage of me since I knew I had given much thought to his complaint and it appeared to me that he had asked for my assistance only so that he could laugh at me and tell others that he had not been hypnotized.

Determined to end the session as quickly as possible, I said, "I went to a doctor who told me that your pain is caused by a calcium deposit between your bones. Therefore, in the future, every time you move your arm a drop of lubrication will be secreted and that lubrication will cover the calcium deposit and remove the possibility of your having any pain or discomfort. When I count to 'seven' I want you to open your eyes." I then counted from one to seven very quickly and left the group. I did not want to give him the chance to tell me that he felt he had not been hypnotized. I knew that I had made no attempt to induce hypnosis after I saw his sly wink and had given him the suggested prescription only because that presented the easiest and fastest way to end the session. After the party, Mr. Preston said, "I don't think you were able to do very much this evening, but I hope you will try again when we have more time and can arrange the proper conditions."

Two days later this friend telephoned and said, "You know, the hypnotic session must have been more effective than we thought. I have not had any arthritic pains for the past two days and I am beginning to think you have cured a condition that has been bothering me for the past few years."

Induction technique used: It had been my intention to use the eye-to-eye technique but when I saw him wink, I decided to end the session as quickly as possible and that was one of the first instances where I used what later was to be known as the "brush-off technique."

Hypnotic prescription used: Arthritis is caused by a calcium deposit between your bones. In the future, every time you move your arm a drop of lubrication will be secreted and that lubrication will cover the calcium deposit and remove the possibility of your having any pain or discomfort.

Additional history: I have continued to see Mr. Preston frequently during the past twenty two years and he tells me that he has had no re-occurance of the arthritic pains.

I have used this prescription on innumerable occasions and always with great success. It is comforting to know that I have an effective prescription for arthritis. Bursitis is different, of course, and I had only one experience with that ailment.

Bursitis

Name: Mr. Pete Pooleon
Age: 66 years old in 1960
Complaint: Bursitis

History: My neighbor, Mr. Pooleon developed this pain in his right arm and he was informed by his physician that he had Bursitis and that they could offer him nothing to ease the pain. Mr. Pooleon's son was a medical student at that time and it was agreed that the boy and I would study the anatomy text books before deciding upon the proper wording of the hypnotic prescription to be administered. We spent one hour reading about Bursitis but could think of nothing which could be incorporated in the prescription specifically for that ailment. Therefore, it was decided to use the same hypnotic prescription which had been so effective in overcoming the pain of arthritis.

Mr. Pooleon responded to the "eye-to-eye technique" and was given the short prescription. At the end of the session he went to sleep in his bedroom. The next morning his wife asked him how he felt and he said, "Just fine." Of course, she was pleased and said, "Well, I guess the hypnosis worked."

"Nothing of the kind," he replied. "The hypnosis had nothing to do with it. I could hear everying that was said and I knew everything that happened. The pain just went away by itself."

Induction technique used: Eye-to-eye technique.

Hypnotic prescription given: Every time you move your arm a drop of lubrication wil be secreted. This will help to make you more comfortable. There will be a slow, gradual improvement, but you will notice the improvement each time you move your arm and you will be well pleased to notice your recovery.

Additional history: Mr. and Mrs. Pooleon are good friends and I am pleased to say that there has been no re-occurance of this complaint during the past eight years.

Recovery From Prostate Gland Operation

Name: Charles W. Preston

Age: 82 years old in 1965

Complaint: Removal of post-operative problem resulting from Prostate gland operation.

History: A few years ago, my friend Mr. Preston entered the Queen of Angels Hospital for a prostate gland operation. His recovery was rapid and he was told that he could return to his home as soon as he was able to learn how to control himself and keep from wetting his bed while he slept. The attending physician reported that this was something that had to be learned after an operation like this one and it was likely to take several days.

After one short hypnotic session Mr. Preston slept the entire night without incident and went home the next day.

Induction technique used: Eye-to-eye technique

Hypnotic prescription given: You will have more will-power and self-control. When you go to sleep tonight you will sleep very well and when you wake up in the morning you will feel refreshed and pleased to find that your bed will be dry. You will be able to control yourself, while you sleep, in the future just as well as you were able to control yourself before you had this operation.

Additional history: Mr. Preston is now 85 years old and has had no problem of wetting the bed since the brief hypnotic session.

CHAPTER FIFTEEN

Prescriptions For Sexual Problems

Very often sexual problems stem from a "fear of failure". Therefore it is important to use the "brush off" approach with a brief prescription that either promises a return to the sexual ability that the patient once enjoyed or an indication that there will be some improvement as to his ability to perform more properly in the future.

Premature Ejaculation

Name: Charles Duvall
Age: 45 years old in 1947
Complaint: Premature ejaculation

History: While sailing from New York to London in the summer of 1947 Mr. Duvall told me that he had the serious problem of premature ejaculation. He explained that he was a professor of French in a Woman's university and found that his young teenage students would often indicate an interest in having sexual intercourse with him. He explained that when he found himself in bed with an extremely young person he became stimulated very quickly and invariablly was embarrassed to find himself unable to exert any control over his emotions and suffered from the frustration of premature ejaculation. He requested that I hypnotize him and make him able to continue with the sex act as long as he desired.

I explained that it was not wise to make such extravagant promises but I did agree to hypnotize him with the understanding that there would be some improvement. I found him very un-responsive to the eye-to-eye technique and he later explained that this was due to the fact that he did not understand English very well. I moved him from the chair to the edge of his bed and when I stood over him and told him that his head and body would feel heavy and tired, he fell back into a slight hypnotic trance.

Induction technique used: Sitting on bed or low bench. (See Chapter Five in Part two of this volume.)

Hypnotic prescription given: In the future you will have more will-power and greater self-control. Also you will feel an increase in your power of endurance to the extent that you will be able to reach one or more satisfactory climaxes. In the future you will be well satisfied with the amount of time you spend in the sex act and will feel less concerned as to when you have an ejaculation.

Additional history: When I asked Mr. Duvall to open his eyes, he rose from the bed, shook my hand vigorously and said, "Thank you very much for removing a great burden from my mind. I won't have to worry about that problem any longer since I know now I can continue for a second time if I should ever ejaculate prematurely again."

Several years later a young man came to me in Tokyo with an almost identical problem but he described it as a loss of sexual power.

Loss of Sexual Power

Name: Joe Brown
Age: 32 years old in 1959
Complaint: Loss of Sexual Power

History: Joe Brown located me at The Dai-ichi Hotel in Shimbashi after reading about my lecture tour in The Tokyo Mainichi Daily News. He told me that he was the son of exiled White Russians who had lived in China and Japan for more than thirty years. He had been educated in Japan and spoke the language fluently. While attending one of the leading universities he had many experiences with the Japanese girls who were his classmates and he constantly was flattered as to his sexual ability and power.

In fact, it was often a matter of concern with them that it seemed impossible for him to satisfy his sexual desire. He insisted that it was possible for him to continue the sex act indefinitely and on several occasions had girls ask him to stop so that they could recover from the exertion. When he was thirty years old he went to the United States and found the girls there indifferent to his physical attractions and unimpressed with his sexual ability. The compliments and flattery that had been showered on him by all his bed partners of Japan were omitted and this caused him to develop a sense of inferiority which he hoped would vanish once he returned to the orient. However, when he did return to the scene of his earlier sexual adventures he found that he had lost much of his sexual power. He found it difficult to maintain an erection and sometimes seemed unable to become aroused sexually once he was in bed. Penetration was often awkward and sometimes, impossible. With effort he would sometimes reach a sexual climax but was aware that the words of praise were no longer forthcoming.

Induction technique used: Eye-to-eye technique

Hypnotic prescription given: In the future you will find yourself concerned about giving sexual pleasure and excitement to your bed partner.

You will be interested in getting her greatly aroused since you realize that you can do so many things that will stimulate and delight her. You will speak to her regarding her charms and tell her how much you enjoy being with her. You will have the same sexual strength and power in the future that you had before you visited the United States. There will be a great improvement in the enjoyment that you will derive from your sexual activities.

Additional History: Two days later Joe Brown came to see me and this time he seemed very happy. He said that he had been with a girl friend the night before and found that he was able to perform in the same manner that he could recall from his University years. "I realize now it was all in my mind and there was actually nothing wrong with me," he declared. I knew that there had been something wrong and the something wrong had been caused by his self-consciousness and fear-of-failure but felt it best for him to forget so easily his previous unhappiness and feeling of being inadequate.

When I sailed from New York to London in 1947 I met a young High School boy who expressed a tremendous fear of being seasick. I tried to reassure him and finally offered to hynotize him and remove any uneasiness or discomfort if he should become ill. One hour later I met the boy in the corridor of the ship and he looked very sick. He said he had been looking everywhere for me as he need me to hypnotize him and remove the seasickness which was bothering him.

He was extremely pale and his brow was covered with perspiration but I found the situation amusing. I insisted he follow me up on the deck and I pointed to the skyline of New York City. I explained that our ship had moved from one pier to another and we were still in New York harbor. The lad admitted our ship might not be at sea but he insisted he was very ill and he pleaded for me to hypnotize him immediately. I could see his discomfort was a reality so I spoke to him briefly and when he opened his eyes he smiled and thanked me for having "cured" him.

Later that week I hypnotized the boy several times as I demonstrated hypnosis for some of our fellow passengers. One day he asked if I could use hypnosis to help him overcome the habit of bed-wetting and I told him I was sure I could.

Enuresis

Name: Ralph Stapleton
Age: 17 years old in 1947
Complaint: Bed-wetting

History: I hypnotized the boy and he appeared to be in a deep state. I told him he would stop his habit of wetting the bed and he agreed, while in the hypnotic state, to follow these instructions. The next morning, however, he reported that in spite of the hypnotic instructions I had given, he wet his bed as usual.

I insisted upon having another hypnotic session and I took great care to proceed slowly and deliberately and I gave him repeated "tests" in order to assure myself regarding the depth of the hypnotic state I had induced. All indications were most favorable and the boy responded nicely to my suggestions, even to his having amnesia and not remembering what had been said or done during the trance. I felt this was certain proof he would obey the post-hypnotic suggestions I had given him that he would wake up during the night, if it became necessary for him to relieve himself.

Again, the following morning, the boy reported my treatment had failed and he had wet his bed as usual. This I could not understand. I felt the boy had every reason to follow my suggestions and I was certain he had been in a very deep hypnotic state and I believed him when he promised, while hypnotized, to follow the instructions I had given.

One of our fellow passengers was a physician who had introduced himself to me and had expressed a desire to discuss with me the use of hypnosis in his medical practice with consideration as to it's uses and possible dangers. I sought out the doctor and told him of the boy's problem and that I had failed to help in spite of my sincere efforts.

This doctor explained that the medical term for the boy's complaint was enuresis and that it was sometimes caused by a sexual problem such as sex frustration or a sex guilt complex. He said, "If we could question the boy, while he was hypnotized, we might be able to learn the cause of his having this habit and then it might be easier to prescribe a cure."

I assured the doctor that I could put the boy into a deep hypnotic state and we could then question him and I was sure he would answer our questions. The doctor agreed to visit the boy as he said the possibility of questioning and treating a person in an hypnotic state would be a new experience for him.

The boy was somewhat embarrassed when I brought the doctor down to his stateroom but he agreed to allow us to question him after he had been hypnotized. I gave the boy several "tests" and I was pleased to see that the physician was greatly impressed to observe the ease with which I was able to hypnotize the youth. Both the questions asked and answers given were surprising to me so I shall attempt to reproduce them him, from the notes I made at that time.

Dr. "Do you have the habit of masturbating?"
Boy. "No."
Dr. "Do you masturbate to some extent?"
Boy. "No."
Dr. "Do you ever masturbate?"
Boy. "No."
Dr. "Why not?"
Boy. "Because I don't want to be an idiot."

Dr. "Why do you think masturbation will make you become an idiot?"

Boy. "That is what my mother told me."

Dr. "Have you ever masturbated?"

Boy. (Pause) "Well, yes, I guess once."

Dr. "Did you enjoy it?"

Boy. "No, it was hard."

Dr. "What was hard?"

Boy. "It was hard to masturbate."

Dr. "Why did you do it?"

Boy. "I wanted to see what it was like."

Dr. "What was it like?"

Boy. "It was terrible and I am never going to do it again."

Dr. "Have you ever had any sexual experiences with girls?"

Boy. "No and I never will."

Dr. "Why do you say that?"

Boy. "Because it is disgusting."

Dr. "Why do you think it is disgusting?"

Boy. "Because I know."

Dr. "How do you know?"

Boy. "I saw."

Dr. "What did you see?"

Boy. "My father."

Dr. "Do you mean you saw your father have sexual intercourse?"

Boy. "Yes."

Dr. "Who with?"

Boy. "My mother."

Dr. "Did this happen in your house?"

Boy. "No."

Dr. "Where did it happen?"

Boy. "Hotel."

Dr. "Were you in the same room with your parents?"

Boy. "No."

Dr. "Where were you when you saw them?"

Boy. "Next room."

Dr. "Do you think about sex very much?"

Boy. "No."

Dr. "Do you ever dream about any sexual activity?"

Boy. "No."

Dr. "Do you ever dream about having sexual intercourse?"

Boy. "No."

Dr. "Have you ever had a sexual climax while sleeping?"

Boy. "No."

Dr. "Have you ever awakened with an erection of your sex organ?"

Boy. "No."

Dr. "Do you ever have an erection of your sex organ during the day?"

Boy. "Yes."

Dr. "Frequently?"

Boy. "No."

Dr. "Once in a while?"

Boy. "No."

Dr. "Very seldom?"

Boy. "Yes."

Dr. "Where do you have the erection of your sex organ?"

Boy. "In school."

Dr. "Do you intend to get married?"

Boy. "Yes."

Dr. "Do you intend to have sexual intercourse with your wife?"

Boy. "No."

Dr. "Why not?"

Boy. "Because it is disgusting."

Dr. "Do you want to have children?"

Boy. "Yes."

Dr. "Do you realize that you will have to have sexual intercourse in order to have children?"

Boy. "Yes."

Dr. "What do you think about that?"

Boy. "It is disgusting."

Dr. "Do you realize that you wet your bed at night?"

Boy. "Yes."

Dr. "Why do you do it?"

Boy. "I don't know."

Dr. "Do you want me to help you stop wetting the bed?"

Boy. "Yes."

Dr. "Did you know that you wet the bed at night because you have a lot of wrong ideas about sex?"

Boy. "No."

Dr. "Would you believe me if I told you which of your ideas about sex were wrong?"

Boy. "Yes."

Dr. "Do you know that I am a doctor?"

Boy. "Yes."

Dr. "I have a son about your age and what I am going to tell you now is what I would tell him because it is the truth. Do you believe me?"

Boy. "Yes."

Dr. "A ten year old boy can get the wrong idea about things when he sees something he does not understand. Have you read any books about marriage relations between a husband and wife?"

Boy. "No."

Dr. "I will give you the names of some books you should read. Will you read them?"

Boy. "Yes."

Dr. "Sexual relations between husband and wife are not disgusting and you will realize that when you read and understand some of the books I will tell you about. The important thing now is for you to understand that the proper sexual relations are not disgusting. Do you understand that?"

Boy. "Yes."

Dr. "Did you know that when a man does not masturbate or have sexual intercourse it is normal for him to have an emission of his sperm while he sleeps?"

Boy. "No."

Dr. "Do you realize that you may have had many such emissions of your sperm while you slept and did not know it?"

Boy. "I don't know."

Dr. "Did you know that many men wake up in the morning with an erection and it has no sexual significance at all?"

Boy. "No."

Dr. "Many men do wake up in the morning with an erection due to the fact that they have to empty their bladder. Did you you know that?"

Boy. "No."

Dr. "Do you know that now?"

Boy. "I guess so."

Dr. "I am going to suggest that you wake up with an erection in the morning. Will you do that since it will signify that you must visit the toilet and empty your bladder and nothing else?"

Boy. "Yes."

Dr. "Do you realize you have been wetting your bed in order to hide the fact that you have been having emissions of your sperm while you slept?"

Boy. "I don't know."

Dr. "If that is the real reason, are you willing to stop?"

Boy. "Yes."

Dr. "I want you to understand and believe me when I tell you that it is perfectly normal for you to have emissions of sperm while you sleep."

Boy. (Silence)

Dr. "If you have night emissions in the future you won't mind?"

Boy. "No."

Dr. "If you have to empty your bladder during the night you will wake up and visit the toilet, won't you?"

Boy. "Yes."

Dr. "If you ever start to wet your bed in the future you will wake up. Do you understand?"

Boy. "Yes."

Dr. "You will empty your bladder before you go to sleep and in the morning when you wake up. Do you understand?"

Boy. "Yes."

Dr. "If you wake up in the morning with an erection, it will mean only that you have to empty your bladder and so you will promptly go to the toilet and relieve yourself. Do you agree?"

Boy. "Yes."

Dr. "Do you have some new ideas about sexual relations?"

Boy. "Yes."
Dr. "What do you think about sex?"
Boy. "I don't know."
Dr. "Will you read some books to get a better understanding?"
Boy. "Yes."
Dr. "Do you realize that you have a great deal to learn about sex?"
Boy. "Yes."

The physician then asked me to awaken the boy from the hypnosis and we were both surprised to see how much time the questioning had consumed. When the boy opened his eyes he said he felt well rested but could not remember anything that had happened. I suspect the self-induced amnesia was due to the fact that the discussion had been embarrassing and therefore it was something he preferred to forget.

Induction technique used: Eye-to-eye technique.

Hypnotic prescription given: You will wake up with an erection in the morning. It will signify only that you must visit the toilet and empty your bladder. If you have night emissions of sperm while you sleep, in the future, you will not mind. If you ever start to wet your bed in the future, you will wake up. You will empty your bladder before you go to sleep at night and in the morning when you wake up.

Additional history: The next morning the boy reported that he had awakened during the night and discovered he was urinating in his bed. Of course, he promptly went to his toilet. He said this was the first time he could recall having awakened during the night.

The following morning the boy proudly told me that he had awakened with an erection and had hurried out of bed in order to visit the toilet and empty his bladder. He said it was only after he had finished dressing that he suddenly realized he had not wet the bed that night. For the remaining ten days of the voyage I was to hear a similar report as to the dry condition of his bed and so we both concluded that he had overcome the irksome habit at last.

In the twenty years since, I have evolved a more direct approach. I feel it is best to eliminate all questions. I simply assume that a boy or girl under twelve is wetting the bed as the result of a habit, often brought about by the parents constantly telling the child what he must not do. The unfortunate compelling force behind negative instructions. When I am told that a teenage boy or girl is wetting the bed, I give them a prescription designed to remove some of the guilt feelings a child might have regarding masturbation.

Bed Wetting

Name: Tomas Johnson
Age: 17 years old in 1962
Complaint: Bed wetting

History: My friend, Marc Cohen of Stockton, California asked me to give a program of hypnotic demonstrations for his favorite charity, The Stockton Orphanage. The lady in charge of this institution asked to see me when I arrived in her city. She told me that the boys and girls in the orphanage were all wards of the court and she tried to arrange foster homes for them whenever possible.

She had found a foster home for one of the older boys who was about to enter his senior year in high school. However, she could not complete the transfer of the boy from the orphanage to this family since the boy was in the habit of wetting his bed each night. A psychologist had been consulted and he suggested psycho-analysis as a possibility but his offer of reducing his standard fee of $1,000 to $500 was still far beyond her meager budget and only a grant from the Governor would make such a medical charge feasable. She asked me to hypnotize the boy and I did.

Induction technique used: Silent technique as described in Chapter Four of Part Two of this volumne.

Hypnotic prescription given: I want you to understand that your body is now developing from childhood to manhood and you are becoming aware of your sexual organs and capabilities. There are things you can do at this time which will make it possible for you to become more effective as a husband when you get married. Every young person discovers that it is possible to stimulate and excite himself to the extent that he reaches a sexual climax. This can be done quickly or slowly. In the future you will have more will power and more self control and you will try to learn how to control your sexual activities to the extent that your partner will receive the greatest possible pleasure. You will give consideration to being in various positions and to doing things that will make your sexual activities exciting for the person you love.

You will go to the toilet before you go to sleep at night and when you awaken in the morning you will find your sex organ in an erection. This will indicate to you that your bladder is full and you must go to the toilet to relieve yourself. This has no sexual significance at all. You will have more self-control in the future and you will find that you can control yourself at night, when you are asleep, as you are able to control yourself when you are awake. If it should become necessary for you to empty your bladder during the night, you will wake up and then go to the toilet before returning to your bed and going back to sleep. You will also have a greater interest in your studies, you will concentrate more intently upon what is said in your classes and what you read in your text books and your memory will improve so that you will be able to more easily recall what you have heard and what you have read. There will be a slight improvement in your school work, but you will find the improvement to be progressive, you will notice this improvement and you will be pleased.

Additional History: Three weeks later I received a letter of thanks from the director of The Stockton Orphanage. She told me that Thomas Johnson had completely stopped wetting his bed from the time when I hypnotized him. After one week of careful inspection of his bed sheet it was decided that he could be placed in the foster home that was willing to accept him as a member of the family during his senior year in high school.

Some people might hesitate to use the above prescription which seems to encourage the practice of masturbation. I have found that a permissive attitude towards masturbation is the most effective way to control this normal activity. The act of masturbation can never be as harmful as the unfortunate consequences of sex-guilt which is fostered by foolish fears and admonishments against excessive self-stimulation.

Masturbation

Name: Howard Adams
Age: 20 years old in 1960.
Complaint: Desire to control excessive masturbation.

History: This is but one of the dozens of instances where college and university students have come to me saying, "I realize that all young men masturbate to some extent and that it is not harmful when performed in moderation, but in my case, I feel that I tend to do this too often and I know it is making me week and I am too tired to do any of my school work because of this."

Induction technique used: Eye-to-eye technique

Hypnotic prescription given: In the future you will have more willpower and more self-control. You will be able to masturbate as often as you wish and you will do so with the intent of increasing your sexual power and ability.

We can give some consideration to the most common sexual problem suffered by married woman in this country and also the most common sexual problem suffered by married men. Medical research indicates that married women most often complain to their physician or marriage counselor that they do not fully enjoy the sexual activity they have with their husband. They report that the sexual intercourse more often leaves them with a sense of frustration rather than a feeling of fulfillment. The most common sexual problem amongst married men is premature ejaculation and it is easily seen that these two are inter-related.

It takes the average woman a period of several minutes or more before she is fully aroused while the average man is able to perform the sex act almost from the instant that he disrobes and enters his bed. Very often these men have a past history of masturbation and a desire to keep this activity secret has caused them to develop a pattern of rapid stimulation with the ultimate climax occuring within a period of less than two minutes. Since the goal in masturbation is the selfish relief gained from the release of tension, the instant of ejaculation becames the terminal point with the immediate loss of sexual interest and desire. Sometimes a period of remourse and shame would occur steming from a mistaken idea that masturbation was somehow indecent or improper or immoral. Anyway, their mental attitude caused them to develop a pattern of behavior which resulted in their having a sexual climax as quickly as possible and then a period of reaction or impotence.

The average woman has built up a sex fantasy that her husband will be constantly full of sexual desire for her and anxious to make love to her the entire night. The married woman must overcome a defense mechanism which her parents and friends created as they taught her during her childhood and early adolescence to beware of sexual intercourse. Therefore, once she is psychologically "set" for this activity she maintains a sustained interest for a longer period of time. In order to be more successful as a bed partner it would be wise for a young man to practice masturbation with a purpose. His goal should be to acquire a greater degree of control over his emotions and by changing his position from time to time he can learn to prolong this activity so that ultimately she will be responsive and then he will find his interest will be directed toward stimulating and exciting her more and more until they both reach the limits of their endurance at almost the same instance. During masturbation the young man should give consideration to the various ways he can indicate his desire to please and satisfy while making every effort to control his mounting passion. Sexual activity becomes more exciting when it is performed with an air of spontaneous impulse. The man should take the active role and demand variety so that the female will feel a sense of accomplishment when she succeeds in causing him to achieve satisfaction.

You can learn to shift your attention and pause occasionally if you find yourself moving with too much compulsion. You can develop various techniques which you will find satisfying and will allow you to prolong the sex act. Knowing that this development is designed for the benefit of the recipient of your affection will cause you to feel that this activity is for the ultimate pleasure of your partner and much more significant than just a brief moment of self-gratification.

Since you will have more will-power and self-control you will vary the time and place that you choose to masturbate so that it does not become a simple routine matter but actually a deliberate course of training for your increase of the power of manhood.

Additional history: I saw Howard Adams two weeks after our brief hypnotic session and I was anxious to hear if he had any improvement to report. However, I know it is unwise for the hypotherapist to question the patient and so I said nothing. He asked me to see his mother and explain to her that he had been too busy to write. He then lowered his voice and said in an earnest tone, "Since I saw you last I met a wonderful girl and I have been so busy dating her and thinking about her that I have been too busy to masturbate."

I have been asked to help young men overcome the habit of masturbation many times since I hypnotized Thomas, the newspaper reporter, in 1947 (see Chapter Twelve of this volume) and in each instance when I was able to meet them after the hypnotic session they always reported to me that they had met a young girl who was then the recipient of all their attention and left them no time or desire to masturbate.

Should a young boy who masturbates be sent to a mental institution? My friend, Ward, who was unable to speak to girls when he was a high school student, (see Chapter Ten of this volume) did not think so and he told me of his helpless frustration over his brother's predicament when I visited him one day.

Excessive Masturbation

Name: George
Age: 15 years old in 1960
Complaint: Excessive masturbation

History: Ward told me that he had visited his mother and step-father and learned that his fifteen year old brother had been sent to a mental hospital. "They caught him masturbating," he explained, "and I think it is all so very wrong that I am at my wit's end. Honestly I wish I could just sit down and cry. I don't know what to do."

"I don't know what to do, either," I told him, "but I do know this. Since you have told me about your concern for your young brother this is no longer your personal problem. It is now our problem. We will drive out to the mental hospital next Sunday and we will visit your brother and speak to the Doctor who is caring for him and we will learn all the facts and find out what can be done and you can be sure that we will then do everything possible for his welfare and eventual release."

We visited the mental hospital and were allowed to take the boy out for a ride. Ward introduced his younger brother, George, to me and as we drove around I had an opportunity to question the lad and study him. He was very short and slightly built.

"How old are you?," I asked.

"Fourteen", he answered meekly.

This puzzled me since Ward had told me the boy was fifteen. "When will you be fifteen?" I asked.

"Next week", was the suprising reply.

"Do you know that you are in a mental hospital?" I questioned.

"Oh yes."

"Do you know why you are in that mental hospital?" I continued.

"Well you see, it was like this," George replied. "My mother came in my room one night and she caught me masturbating."

"How did she know what you were doing?"

"Well, I don't want this watch to get dirty and so I always hold my left hand up in the air when I masturbate and when she came in my room she saw my left hand was up in the air and that is how she knew what I was doing."

"I see you value that watch greatly. Who gave it to you?" I inquired.

"Santa Claus gave it to me. Do you believe in Santa Claus?"

"Yes," I told him, "I certainly do believe in Santa Claus".

George turned to his brother and asked, "Don't you think I am getting better? Can you see an improvement in me? I think I am getting better. Don't you think they should let me out of there since I have made an improvement?"

Ward looked at me and I said, "No, I don't think they should let you go home at this time?"

"Why not?"

"You said that you notice some improvement in your condition and you have been there for less than two weeks. I think you should stay there a few weeks more and perhaps there will be a bit more improvement. Right now you can afford to spend a few weeks. If you go out now and then have to come back in a few years for a few weeks, you might find that you can not afford to take the time from your school or other activities."

"Everyone in that place wants to get out," George informed me.

"Yes," I agreed, "and those fellows in there are all sick."

"I know," George said, "they are nuts."

"The doctors and nurses in the hospital are trying to help you get well," I continued. "They are not keeping you to punish you. They want to help you get well. When you tell them that you feel fine, they will make you leave. They are giving you vitamins and other things to help you get well so that you can leave."

Ward asked me to hypnotize his brother and I did. On our way home I said to Ward, "You know your brother is mentally retarded, don't you?"

"Yes," he replied, "but he is so sweet and kind and innocent I hate to think of him being locked up in a place like that with a lot of older kids who might bully him."

Induction technique used: Back-against-the-wall technique as I felt it best to treat George according to his mental age and to disregard his chronological age. George was mentally about ten years old and he responded to this induction method.

Hypnotic prescription given: You will realize that the doctors and nurses are your friends and they are trying to help you get well. You will follow all their instructions and do all your school work since you are in a hospital and if you act like you are sick, you will have to remain in the hospital, but if you study and get good grades and do everything you are told, then they will see that you are getting well and as soon as you get well and act like you are well, they will insist that you must leave.

Additional history: Before the hypnotic session George had mentioned that he was afraid to do his school assignments or obey any of the instructions given to him for fear that the doctors and nurses might think that he was happy and therefore keep him in the place for a longer period. After the hypnotic session George turned to Ward with a sudden inspiration and said, "Do you know what I think? I think I should go up to the doctors and nurses and thank them for trying to help me get well. They are not trying to hurt me. They are trying to help me. They are all my friends. I think I will go up to them and I will tell them that I know they are trying to help me."

I think he did. The following week he was transferred to a state hospital near his home where he was treated as an "out patient" and allowed to attend the neighborhood high school several miles away and he was eventually placed in a foster home where he made great progress and there was a fine improvement in his mental condition as well as his adjustment to his environment.

Supressing an urge to masturbate can have unfortunate consequences as this young college student discovered.

Indecent Exposure

Name: Bobby Smith
Age: 22 years old in 1965
Complaint: Indecent exposure.

History: When Bobby was nineteen he entered a University run by a religious denomination and was given to understand that he was receiving his education from his church and was therefore under the moral obligation to live according to the teachings of his church. He resolved to live without any vices. He stopped smoking and he stopped drinking alchoholic beverages and he stopped masturbating. One day he "snapped". He put a large kitchen knife in his car, drove down the street and forced the first girl he saw into the front seat. He knew that he intended to rape her but was uncertain as to the procedure. While trying to decide where to begin, he stopped at a traffic signal and the young lady opened the door, ran away and reported him to the police who arrested him less than one hour later. He was found guilty of attempted rape with a deadly weapon and given a sentence of from one to ten years. He spent the first two years of this sentence in a state mental hospital where he was in a program of group therapy.

146

All the other boys in his group were admitted homosexuals and so he could not bring himself to relate to them. He was relieved to learn that all the boys felt periods of frustration as far as their sexual desires were concerned and he was taught that masturbation was the medically accepted outlet for this cause of tension.

He was then paroled and went to work as a truck driver. While returning from having made a delivery he decided that it would be wise for him to park on a side street and wait for ten or fifteen minutes so that it would be more likely that he would be dismissed rather than sent on another trip. He saw no one on the street and therefore he opened his pants and proceeded to masturbate just as a small girl ran by, in pursuit of a ball, and observed him. She reported him and this time he was arrested for indecent exposure.

The judge said, "I do not think you are guilty as charged. However, I do believe you are guilty of using very poor judgement and so I will find you guilty and sentence you to six months in the country jail with one day suspended."

Bobby was transferred to the Honor Farm and his parents asked me to help him. I knew that there was no way for me to hypnotize him while he was confined but I decided to visit him to show my interest and concern and thus established rapport which I knew was so necessary before I could treat him when he was released. Bobby told me that he did not mind spending the six months but greatly regretted the fact that he would be unable to register for the coming school year. He had decided to return to his University and his being in jail might result in his losing another year before he could resume his studies.

I contacted Bobby's parole officer who told me that the sentence had been worded in such a fashion that it could no longer be reduced and that only the judge who had passed the sentence could dismiss the case and otherwise the full time would have to be served. I was told that the judge had refused to discuss the matter with anyone and I could contact him only by sending him a letter. I wrote as follows:

Dear Sir:

I have discussed this case with Bobby's parole officer who agrees with me that you will be making a real contribution towards his rehabilitation by allowing him to return to college and resume his studies at this time. Also, we have arranged for him to begin receiving thereapeutic treatments as soon as he is discharged. I will be happy to discuss this with you at your convenience.

Two days later I received a letter asking me to appear in court the following day.

The judge asked me to explain my connection in the case and I told him that the boy's mother and father had been my friends for many years.

"What treatment do you propose to have the boy receive?," the judge asked.

"I have written books and lecture on the subject of hypnotherapy," I began, and then the judge interrupted me. saying, "I know all about hypnosis and I do not go for that at all."

As the judge threw the case file towards the court clerk I said, "You realize that hypnosis is just an effective way of giving instructions. In this instance the instructions the boy is to receive will be prescribed by a medical doctor."

"That is different," the judge replied, "case dismissed."

The boy and his mother thanked me for my help and it was decided that the boy would come to see me two times a week for several months so that they could honestly state, if questioned, that he was receiving a course of treatment.

I told Bobby I would give him some hypnotic suggestions that would enable him to concentrate better and improve his memory and make it possible for him to do his school work with less effort . Bobby indicated that he thought that might be all right. He insisted that he had no sexual problems and was well adjusted as far as his various interests and activities were concerned.

After several visits he told me that it was his intention to become the most Christlike christian that ever lived. "When I die", he boasted, "I will sit on Jesus Christ's right hand."

I then realized the extent of his religious zeal and knew that I could not try to present to him anything under hypnosis that might be contrary to his dogmatic code. I did suggest that he would be able to sing better and speak with more sincerity and earnest concern when he taught Sunday School or delivered sermons and that he would become more capable and effective when performing his church duties. However, I also suggested that he would be a bit more tolerant towards others while trying to help them to follow his good example as to the proper way to live.

One day I mentioned that some churches were changing a bit and were uniting together with a common approach to the teachings of Jesus Christ. Bobby became almost hysterical as he denounced such proposals and insisted that he would adhere to each word and each comma to be found in the bible and he would rather die than accept the concept that anything could be altered or changed as far as its interpretation was concerned. During the hypnotic sessions I spoke to him only about being a good student and a more capable Sunday School teacher and more effective with his church duties. Also I tried to suggest that often moderation is the best policy.

Induction techniques used: Eye-to-eye technique

Hypnotic prescription given: You will concentrate more intently on what is said by your professor and you will concentrate upon the assignments given to you for home work. You will have a greater interest in your studies and you will have a better memory and your singing will improve along with your ability to speak easily and effectively to others regarding the teachings that are to be found in the bible. You will find more understanding in your heart towards the shortcomings of others and be tolerant towards those who do not have the capacity to understand matters as well as you. You will find yourself better able to adjust to the various situations in life and to the people with whom you come in contact.

Additional history: Later I learned that Bobby had met a young lady who was a divorcee and he married her and is now the father of two children. His family reports that he seems to be very happy and working hard at his job and is busy with his various church activities.

Frigidity

Name: Mrs. Renolds
Age: 32 years old in 1962
Complaint: She told her friends that she had a problem of incompatability. I decided it could more properly be termed, frigidity, since she was not interested in having sexual activity with her husband while he was desirous of being in bed with her.

History: Mrs. Renolds made it a practice to visit her neighbors every day and complain to them about her husband's desire to have sexual intercourse. She insisted that she found no pleasure in the sex act and therefore tried to find excuses to refuse his nightly demands. One of her neighbors asked me to meet Mrs. Renolds. I found her to be very overweight. Without make-up, uncombed hair and bare feet in well-worn house slippers, she was most unattractive. I wondered if this might prove to be a case of "third-party intervention". She had not asked for my help. The "brush-off technique" seemed appropriate for that reason and aside from the fact that it is the usual approach to almost all sexual problems.

Induction technique used: Eye-to-eye technique with brush-off technique.

Hypnotic prescription given: There is only one good reason for you to have sexual activity with your husband in the future. That is so that you can give him pleasure. Your husband does not always feel like getting up in the morning and going to work, but he does get up and he does go to work as that is part is part of his contribution to your marriage. You do not always feel like cooking or cleaning the house, but you do these things because it is part of your contribution to your marriage. If you have sexual activity with your husband for no reason except your desire to make him happy and when you feel that you have succeeded, then you will have a sense of accomplishment and the knowledge that his excitement and ultimate climax bringing about a release of his emotional tension was due to your presence and stimulation, will give a sense of satisfaction to you and your efforts will seem worthwhile.

There is a sympathetic response which comes from being near a person who is sexually aroused. By doing things that you know will cause your husband to become aroused and excited and by contriving to keep the sexual activity interesting with variety as to time and place and position you will discover a certain sexual pleasure which you may not have experienced before.

Additional history: Mrs. Renolds comment was the oft-repeated phrase, "You know, I could hear every word you said. This was nothing like the way I thought being hypnotized would be." After Mrs. Renolds left I told her friends that there was no way for us to evaluate the hypnotic session except to wait and see what degree of improvement might be experienced by Mrs. Renolds after a period of time. Four years later I met Mrs. Renolds' neighbor and I was given this report. Mrs. Renolds went to a beauty parlor the day after our hypnotic session and had her hair set in a permanent wave. She bought expensive dresses and eventually lost more than twenty five pounds. She went out shopping often and seemed to be busier than formerly since she no longer visited her neighbor. She seemed happier and looked much more attractive when she moved from the neighborhood a year later.

Frigidity

Name: Mrs. Bill Price
Age: 39 years old in 1960
Complaint: She asked me to hypnotize her so that she could be warmer and more affectionate towards her husband.

History: One day my neighbor, Bill Price, came over with an invitation to have dinner with his family. It was one of the most honest invitations I have ever received.

"My wife wants me to invite you to have dinner at our house," Bill began, "but I know what she has on her mind and therefore I am going to warn you so that you will be able to consider this matter carefully before you accept. I told my wife about the books on hypnosis that you write and I know she is going to ask you to hypnotize her. She won't tell me why she wants to be hypnotized but I do know that she has a lot of respect for you and I would appreciate your talking to her, but I don't see how you can decide if you will hypnotize her or not until you know why she wants to be hypnotized."

Bill is a good friend who has helped me greatly with the printing of my books and I was pleased to accept his invitation and was anxious to help his wife since I think of her as a personal friend.

"Will you hypnotize me so that I can be warmer and more affectionate towards my husband?" was the first thing Mrs. Price said as soon as we were alone in the kitchen after dinner that night.

150

Induction technique used: Eye-to-eye technique

Hypnotic prescription given: You will have more will-power and self-control in the future. When speaking to your husband you will try to express your opinion in such a way that he will understand that you are trying to be helpful and not argumentive. When you can think of something to say that will be complimentary or flattering, you will try to speak in a soft, sincere manner so that he will be able to accept your remarks without embarrassment or question the motive behind your statement. In the future you will treat your husband in such a manner so that he will feel that he is necessary and important to you and your family.

Additional history: Several months later, Bill came to see me and asked for my help. He explained that his wife had been visiting a psychiatrist for several years and had received expensive hypnotic treatments from time to time. Recently his wife had seemed more upset than usual and Bill was not suprised to learn that the psychiatrist suggested another series of hypnotic treatments. However, his wife insisted that the psychiatrist took too much time to induce the hypnosis and she had more faith in my ability.

Of course, I accepted another dinner invitation and this time the hypnotic prescription was the usual general instructions: "You will notice some degree of improvement in your condition. The improvement will be progressive. You will notice the improvement and you will be pleased."

One week later Bill asked me to come to his office and he seemed greatly upset. "I guess it was all my fault in not telling you the entire history concerning my wife's problem," he began. "You see, she had so much faith in you and you seemed to feel that you could help her so easily . . . you know, just one session and just a few minutes . . . so I thought I would let you hypnotize her and perhaps it might help. I didn't see how it could do any harm and now she has had a relapse and I know it is my fault."

"This time you are going to hear the entire story", Bill insisted. "When I married my wife I knew she had been married before and had suffered a nervous breakdown after the divorce. I knew I loved her and I wanted to be with her and nothing else mattered. When I courted her I found that she was willing to kiss me but became greatly upset if I tried to do any 'petting' or tried to get her to touch me.

"Of course, I knew that would all change after we got married, but it didn't. We would eat dinner when I got home and sit next to each other, holding hands with an occasional kiss during the evening. Once we got to bed her body became rigid and her breathing became difficult until she was gasping for air and she was able to relax and go to sleep only after I had left her room and she had bolted the door.

"She had explained to me how she had been married to an older man while she was a student in High School. She had signed her property and inheritance money over to her first husband who then left her and finally the marriage was annulled by her church.

"My wife and I went to our family doctor and our priest and finally to a psychiatrist. We knew we loved each other and we agreed that we wanted to have children and were willing to do anything which would permit us to enjoy sexual activity. The psychiatrist finally came up with a suggestion which solved our problem.

"The psychiatrist told me to get some "stag films". You know, the sort that are shown at fraternity "smokers" and "private showings" that the taxi drivers can locate in such places as Tia Juana and Juarez in Mexico. I was able to rent some of those films and I found that my wife could enjoy seeing them; she would get fully aroused sexually and we were able to enjoy marital relations as long as the films were projected. In fact, we found that it was impossible for her to relax and allow me to touch her unless the films were being projected.

"We do not go out to shows or watch television as any violence on the screen causes my wife to become ill.

"However, since your hypnotic session last week, my wife seemed like a new person. When I came home each evening I found her singing and she seemed so happy that I decided you must have cured her. Last night I asked her if she wanted to go to a movie and she agreed. We found that a Studio Preview Film was substituted for the advertised comedy and I noticed that my wife became very tense during the scenes of rape and brutality. When we got home my wife began to vomit and had convulsions so I sent for the psychiatrist who gave her a sedative and now she must have a nurse in constant attendence and I guess we will have to start a whole series of treatments again.

When I saw Bill's wife that evening she insisted that she felt fine and was sure that she would be happy if I simply hypnotized her to forget the motion picture which had upset her.

During the hypnotic session I told Bill's wife that we all "identify" with the people we see in motion pictures. It is perfectly natural for the young men to "identify with the leading man" and for the teen age girls to "identify with the leading lady." However, as we become mature we are able to control our emotions and we have in back of our minds at all times the understanding that we are viewing a play or motion picture and thus do not allow ourselves to become too deeply involved in the action we are seeing portrayed. Many people go to a show and "enjoy a good cry" but they dry their tears as they leave the theatre since they understand the presentation they had seen was for their entertainment and was not "reality". I concluded by telling her in the future, she would be able to recognize the difference between "make believe" and reality and have a greater control over her emotional reactions to these various presentations.

A short time later Bill told me that his wife was improving nicely as the new series of treatments progressed. "In fact", he added, "she is so much better that she has asked me to stop running the stag movies in our bedroom and yet we both seem to be enjoying sex as much as we ever did in the past."

I saw Bill's wife one year later and this time she seemed very embarrassed as she explained her reason for requesting the hypnotic session. "I don't know if this is much of a problem," she said, "but Bill is able to reach a climax so easily when we are together and I can not reach a climax unless he resorts to some un-natural sexual activity."

When I explained that there was no sexual activity performed between a husband and his wife which could be classified as 'un-natural', she seemed greatly relieved and left the room quickly, saying, "I told you it wasn't much of a problem."

Homosexuality

Name: Stan Fleming
Age: 32 years old in 1957
Complaint: Stan said to me, "I want you to hypnotize me so that I will never be able to have any sexual activities with boys the rest of my life."

History: Stan telephoned to me one evening. He explained that he had been arrested on a morals charge. He was accused of having had sexual relations with a twelve year old boy. He asked for my advice.

"My advice is to get a good lawyer", I replied.

"I know that", Stan agreed, "but I don't know any lawyers".

My father had passed away a few months previously and a former college classmate, Alan Selznick, was helping me settle my father's estate. Therefore, I offered to call Alan and I asked him to accept the case.

Alan arranged for Stan to receive psychiatric treatment and upon the recommendation of the local Probation Department, was put on probation for a period of three years and released. I was pleased to learn that the court had been so lenient, but Stan came to see me that evening insisting that he needed more help; help which only I could give.

"I guess it all started when I was fourteen years old", Stan began. "I lived on a farm in Iowa and we boys would swim in a swimming hole in the woods. Sooner or later someone would pull another boy's swimming trunks off and then we would all be swimming in the nude. Of course, one thing led to another and we would masturbate together and often attempt anal and oral intercourse. That was the only form of sexual activity I had until I was seventeen years old and went into the army.

"Once I got into uniform I discovered it was easy to meet girls and then all my sexual activities in those days were strictly with girls. I went with girls from the time I was seventeen until I was thirty.

"I started going with this school teacher who was about my age and I had a date with her each Friday and Saturday evening. One Friday afternoon I came to her house and she was not home but her seventeen year old nephew invited me inside and we talked and he showed me his bedroom with his various school pictures on the wall and then he got closer and closer and I understood what he wanted. I agreed to meet him the following Friday and he took me to a coffee shop where the homosexual boys and men gathered.

"For several months I would spend my Friday evenings with the boy and my Saturday evenings with his aunt. I told her that it was necessary for me to work on Friday evenings and she believed me. When the boy told me one day that he had made arrangements to see someone else, I didn't mind as I rather looked forward to going into the bars and meeting some new girls.

"However, I soon found that I was spending my entire Friday evening going into one bar after another and when I was able to meet a girl that was attractive and I invited her to have some coffee and a sandwich when the bars closed, more often than not, she would have some excuse for not inviting me to her home and I would have to return to my room alone.

"One Friday evening I went to the coffee shop and an older man invited me to his house. We had a fine meal and many drinks and I slept with him that night and the next morning he served me breakfast in bed before I left. I soon got into the habit of going to the coffee shop on Friday evenings and I always ended up sleeping with some man. Of course, I still had my regular Saturday evening dates with the teacher.

"I figured as long as half of my sexual activities were with women I had nothing to worry about.

"Then the teacher left this state and I tried to find girls each Saturday evening but it was so uncertain and I had to buy them drinks and take them to a restaurant and it would get later and later and we would talk and argue but most of the time I would be sleeping alone and feel that my time had been wasted.

"Well, finally I got into the habit of going into the Coffee Shop on both Friday evening and Saturday evening and for the past year all of my sexual experiences have been with men. I told my lawyer and the psychiatrist that I had just talked to the 12 year old boy about masturbation and they believed me, but actually I did touch the boy and I want to stop being a homosexual. The psychiatrist has said that he does not know how long his treatment will take, but he did say it will be likely to take some time. I don't care how much it will cost me, I am going to continue his treatments until he says I am cured, but I am worried about what I might do next week or next month. I want you to hypnotize me so that it will be impossible for me to have sexual relations with men."

Induction technique used: Eye-to-eye technique. Stan had seen me hypnotize others and he responded instantly.

Hypnotic prescription given: "In the future you will have more will-power and more self-control. You will understand that you are not a homosexual just because you have been limiting your activities lately. You are a bisexual person since you have enjoyed sexual activities with men as well as with women in the past and you know that you could enjoy such experiences in the future. The important thing for you to realize is that you have the ability to eat the food you wish and to avoid eating food you do not want. You have the ability to seek and find girls and by dating girls you will develop meaningful relationships that will be more significant than "one-night stands".

Additional history: When I asked Stan to open his eyes at the end of the brief hypnotic session which we feel is adviseable with all sexual problems, he voiced his disappointment. "I wanted you to tell me that I could never do it with men again," he insisted.

"Do you want to do it with men?" I asked.

"No. I want to go only with girls", he shouted.

"Well," I assured him, "you now have the will-power and self-control to limit your sexual activities to girls."

Stan came to visit me a few weeks later and reported that a young man was sent to him by one of his former friends and he found it was very easy to turn the caller away.

Stan was married in 1960 and is now the father of two children.

Molesting 12 Year Old Girl

Name: William Franklin
Age: 29 years old in 1957
Complaint: I had been asked to meet William Franklin because he told his lawyer he wanted to be hypnotized so that he could stop drinking. He told me that his problem was that he was not interested in being with his wife except when they were in bed.

History: While he was serving in the United States Army in Germany, a young lady contacted Wililam and asked him to marry her so that she could immigrate to the United States. She promised him a sum of money and assured him he could easily obtain a divorce, if he so desired. William agreed and found the young lady to be an excellent cook; an efficient housekeeper and a pleasant bed companion. Unfortunately, she spoke very little English and he could not speak or understand German.

155

Upon his discharge from the service, William got a job as a carpenter sent out by the Carpenter's Union. He went to the Union hiring hall every morning and earned a very fine income, although he often was finished working early in the afternoon. He did not know how to explain his irregular working hours to his wife and therefore he always returned to their apartment at 6:00 p.m. and visited bars and cocktail lounges on his free afternoons. In one of the bars he met a woman in her mid-thirties who invited him to her apartment and they were intimate.

One day this women suggested to William that he obtain a divorce and marry her. This proposition embarrassed him and he felt foolish as he mumbled an inadequate, "No, thanks."

"Why not?" she insisted. "You told me that you have no one to talk to when you get home at night. Your wife can't be any better to you in bed than I have been. After all, we have done everything you suggested and I bet we did a few things you didn't know before. I know I can satisfy you. Can you think of anything we have not tried?"

Anxious to change the conversation, William replied, "Well, I have been reading about the book called, 'Lolita' and I have been thinking that would certainly be different. It would sure be exciting to be in bed with a girl that was just 12 years old."

"If you think that would be any better than being with someone who has had a great deal of experience," the woman scoffed, "I can arrange for you to be with a 12 year old girl and then you will see for yourself. I have a daughter from my first marriage who is 12 years old and if you come here tomorrow afternoon, about 4:00 p.m., when she gets home from school, I will fix you up with her. After all, she will have to learn about sex sometime. I would rather her first experience was with some one like you."

Puzzled by this strange offer, William concluded that the woman was lacking in maternal instincts and he decided to return the following afternoon, if for no other reason than to ascertain her sincerity.

The next day he was ushered into the bedroom where a young girl sat on the large bed. "This is Angelita," the mother said ,"I'll now leave you two alone."

William sat next to the girl and when he put his hand on her knee he asked if she had any objections and she said, "I don't mind."

She was equally permissive when he put his hand under her dress and then slowly moved his hand upwards along the inside of her leg until he discovered she was wearing no undergarment beneath her dress. His excitement increased when he asked if anyone had ever touched her where his hand was resting and she replied, "No."

William lifted her dress and looked at her naked body as he slowly spread her legs apart. He dropped to his knees between her out-stretched feet and lowered his head between her legs. At that moment two men from the vice detail of the local police department stepped from the closet where they had been hiding and they arrested him.

In the state of California the law enforcement agencies are permitted to use entrapment only when trying to apprehend sexual offenders. William went to Alan Selznick who agreed to act as his attorney. He confessed to Alan that he had stopped in at a bar for several drinks on his way to the 4:00 p.m. appointment and insisted that his unfortunate situation was caused by his drinking habit. "After all," he reasoned, "if I had not gone into the bar I would have never met Angelita's mother. I wish I could stop drinking."

When William was told that hypnosis might enable him to stop drinking, he agreed to having me called in to treat his drinking problem. Alan told me that he did not feel William had a drinking problem. However, he wanted to request a postponement of the hearing on the grounds that the defendent was receiving some "treatment" at that time.

Mouth-genital contact is recognized as a form of insanity according to the California Penal Code. Alan explained that ordinarily, his defense would be a plea of insanity and his client would be admitted to one of the State's Mental Hospitals. After the defendent had been in a mental hospital for more than one year, his lawyer could petition the court to have him re-examined by competent psychiatrists who might be expected to find him sufficiently recovered to justify his being released. However, since the client had voiced a desire for immediate treatment, his attorney felt that a request for postponement of the hearing would serve to inform the court he was receiving some therapy and in this instance the plea might be "temporary insanity" and he would request the judge to arrange for psychiatric examinations to be made and presented at the hearing. This might accelerate the wheels of justice and cause the judge, with the approval of the probation department, to free the defendant on a probationary basis.

Induction technique used: Eye-to-eye technique.

Hypnotic prescription given: "You will have more will-power and more selfcontrol in the future. You know that you are able to eat the food you like and you do not eat food you do not like. In the future you will be able to drink the liquids you want to drink and you will have the ability to not drink liquids, if that is your desire. You know that it is difficult to eat just one peanut if a bowl of peanuts are sitting in front of you. It is difficult to drink just one Dry Martini. However, the longer you go without eating peanuts, the less interest and desire you will have to eat peanuts. This is also true as far as drinking is concerned. The longer you go without a drink, the less need or desire you will have for a drink.

"You have lived with your wife for more than one year and she has come to mean more to you than an instrument to satisfy your sexual needs. When you have sexual intercourse with your wife it should be as the result of your desire to stimulate and excite her and your pleasure will be a sympathetic response, for as she becomes aroused you will also become aroused. A boy who has had no sexual experience is often so anxious he is willing to pay a woman to go to bed with him. This can be disappointing since he is using the prostitute's body as a device for his own pleasure or self-gratification.

"In order for you to enjoy sexual activity to the fullest extent you must feel that you are needed and necessary for your partner's ultimate satisfaction. Your relationship then becomes significant. If you touch a person who has had no previous sexual experience, this is lacking and you will recognize the futility.

"In the future you will have a greater desire to be with your wife than any other person. You will devise ways to keep your sexual activity fresh and spontaneous. Variety as to the time and place and position will keep your interest alive and your feeling towards each other will grow as you discover so many things you have in common."

Additional history: The attorney asked me how many additional hypnotic sessions were needed and he was genuinely disappointed when I told him that one hypnotic session was sufficient. He insisted I had to see his client at regular intervals during the following three months as he felt William might be questioned by the judge or probation officer as to the extent of the treatment he had received and he did not want it to appear that the therapy had been superficial. Therefore, at the next session I hypnotized William and told him he would be able to concentrate and have a better memory. Each hypnotic session was for a different purpose.

At our last meeting, William told me that his wife had enrolled in a Night School class in order to learn English. He did not like the idea of her going to the school alone so he enrolled in the class with her. He had traded his late model automobile in on a much older car and with the money he received he made a down payment on a house. He reported that he was anxious to get home from work each night as there were closets to construct and shelves to build. He went to work for a contractor although the wages were a bit less than he had been earning. It did give him regular hours, and also, it provided him with health insurance; a pension fund and security for the future. The reason he needed to build the closets and have the job security, he explained, was that his wife was pregnant.

The judge arranged for William to have three psychiatric examinations and the consensus opinion was that it would be impossible for him to have any sexual interest in a small girl, in the future, since he was so much in love with his wife. Of course, he was an excellent risk for the probation department since he felt it was inconcievable that he would ever be attracted to a 12 year old girl or to any person other than his wife.

Molesting Nine Year Old Girl

Name: Ralph Wester
Age: 39 years old in 1957
Complaint: Molesting 9 year old girl.

History: Ralph lived in a small desert community. His wife returned from the hospital after an operation for the removal of her uterus, oviducts and ovaries and informed him that she would be unable to have sexual relations with him for several months. To escape his advances, she moved to another city. Ralph was building a patio one morning when his neighbor's nine year old daughter asked if he wanted her to bring him a can of beer from the refrigerator in his kitchen.

"Not unless you also bring me a can opener", was the reply which sent the small child laughingly into his house.

"Do you want another beer?" the girl asked a few minutes later.

"Not unless you open the can before you bring it to me."

"Do you want another beer?" was asked shortly thereafter.

"Not unless you open the can and pour the beer into a glass", Ralph replied and thus the game was established. With each can of beer consumed the conditions were more challenging and the little girl was pleased with her ability to satisfy the conditions which became progressively more involved.

"Do you want another beer?" she asked.

"Not unless you open the can of beer and bring it into the bedroom and sit on the bed next to me while I drink it," was his reply.

"Do you want another beer? she finally inquired.

"Not unless you bring the beer into this bedroom and take off all your clothes and lie down next to me as I drink it", he insisted.

Ralph had disrobed anticipating the child's return and was lying on the bed, fully aroused. However, he found that he could not insert his forefinger and soon lost interest in the giggling girl who reminded him so much of his own daughter. "In fact," he confessed to me, "I did it all to get even with my wife who went with our children to stay with her parents, just because I wanted her to have a little sex with me from time to time."

"When she came back from the hosptial, I showed my wife my organ in an erection one morning and she offered to masturbate me, but I had been taught that masturbation was dangerous and I refused to allow my wife to do it to me for fear that it might become a habit."

"My lawyer asked me to see you and have you hypnotize me for my sexual problem," he explained, "but actually, I do not have any sexual problems. When we were overseas during the war, I always went to bed with another fellow and this way we were able to have intercourse with each other rather than masturbate."

"Of course, the only exception I make to this rule against masturbation," he added, "is when I am driving down a deserted street and I see a beautiful girl walking ahead of me. I park my car next to the sidewalk about half a block in front of her and I open my pants and I play with myself, not caring if she can see what I am doing or not. On three or four occasions they have returned with policemen but I have always been able to explain to the officers that I was driving home from work and had stopped to change my clothes as I had to attend a church function and was late."

We agreed that the hypnotic session would be primarily for the lawyer's benefit since he had indicated it would be helpful if he could inform the court that his client had sought and received hypnotherapy.

Induction technique used: Eye-to-eye technique.

Hypnotic prescription given: In the future you will sleep better and you will feel stronger, healthier and more alert. You will be able to perform your duties at your work more efficiently and effectively and when you come home at night, you will feel more rested and eager to spend more time with your family.

I would describe masturbation as self-stimulation for your own sexual gratification. When your wife offered to put her hand on your organ this action would be properly classified as a form of "petting". You could have accepted her offer as a generous indication of her love for you and her awareness of your needs. However, you should also realize that the action your wife suggested would have been stimulating and exciting for both parties and therefore she would have made a novel sexual experience as well as having felt that she had made a contribution towards your ultimate pleasure and release of tension.

The honest man will admit that he does derive some degree of pleasure on occasion from being a voyeur or "peeping tom" and on other occasions he might enjoy exhibiting himself, in one way or another. However, you must understand that sexual pleasure is dependent upon the sexual activity being mutually enjoyed by both participants. It is exciting to bite your wife on her shoulder during intercourse if you know that she is being stimulated and more aroused when you bite her. Sitting in your car with your pants open is stimulating only because you imagine that the passing young lady will be excited and pleased when she observes you in the act of masturbating. The fact that several have called your actions to the attention of the police shows that this has not always been the case.

Your sexual actions should be in response to the needs of others. Then you will feel that you have made a contribution towards their happiness and your satisfaction and pleasure will be so much greater. You will realize that your wife's sexual needs will be greater in future

160

and you will devise ways to keep your sexual activity fresh and spontaneous with many changes as to the time and place you select. By keeping her interest alive you will both receive increased enjoyment from your relationship together as the years go by.

Additional history: My friend, Alan Selznick, informed me that Ralph's wife returned to live with him and she testified at the hearing that their family relations were frequent and enjoyable. The court appointed psychiatrists stated that their examinations revealed that Ralph was unlikely to commit further sexual crimes and his three year probationary period passed without incident.

Molesting Seven and Eight Year Old Girls

Name: Lawrence Brown
Age: 24 years old in 1957
Complaint: Second occasion that he was arrested and charged with molesting little girls.

History: Alan Selznick called me to his office to discuss this case. Lawrence had been arrested three years previously when a seven year old neighbor reported that he had molested her. Lawrence insisted he was innocent but it was decided for reasons of legal expediency for him to plead guilty and be placed on probation for a period of three years. This probationary period was about to be terminated when Lawrence was accused by two small girls and was again arrested. Lawrence insisted he was innocent as before but there were some doubts the lawyer had as to the proper way to handle this case. Much depended upon knowing if the defendent was actually guilty or innocent.

Alan told me that he realized I could not hypnotize Lawrence into testifying against himself, but he did want me to report to him my opinion as to whether he was or was not telling the truth.

I saw Lawrence that afternoon and he seemed most straightforward. "I came to see you at Alan's request," he explained, "but I don't see what you can do for me as I am happily married and I have no sexual problems."

I offered to hypnotize Lawrence so that he would be able to testify at his hearing with simple statements which would reflect his sincerity.

Induction technique used: Eye-to-eye technique.

Hypnotic prescription given: When you are called upon to tell your story, you will be able to speak slowly and carefully. Your statements will be honest and sincere. You will answer all questions put to you in such a manner that it will be apparent that you are trying to assist the court in it's efforts to learn the true facts.

Additional history: After the hypnotic session I returned to Alan's Law Offices and I told him I felt Lawrence was innocent of the crime since he had responded so readily to the hypnotic induction technique and he accepted my suggestions that all questions put to him in the future will be truthfully answered.

At that moment the telephone on Alan's desk rang and when he lifted the instrument he was informed that Lawrence had driven to his parent's house after our hypnotic session and had confessed to them his guilt.

I was embarrassed for never before had my opinion of someone's character been so rapidly disproven. However, Alan asked me to accept his thanks for my help which he assured me had been of the greatest value and he reminded me that my suggestions that Lawrence speak truthfully in the future, had been accepted and was very likely the cause for the sudden confession.

Loss of All Hair From Head

Name: Jim Mayer
Age: 22 years old in 1957
Complaint: Loss of all hair from head and subsequent lack of growth of hair.

History: I arrived in San Francisco on Easter Sunday in 1957 and was invited to a buffet supper my friend, Larry Ferreire was hosting for some of his classmates at San Francisco State College. At that time I was introduced to Jim who informed me that no one knew why he had lost his hair, and he was told that it was psychological in origin and not due to any physical infection or disease. I agreed that hypnosis might be effective in this case and I was anxious to talk to Jim who was obviously eager to be treated. In order to escape the noisy party we sat in the front seat of my car which was parked in front of the house.

Jim told me that he had enlisted in the U.S. Marine Corp when he reached his seventeenth birthday. After five or six months he suffered a minor nervous breakdown and was sent to one of the State Hospitals for observation. At the termination of his four year enlistment, he was called before a medical board who informed him that he was about to receive his discharge from the Marine Corp and they asked him if he had any plans for the future. He indicated that he would go to college and complete his education. The medical board seemed pleased with this answer and agreed that he could leave the State Hospital when he received his service discharge.

Thereafter his hair began to fall away. He awakened in the morning and found he could run his fingers over his head and withdraw an alarming amount of loose strands of hair. Combing and brushing thinned his hair further. At the end of one week he was completely bald. The medical and psychological staff examined him extensively and pronounced him free of infectious, contagious or communicable disease. Once again he was summoned before the medical examining board and asked his plans and he replied that he intended to enroll in college

162

since he knew of no courses which had a prerequisite that the student have a full growth of hair.

When Jim finished telling me of the circumstances relative to the sudden loss of his hair I agreed to hypnotize him and his response was immediate. The hypnotic prescription was brief and he opened his eyes when instructed to do so and stated, "I know I was hypnotized deeply and I am certain my hair will return. Thank you."

I then explained that my primary interest had been to cause a new hair growth. "Ordinarily, a psychologist would be interested in learning what brought about this condition", I explained. "This would take a bit more time and perhaps a deeper hypnotic state."

"I don't mind," Jim agreed. "I want you to take as much time and you can hypnotize me as deeply and as often as you think best."

The second hypnotic session then took place and Jim responded like a person in a deep hypnotic state. He spoke in a mono-tone and it seemed an effort for him to form each word. His answers were barely audible and given very slowly.

Question: "Why did your hair fall out?"
Answer: "I was afraid I would have no girl friends when the students at the college learned I had been in a State Hospital."
Question: "What difference would having hair make?"
Answer: "I wanted people to think I had no girl friends because I had no hair."
Question: "Have you made any girl friends at college?"
Answer: "Yes, I have girl friends."
Question: "Have you had dates with girls?"
Answer: "Yes."
Question: "Have you had sexual intercourse with the girls you met at college?"
Answer: "Yes."
Question: "Have you found that the students at the college accepted you and your being without hair made no difference?"
Answer: "Yes."
Question: "Then you realize that your fears were unfounded and it is not necessary for you to be without hair any longer?"
Answer: "Yes."

At the end of this questioning I told Jim to open his eyes at the count of seven. "This time I was hypnotized much deeper," Jim stated. "I know you asked me some questions, but I don't remember what they were and I can't remember if I answered you or what I said." He then returned to the party and I drove away as he thanked me again for my help since he was firmly convinced his hair would return.

I was back in San Francisco six weeks later and I telephoned my friend, Larry Ferreire to learn if Jim's confidence in our hypnotic session had been rewarded with some signs of a new hair growth.

"Oh yes," Larry informed me, "the hair is coming back on Jim's head, but it looks very strange. There are dark patches and light patches and some of the hair looks blonde or white and other places it seems brown or black."

I asked Jim Mayer to see me at my hotel and he came over a few minutes later. As soon as he entered the room, he pulled off his cap and stood in front of the mirror and with enthusiastic vigor combed what appeared to be a quarter inch growth of hair over his entire head. I looked at him critically and I had to admit there was a great improvement in his appearance for now the hair line was clearly defined and he seemed so genuinely happy as he looked at his reflection.

I told Jim it might take a few more months before we would know if the coloring would become an even shade or the various tones now so apparent would remain and perhaps he might have to get his hair dyed and thus regain his former appearance.

"Don't worry about it at all," Jim insisted. "I am so pleased the way it has all returned and I am completely satisfied."

I was not satisfied, however, and proposed another hypnotic session. As before, Jim was most responsive.

Question: "Why do you think your hair has returned with the uneven coloring?"

Answer: "I was afraid that it might all fall out again, if it came back looking as good as before."

I considered this answer and decided that there might be a deeper basis for Jim's problem. I had given much thought to the statement Jim had made about his fear that he would lack girl friends and the idea that by losing his hair this might insure his not having any girl friends and the reason for his lack of girl friends would be more acceptable. It occurred to me that he might want to have boy friends.

Question: "Did you have any homosexual experiences while you were in the State Hospital?"

Answer: "Only once."
Question: "What happened?"
Answer: "Well, there was this gardener who worked at the hospital. He offered to give me some money if I would have intercourse with him."
Question: "What did you do?"
Answer: "I told him that I had been paid only once in my life to have intercourse and that I was never going to do it again."
Question: "Then what happened?"
Answer: "He went away and that ended the matter."
Question: "How old were you when you were paid to have intercourse?"
Answer: "Seventeen years old."
Question: "Where did this happen?"

Answer: "In San Diego. I had just finished my 'basic training'. I was standing on a street corner when this older woman came up to me and she offered to give me ten dollars if I would go to bed with her. I agreed since it seemed like such an easy way to earn so much money. When we took off our clothes and got to bed it was no fun at all. She kept telling me to do one thing and then another. It was the most horrible experience I ever had. When I was getting dressed she told me that she had approached me because she was attracted by my wavy hair."

At the end of the hypnotic session Jim opened his eyes and said, "I don't remember anything that happened that time, but I do have a headache and also I must return to my studies."

Two months later I returned to San Francisco and called Larry for a report. "Jim's hair has come back," Larry told me, "but he goes to the barber shop every week and he gets the barber to shave his entire head. So he looks as bald as ever. He says that the girls insist that he reminds them of Yul Brynner and they prefer him without hair. However, he no longer wears that skull cap pulled down over his ears and he seems to be doing very well with his studies although I don't see where he finds the time to do his assignments since he is kept so busy with various social activities."

Induction technique used: Eye-to-finger technique since we were in the front seat of my automobile and that was the most convenient technique to use, considering our position. I used that technique at each subsequent session since I felt Jim had responded so well to that technique in the past and might find a different technique confusing. I felt that he had been somewhat conditioned to respond to that particular technique.

Hypnotic prescription given: The sebaceous glands in your scalp will be stimulated and this increased secretion will cause an improvement in the condition of your hair and scalp and will result in a growth of new hair during the next few months. There will be some degree of improvement at first, but it will be a progressive improvement which you will notice and the amount of improvement will please you as you will then realize that a desired change is taking place. You will have a greater interest in your studies and you will be able to concentrate better when you read your text books and when you listen to your lectures. Your memory will improve and you will be better able to recall what you have read and what you have heard in your various classrooms. When you speak to your classmates you will talk to them about their experiences and the plans they have for the future. You will ask them for their opinions and you will realize that the more you talk to others about themselves, the more they will want to be with you. You will sleep well and have greater strength and energy and feel a sense of accomplishment as you continue your studies.

Additional history: I feel that the questioning did not contribute much towards the solving of Jim's problem. I suspect that Jim did not give me the correct reason for his having lost his hair and for it having returned with such a 'blotched appearance'. My theory is that the traumatic experience with the older woman may have been the cause for his nervous breakdown and since this proposition was unlikely to be made to him as long as he remained in the State Hospital his physical condition was unchanged. However, once he was informed that he was going to be discharged, the thought occurred to him that other individuals might approach him after being attracted by his wavy hair. It is interesting to note that although he was told at the first hypnotic session that his hair would return and he was told at the last hypnotic session that his hair would eventually all be a uniform shade, he has continued to have his head shaved every week so that he is still without any hair on his head. He is happier now since he feels his hairless appearance is his own decision.

Impotency

Name: John Wright
Age: 22 years old in 1956
Complaint: Impotency.

History: When I returned from Europe in 1956, John Wright, a friend of long standing, came to visit me and he introduced a most attractive young lady to me as his fiance. I told them that I was going to write a book with Dr. Lester Kashiwa about hypnotherapy.

"Do you really believe in hypnosis," he asked, "and do you think you can hynotize me?"

"Yes," I said, "I think I can." John became somewhat excited and declared, "I must take my girl friend home. However, I will be right back as I have something very important to discuss with you."

When he returned to my house a few minutes later he told me that he had been in the U.S. Army and was stationed for more than one year in Korea. He was warned against the venereal diseases common in that country and also the girls seemed to him to be most unattractive. Some of his friends told him about Heroin and he discovered that when he took Heroin, he could lie in his bed and enjoy all the sensations of sexual intercourse and reach a climax without using his hands. When his unit was returning from Korea, they sailed to Kobe, Japan and he was invited to go ashore with one of the servicemen who said he knew a place to go to obtain some Heroin.

John rejected the invitation saying, "I have no more need for Heroin. I am on my way back to the states where I can find nice girls and I will go back to the sexual activity I had before I entered the service, I think." He had been warned against allowing himself to become addicted to the use of Heroin or other drugs and so he discontinued their use completely.

After returning to his home, he met the young girl who was a member of his church and they became engaged to be married. After the invitations had been mailed and the wedding arrangements completed, they decided to spend a night together in a roadside Motel but he found that he was unable to perform the sex act since it was impossible for him to have an erection. He visited his family physician who sent him to a psychologist who in turn referred him to a hypnotherapist.

This man offered to "cure" him by the use of hypnosis but was unable to hypnotize him. He visited two other hypnotherapists and they also told him that he was a "bad subject" and they could not help him.

"Now that you know my story, do you still think you can hypnotize me?" he asked. I reassured him and he promised to return later that evening.

As I ate my dinner, I gave this matter some consideration and I was prepared for John who marched through my front door, pointed his forefinger at me and challenged, "How do you expect to be able to hypnotize me when I am sure there is no such thing as genuine hypnosis?"

"I have no intention of having an argument with you about hypnosis," I said, "instead, I will take the next few minutes and teach you how to hypnotize others. After you have learned what hypnosis is and how to use it, you will understand that hypnosis can be induced when the conditions and motivation are proper and then I will hypnotize you."

I knew John as an ardent amateur magician; a fine athlete and capable swimmer and I understood that he was then earning his living as a salesman. I took all these facts into consideration as I began the briefest lecture I have ever delivered on the broad subject of "Hypnosis —what it is and how it is induced."

"Let us agree that swimming can be described as self-propulsion through water," I began. "Hypnosis is self-induced as the result of instructions received from someone else."

"Let us continue by comparing hyposis with swimming as I think that will make it easier for you to understand. If you met someone who wanted to learn how to swim, it might be possible for you to teach him . . . but you could not force him to swim. You know that he would float if he allowed his body to relax and rest with his full length extended. However, he might be afraid of being in the water and double-up his body. Therefore, it would be necessary for you, as his swimming instructor, to use your ability as a salesman to keep him relaxed and following your instructions.

"If the swimming student did succeed in floating or swimming, it would be due to his having followed your directions but you could not say that you had "made him swim" or that you had any "control over him" or had "forced him into following your instructions". You had, however, been able to show him that you understood what you were talking about and thus succeeded in gaining his confidence so that

167

he had "faith' in you and he allowed you to tell him what to do, only because he was certain that you were anxious to help him and he felt that by following your instructions he would eventually gain the ability to swim.

"Now, after a period of time, this swimming student might tell you he could only swim so fast and no faster. You might know that he could swim faster and, therefore, the problem would be for you to get him to take a greater number of strokes per minute. If you gave the student the instructions to 'swim faster' he might very likely say to you that he could not swim any faster. However, you could get him to swim faster by asking him to take a stroke each time you counted and by very slowly increasing the speed with which you counted, you might cause him to increase his speed and thus he would be swimming faster. If he had been timed and shown the proof, he might accept that as a 'fact' and thereafter continue to swim at a faster speed.

"In that instance, your 'trick' of counting faster was responsible for his swimming faster but actually, you did not make him do anything that he could not have done, excepting that he did not realize the full potential of his abil.ty. You simply made it possible for him to use his own ability.

"Hypnosis is one way you can get others to use the ability that they do not realize they possess. This can be done in many different ways other than by hypnosis. It can be accomplished entirely by salesmanship or persuasion. You have heard people say they were 'talked into doing something'. Even military orders or commands are not as effective as hypnosis since the soldier is always aware that he can do as he is told or he can accept the punishment. Hypnosis is so effective because the person who is hypnotized feels that he has no choice other than follow the directions he receives from the hypnotist.

"Let us get back to our imaginary swimmer that you are teaching. You might urge him to dive from the top diving board and he might say to himself, 'Yesterday, I did not think I could swim any faster, but my teacher proved to me that I could. I now have faith in him and can accept all his instructions without hesitation. In that case, you would have succeeded in gaining the student's confidence and caused him to trust you and this 'faith' would make it possible for you to cause him to use the fullest extent of his ability.

"Your mind has a great deal of ability that you do not use. If I can show you that your mind has ability that you have not been using, you might be willing to allow me to give you other instructions which would thus enable you to put more of your un-used ability to work. In order for you to increase the ability of your mind, it is only necessary for you to concentrate a great deal of your attention on the part of your body that you wish to influence. We are taught that we have no control over various parts of our body, but we know that our body will sometimes by influenced by our thoughts as well as by the actions of others.

"We are taught that we have no control over our salivary glands and that they secrete only when we are eating. However, it often happens that our saliva is secreted when we think of a favorite food. Also we have had the salivary flow begin only because a friend was talking about food. We must admit that our friend had influenced us and caused the saliva secretion by speaking of food in such a manner that we had put a great deal of our attention or concentration on the idea of food.

"For hypnosis you must capture the individual's attention and direct it from one part of his body to another part of his body. After you have done this and he has responded according to your directions, you can then direct his attention to other matters and he will be receptive and believe that he must follow your instructions, as long as your instructions are designed to help him and he knows that your interest and concern is for his welfare and benefit.

You have a great deal of ability as a salesman so you will have no trouble in capturing the attention of your subject. In order for you to direct his attention it will be necessary for you to know exactly what you are going to say and be prepared to repeat or modify your instructions until it has the desired effect. Usually, all you are trying to do at first is see if the subject will follow your instructions and then you try to direct his atention to some thought which you feel will bring about a re-action. After the subject has re-acted you can expect that he will continue to follow your instructions as long as they are properly expressed and voiced by you with firm assurance. Of course, we understand that hypnosis is a skill and you will have to practice this skill a number of times until you acquire some degree of proficiency.

I then explained the "reflex technique" to John. It was easy for him to learn and I needed some induction technique which could be described as novel and different from the usual concept of hypnosis which is based upon repetition or fatigue.

I had hypnotized the High School boy who lived across the street on several occasions and I knew he would be very responsive. He knew John by reputation and admired him. This boy was watching a television program with my father so he was readily available and convenient for me to present to John as his first hypnotic subject.

I told the boy John had learned a new hypnotic technique he wanted to show me and I asked him to allow us to use him as a subject. John spoke to the boy as I had instructed and the boy responded by falling forward. John and I eased the boy's body on to a couch and then John told the boy his arm would become rigid. The boy was most responsive and put forth a great deal of effort while trying to bend his right arm which was obviously rigid and unyielding. John seemed to be pleased with his success but puzzled by the ease with which he was able to influence the boy and he kept asking me if I thought the lad was actually hypnotized or just pretending. I assured John the boy was in a genuine hypnotic trance.

I allowed John to give the following post-hypnotic suggestion since he insisted upon more proof of the hypnotic trance. He told the boy to give us his High School ring and upon awakening not remember having removed it from his finger. John then aroused the boy and dismissed him. We called him back in order to return the ring and the obvious suprise on the boy's face was enough to convince John.

I then told John I would hypnotize him as I felt it is most important for all hypnotists to be hypnotized on several occasions so that they will have a better understanding of hypnosis and the hypnotic trance.

To my pleasant suprise, John was very responsive and he went into a light hypnotic trance instantly. I told him his right arm would become rigid and stiff as he pushed it away from his body. I had him close his fist tightly when I said, "One" and I told him to push his clenched fist out away from his body until his elbow locked into place as I counted, "Two". I counted "Three" and he exerted a great deal of effort but his right fist continued to be thrust forward and of course, he was unable to bend his right arm.

"I can talk to you," he said. "Does that mean anything?"

"Only that you are not in a very deep hypnotic state and that you feel it is important to speak to me right now," I answered. "You are hypnotized, but you are also awake and that is something neither of us should forget."

"I wanted to tell you that I can feel my arm get very stiff and yet I think I could bend it, if I had to, but I feel I would rather keep pushing my right fist away from my body because I prefer to feel the stiffness in my right arm," John explained.

"Just as your right arm is stiff and rigid," I said, "that will be the condition of your sex organ during intercourse. In the future you will have more sexual power and control and you will soon have the some capability that you had before you went to Korea. You will be well satisfified with your sexual ability in the future and it will give you no further concern. As time goes by you will have greater control and enjoy all your sexual experiences."

When I asked John to open his eyes he said, "I wonder if I was really hypnotized. I did not feel very different at all. I could hear everything and I felt that I was doing what you asked only because I wanted to please you. Do you think you could hypnotize me like I hypnotized the High School boy? I would like to be put into a deep trance so that when I was awakened I would not recall what had happened. If you did that to me, then I would be convinced I had really been hypnotized."

170

I did not try to explain to John that he felt exactly as all persons who are hypnotized feel. When there is a great deal of rapport and the hypnotized person knows the hypnotist will be pleased if he acts as though he were not aware of his actions while hypnotized, then the subject will ACT as though he does not remember what he did while he was hypnotized. Sometimes the patient will report that he can not recall what was said or what he did while hypnotized and this is not due to his desire to please the hypnotist but rather caused by a need to hide his embarrassment.

As I walked with John to the door I reminded him that his arm had felt rigid and stiff and that his head had felt heavy as it fell against his chest and that his entire body did fall as I had suggested. I told him he had been in a slight hypnotic trance and that was sufficient for treating his sexual problem, which after all, was our primary concern. However, I promised him I could induce a much deeper hypnotic trance after several sessions and I invited him to return.

John insisted he would not be satisfied until he had been deeply hypnotized and he arranged to see me the following week and he indicated his willingness to endure hundreds of sessions until this goal had been reached. I was pleased that he wanted to come back since I was interested in the report I expected to receive from him as to the return of his sexual power.

However, John did not come to visit me the following week and I did not see him for several months. I thought of him and wondered if there had been any change in his condition. The session had been brief, but I had invited him to return and since there was no fee, I expected him to be giving me progress reports for a period of many months. I could not bring myself to telephone to him as the hypnotherapist must never ask the patient if there has been any improvement. This is an admission that the hypnotist is not completely confident as to the outcome of the hypnosis.

I saw John five months later at a banquet. He came over and told me he had been having a great deal of success as a hypnotist at parties. I said, "How about your problem?" He answered in a fit of impatience, "Oh never mind that."

His problem had been in my thoughts a great deal and I refused to allow him to dismiss the entire matter. "Are you having sexual intercourse with girls?" I demanded.

"Certainly, of course," he replied and the implication was that my question was naive and foolish.

I wondered if there had been a psychological "block" due to the fact that his fiance was so extremely beautiful. "Have you had sexual intercourse with the girl you introduced to me as your fiance?" I persisted.

"Yes, several times, however she changed her mind about getting married at this time and so I have other girls I can go to bed with, when I choose."

Thus assured that his problem of impotency had been overcome, I felt he owed me some gratitude and should be thanking me for my help. I wanted to say, "Why didn't you come back and thank me?" however I did ask, "Why didn't you come back?"

"Well," John said, "when I realized that there was nothing wrong with me and that I had been bothering people about a problem that did not exist, I was so embarrassed I just wanted to forget about the entire matter."

John was wrong. He had gone to bed with his fiance on several occasions before I hypnotized him and on these occasions he could not maintain an erection, so he had a problem which did exist. However, the reason for this problem was not his having taken Heroin as he suspected, but it was due entirely to his "fear of failure". John, like so many others feel that a psychological problem is not a "real" problem and that it is somewhat of a disgrace to be troubled by a disorder which is "all in the mind".

Additional history: This case was in our book, CASE HISTORIES IN HYPNOTHERAPY, and I have included this case in my lectures at Keio Medical University in Tokyo and elsewhere. Often I was asked for additional information and I regretted that the "brush-off technique" did not allow me to question John at length regarding his use of Heroin as I wanted to give the impression that his unfortunate activities in Korea could be lightly dismissed and that his problem would respond readily to the hypnotic prescription I administered.

In 1965 I saw John when he returned to California for a brief visit. I then asked him how many times he had taken Heroin while he had been stationed in Korea and he replied, "Oh, I don't know. Two or three times, I guess."

Hypnotic technique used: Reflex technique.

Hypnotic prescription given: You will have the same sexual power in the future that you had in the past before you went to Korea.

PART II

CHAPTER ONE

Understanding Rapid Induction Hypnosis

Hypnosis is simply a most effective way for one person to give instructions to another person. Hypnosis is the giving of instructions in such a manner that the person receiving the instructions feels compelled to follow them due to a desire to please the hypnotist. Therefore a special situation must be created and a special relationship must exist between the hypnotist and the subject.

Hypnosis is a skill which can be learned by those who are meek and unassuming as well as those who are dominating and agressive. Like all skills, proficiency in its use can be gained by practice and experience. Professional entertainers deliberately try to give the false impression that they have a "remarkable power" over their subjects and can cause the hypnotized person to do anything the performer desires, without having any knowledge or ability to control his actions.

The hypnotherapist understands that the patient is at all times awake and fully aware of everything that is taking place. Although the word, hypnosis is derived from the Greek root for sleep, hypnosis is not a form of sleep. Medical scientists have twenty six methods of determining if a person is awake or asleep. From the use of the electrocardiograph and other devices to the study of the reflex responses it can be proven that a patient who is hypnotized is fully awake. The person who is asleep can not hear what we say and can not answer us. He is not conscious of his movements and can not control his actions. When he is hypnotized, the subject is more keenly aware of what is taking place since his senses are sharper and he can think more clearly. The patient can only be hypnotized by someone he trusts. Once he is hypnotized he can summon unusual strength and exert remarkable control over his body. He is not as helpless as he appears, for if the hypnotized person is ever asked to do anything he does not want to do, he can either open his eyes, look about and thus indicate that he is no longer hypnotized, or he may simply keep his eyes closed but go asleep and then there will be no line of communication and a state of hypnosis will cease to exist.

There are many different ways in which one person can give instructions to another. We shall consider here a few in the order in which they might prove to be least effective.

Repetitous Persuasion: Giving the instructions over and over is not always wise. Anyone who has lived with a nagging wife or mother will agree that the constant repetition of a request is likely to cause a negative reaction and most certainly will not bring forth the prompt compliance desired.

Salesmanship: By giving one or more good reasons, the person follows the instructions since he feels that he is acting in the manner desired because it is to his advantage. However, he is aware that he can accept or reject the offer given for his consideration.

Psychological Persuasion: This is the same as "salesmanship" except that the motivation presented is directed to a greater degree towards our subconscious desire. For example, merchandisers know that they will sell more "cold cream" if they present it to their customers as a "beauty cream" rather than a "cleansing cream". "The Hidden Persuaders" by Vance Packard is an excellent book on this subject of motivation research.

Suggestion: This is the presenting of instructions in such a subtle manner that the person following the instructions is not aware of the reason for his action. This explains why others in a crowded room will yawn after seeing a neighbor yawn. Suggestion alone is not hypnosis although the hypnotist will use a combination of suggestion and salesmanship and conditioning in order to induce hypnosis depending upon the induction technique selected.

Conditioning: This is the manner of training a person to repond to instructions automatically. It is the way all military persons are taught to respond. It is perhaps the most effective way of giving instructions to a group of individuals while hypnosis is the most effective way of giving instructions to one individual. The serviceman is at all times aware that he has the ability to follow the orders or commands given to him or he can accept the punishment.

Hypnosis: This is so effective because the person receiving the instructions feels that he has no choice and must do as he is told. He feels a lack of responsibility for his actions and will often insist that he tried to resist but found he lacked the power and he will sometimes try to hide his embarrassment by declaring his inability to recall what transired.

We must also realize that there is a tremendous compelling force behind negative instructions. For example, if you are asked to NOT think of this page during the next thirty seconds you will find your attention returning here no matter how you try to direct it elsewhere. Equally foolish is the custom of saying the exact opposite of what we wish others to do. The Judge said to the prisoner, "I will let you go this time but I know you will go right out and get drunk again." When the man was arrested later that day he explained, "What the judge said kept running through my mind and it seemed like there was nothing left for me to do but get a drink."

In view of the fact that hypnosis obviously is the most effective manner of giving instructions, it is suprising to find so many of the traditional methods of inducing hypnosis are dependent upon the less effective form of repetitious persuasion. The hypnotherapist is careful to prepare the hypnotic prescription as explained in Part One of this book and he is careful to avoid being repetitious since each time he repeats his instructions the patient recognizes a lack of self-confidence and he tends to become impatient. When simple instructions are given briefly and without hesitation, the subject realizes that the hypnotist fully expects them to be obeyed and so the problem is diminished in importance and the idea of an improvement occuring is more readily accepted. Thus it becomes apparent why the "brush-off technique" and other rapid induction techniques are so much more effective when used by the physician, dentist and hypnotherapist.

All persons who can understand such simple instructions as stand up; sit down; close your eyes; and turn around, can be hypnotized. You can not hypnotize a baby that is three weeks old and you can not hypnotize a person whose mental capacity is so week that he can not follow simple directions. Of course, certain induction techniques likely to be effective when speaking to children, would not be used on persons who were much older. The proper technique must be found for the situation and individual concerned.

Having a knowledge of a grest variety of hypnotic techniques is important for two reasons. Primarily, it enables the hypnotist to select the technique which best suits his manner and personality. Secondly, it makes possible the use of a great variety of techniques when a subject fails to respond at once. The hypnotist should be prepared to change from one technique to another since sometimes the changing of the position of the patient from sitting in a chair to standing against the wall will make the difference between success and failure.

When you realize everyone can be hypnotized, under certain conditions, to some extent, by one hypnotist or another, you will not accept failure without having exhausted a wide range of techniques and you will be well pleased with your percentage of successes.

Four conditions must exist before one person can be hypnotized by another. They are as follows:

Rapport: This is the condition which does exist between the physician and his patient and between the dentist and his patient and between the teacher and his student. This condition does exist when the hypnotherapist speaks to his patient. The hypnotist who attempts hypnosis at a party must speak to his subject and by his considerate manner develop some degree of rapport.

Confidence: The person being hypnotized must know that the therapist has the ability to hypnotize others. Modesty has no place here.

Attention: The hypnotherapist need give this condition no consideration. However, it may serve to remove some foolish fears or superstitions concerning hypnosis. It is a fact that you can not hypnotize a person unless that individual knows that you are speaking to him. You can not hypnotize a person by accident or inadvertently cause a bystander to become hypnotized. We have all read of such incidents and must understand that some unfortunate individuals are so desireous of attracting attention they report such myths.

Motivation: Before one person can hypnotize another person there must exist a good reason. A husband can not hypnotize his wife in order for her to not spend so much money in the future. The dentist must offer hypnosis to his dental patient, not in order to lessen the possibility of pain, but he must suggest hypnosis with the understanding that when the patient is hypnotized it will be easier for the dentist to do his work.

After effective motivation has been offered and a feeling of rapport has been established and the patient has placed his confidence in the ability of the hypnotist who he understands is speaking to him, then it is necessary for the hypnotist to direct the subject's attention from one part of his body to another part of his body and we can consider him to be hypnotized.

Usually, this is when the hypnotist says to the patient, "When I count to 'three' your head will begin to move down to your chest." As the head slowly descends, the patient's respiration will change and this is perhaps the most common and most easily identifiable indication that the technique is effective and a state of hypnosis is being induced.

CHAPTER TWO

The Eye-to-eye Technique

The hypnotic induction technique referred to most frequently in this book is the "eye-to-eye" technique. It has the greatest value to the beginner since it incorporates the most basic principles of psychology and yet takes a short time and it is easy to learn. Most important is the fact that it allows the hypnotist to watch the subject intently and judge his response or resistance and it offers so many "check-points" or instances where the hypnotist can evaluate the acceptance of the suggestions as they are being given.

After the hypnotist has talked to the patient and explained his various reasons for desiring to induce hypnosis and he feels that the patient is receptive to the idea and that a feeling of rapport has been established, he then tells the patient to sit in a firm chair which is moved into position. The chair is moved so that it is directly under a light or so that the light from a window is at the patient's back. The actual position of the chair is not important, of course. but the act of moving the chair into a desired position is an effective way of indicating to the patient that the hypnotist does know what he is doing and this helps to create a feeling of confidence.

The hypnotist says, "Since being hypnotized is nothing like being asleep, I want you to sit in this firm chair so that you will be alert and better able to concentrate and follow the instructions I am about to given you. I don't want you to feel sleepy and tired. I am going to make you feel stronger and more capable in the future."

The hypnotist stands in front of the patient, with his right foot in between the subject's two feet which are resting flat on the floor The subject is not likely to feel as uncomfortable as he would be if the hypnotist stood directly in front of him. No one likes the feeling of being "enclosed" or "confined". The hypnotist is standing with his right foot forward and his body is actually in front of the right half of the subject's body.

The hypnotist lifts the patient's hands and gently turns them over

179

so that the palms are turned up. This is important for two reasons. The subject has a feeling of insecurity and helplessness when his open palms are turned up in his lap. Secondly, it affords the hypnotist the opportunity of lifting the hands and he can thus feel if the subject is tense or is relaxed and offers no resistance. If the hands are firm and unyielding, it is well for the hypnotist to say, "Just relax and follow my instructions as you listen to my voice."

A common reaction at this point is for the subject to smile or laugh. I always say, "It is perfectly all right for you to smile or laugh as there is nothing serious about what I am going to do and there is no reason for you to be frightened or concerned." In some instances the laughter is actually caused by a desire to disturb the hypnotist and the giving of permission at this point is enough to stop it completely. Also, the "negative suggestion" is deliberately used to cause the subject to become concerned and take the instruction seriously.

The hypnotist then brings his right forefinger up to his right cheek, under his right eye, and says, "Look into this eye and listen to my voice." Once you have the un-divided atention of the subject you breathe slowly and deeply as that is the manner in which you want the subject to breathe and there is bound to be some degree of "sympathetic response" between you and the subject.

Speaking in a soft voice, you say, "When I count 'three' I want you to allow your eyes to close; your eyeballs to roll upwards and your head will begin to feel heavy and tired. You will not go to sleep. You will hear everything I say and will know everything that takes place. One . . . two . . . three." When you see the subject's head begin to nod, you say, "When I count to 'three' your head will begin to nod and slowly begin to fall down towards your chest. One . . . two . . . three."

For our purpose we can consider that you have succeeded when the subject's head begins to nod and eventually falls against his chest. If the response is slow, you can say, "You will notice that your head seems to be moving very slowly and it seems to you that it has a long way to go."

There are several negative reactions from the subject which might have occurred. These take place during the first few seconds and they enable the hypnotist to judge how responsive the subject will be. First of all, if the subject does not look directly into your eye, he is asked to follow your instructions. Next indication that is noted, would be if the patient did not close his eyes at the count of 'three'. You are prepared for this bit of resistance. As you ask the subject to close his eyes, you slowly raise your right hand with the forefinger and middle finger extended and after a brief pause, to assure yourself that the subject is not about to respond willingly, you bring these two extended fingers to the subject's eyelids and you close his eyes for him. If the subject opens his eyes when your fingers are removed, you say, "No, I want you to allow your eyes to remain closed until I ask you to open them."

Another possible reaction to your having deliberately closed the subject's eyes would be for the eyeballs to roll upwards as you close the lids and then you can consider that you have succeeded as the rolling upwards of the eyeballs is an indication to be desired as it shows some degree of co-operation. If the subject just stared at you as you pulled his eyelids down, you can consider you are in the same position you were in when you started. The subject has not responded, but you do not know how soon he will begin to react. Therefore, you continue as before, suggesting his eyeballs will roll upwards and his head will become heavy and tired.

When the airplane pilot is about to bring his airplane in for a landing he can refer to many dials and gauges and lights on his instrument panel. He can thus "check" to learn if his landing gear is down and if the plane is ready for the landing he is about to attempt. If the indications are not favorable, he can take the airplane around the landing field once again and try to bring about any changes which he feels is necessary. In this same sense, the hypnotist has "check-points" that help him to decide if the subject is responding. All the rapid induction techniques described in this book have one or more "check-points".

The eye-to-eye technique has five primary "check-points" and thus it can be used so effectively by the beginner. First is the resistance you meet when lifting the hands slightly as you turn them over with the palms up. Secondly, when you ask the subject to look into your right eye. Third is when you ask him to close his eyes. Fourth is when you see if his eyeballs are turning upwards and fifth is when his head begins to nod. If these are all negative you may wish to attempt to induce hypnosis by another technique or simply state the hypnotic prescription and then ask him to open his eyes at the count of 'seven'. When the un-responsive patient opens his eyes he is told that he had been caused to relax slightly and the instructions given will bring about some improvement as far as treating his problem is concerned.

This eventuality is very remote, but if it happens do not be discouraged. I have had several experiences in which I felt I had not influenced the subject at all and yet later I received reports of complete and lasting results derived from those sessions which I had considered to be so unsatisfactory.

If the subject responds and his head falls against his chest, the hypnotist has a choice of "testing" the subject or just giving him the hypnotic prescription. The "testing" is often done for the benefit of the subject who wishes to feel that "something" has happened and also it is valuable to the beginner who wishes to assure himself that he has succeeded and is not able to recognize the lethargic breathing of the hypnotic state as readily as the experienced hypnotist.

Under no circumstance should it be possible for the subject to feel that he was not "a good subject" or not influenced by the hypnotic suggestions. To tell a subject that at the count of 'three' his head will fall against his chest makes it possible for him to resist and declare that his head did not fall as the hypnotist had predicted. Instead, the hypnotist should tell the subject he will feel his head get heavy and tired. The hypnotist should then watch carefully to see if there is any movement or lowering of the head. If the hypnotist sees the subject raise his head defiantly at this point he should change his tactics instantly. If the subject's head does move slowly downward or nods slightly it would then be wise to say, "At the count of 'three' your head will begin to nod slightly."

After the hypnotist sees the desired indication that the subject's head became heavy and tired and was lowered, he can give the subject one or more "tests" such as the "rigid arm" or "dry lips" or "hand-rising test" or the simple test of "being unable to open the eyes". The "tests" themselves can also be used as induction techniques and we prefer to use them as such. These "tests" will be found in Chapter Four as rapid-induction techniques for they can serve so well to induce hypnosis when you are talking to those in the particular age category indicated.

CHAPTER THREE

How To Awaken The Subject

A young lady recently told me that she greatly enjoyed being hypnotized but added that one of my suggestions upset her and made her very unhappy. I am sure I appeared very puzzled as she explained "Yes, I was very angry when you told me I would open my eyes at the count of 'seven'. Being hypnotized was so pleasant I wanted the hypnotic session to last much longer."

When you realize how pleasant a person feels in the hypnotic state, you must accept the possibility that some of the subjects will refuse to open their eyes when you give them such instructions.

The person who is hypnotized feels that he wants to follow the instructions given to him and he wants to respond promptly. If you say to a hypnotized subject, "You will raise your hand," this causes him to feel frustrated as he does not know WHEN you want him to raise his hand. If you start a group of school boys in a "foot race" and tell them to start running when you say 'one', many will be left at the starting point. Starting the boys by counting to 'two' will not improve matters as they have no idea how much time you will take between 'one' and 'two'. Therefore, to give the young racers an opportunity to become psychologically "set" for this race, you must count from 'one' to 'three'. To count further will serve no useful purpose and might result in confusion.

The hypnotist establishes a pattern and gives all of his instructions with the preliminary, "When I count to 'three' you will do this or that." This makes it possible for the subject to feel that he is responding at the proper instant. Finally he is told that he will open his eyes at the count of 'seven' and this additional few moments is a subtle indication that the hypnotist is considerate and allowing the subject to have a bit more time in preparing himself for the awakening from the hypnosis.

When the instructions for opening the eyes are preceeded by a few sentences of a beneficial nature, it is very likely that the subject will respond. I terminate the hypnotic session by saying, "When I count to 'seven' you will open your eyes and you will feel wide awake and well rested and refreshed. You will realize that you had been relaxed while able to hear me and you will look forward to the improvement that we have just discussed. You will be pleased to notice the changes and you will realize that it is all due to your using the ability that you have always possessed. You will sleep well tonight and tomorrow you will feel stronger and more capable. One . . . two . . . three . . . four . . . five . . . six . . . seven."

Situations where a subject responds nicely to all suggestions given him and yet insists he was at no time hypnotized or under the influence of hypnosis are by no means rare. The subject is conscious of having heard everything and he feels that he acted in a completely voluntary manner. He is likely to rationalize his actions and say he followed the instructions only because he wanted to see what was going to happen and he will tell you that he knew all the time he could open his eyes or refuse any of the suggestions, if he had so desired.

It is much easier and wiser to prevent the subject from feeling this way than to try to remedy or correct this impression after the hypnotic session. As soon as it is apparent the subject has responded to some extent, he should be told he will be able to hear every word spoken. Next the least change in his condition is called to his attention and he is asked to be conscious of the fact that his head feels heavy and tired. He is asked to be aware of all "tests" that take place. For example, the hypnotist should say, "I want you to realize your arm does feel stiff and straight and it is impossible for you to bend your arm no matter how hard you try."

The hypnotist might say, "When you awaken you will feel like you had a very pleasant little nap. You will realize you had been hypnotized because your head and body felt heavy and tired and when you open your eyes you will feel so much more rested and refreshed. You will want to be hypnotized again because it is such a pleasant feeling."

Since the hypnotist used the term, "nap", it sometimes happens that the subject will report a partial amnesia as he may consider a "nap" to mean he was asleep and so he will declare he could not remember anything that took place. The precautionary suggestions will at least cause the subject to say, "I could hear everything that was said, but I did feel heavy and tired and I do know I was hypnotized."

Sometimes the subject appears to reject the suggestion that he will open his eyes at the count of 'seven'. This may be due to his feeling happy and comfortable in the hypnotic state or it may be caused by the subject realizing that he can get a great deal of desired attention by keeping his eyes closed. There is absolutely nothing to worry about if the subject does not open his eyes when instructed to do so. Don't forget, he is awake.

If the hypnotic session has been very long and the subject appeared to be in a deep state, it would be wise to say, "When I count to 'seven' you will open your eyes as you are so well rested and you are eager to see the improvement that we have discussed and you want to do so many things, now that you feel so much better and more capable."

When the subject fails to open his eyes and you suspect it is because he is trying to cause you some concern or wishes to gain additional attention, it is very easy for you to poke him gently in his ribs and remind him that although he was hypnotized . . . . he was awake.

CHAPTER FOUR

Rapid Induction Techniques

On various occasions I found it possible to devote only a minimum amount of time to an individual and learned later that the hypnotic instructions had been accepted and the subject was quite well satisfied with the results. On the other hand, when the hypnotic session extended over a period of half an hour or more, the outcome was less successful. This has led me to adopt what I call a "brush-off" technique. I try to assume a casual manner and treat each complaint presented as being very easily treated by hypnotherapy. Frequently, I explain that I can not hypnotize the patient at that time due to an appointment I suddenly remember and then I re-consider and offer to have the hypnotic session anyway, explaining that his particular problem responds to hypnosis so readily that the entire session need take no more than a few minutes. After that introduction, I have found the subjects respond quickly and the results from these brief sessions have always been most satisfactory.

I believe that hypnotherapists help to defeat themselves when they have a long preliminary talk with their patients regarding hypnosis and the patient's pre-conceived ideas on the subject. By asking questions and trying to describe the sensations of hypnosis, the impression is created that the hypnotist is lacking in self-confidence.

The therapist should have a good understanding of the patient's problem and secure as much background information as possible. He should know the patient and the patient's interests and activities. Thus he can better create the warm feeling of rapport and present effective motivation. However, once he has this information, he should state in a matter-of-fact manner, "I will hypnotize you as that is the best way to bring about some improvement in your condition."

Ink Spot Technique

Age category: Three to six years of age.

Dr. Lester Kashiwa has used this technique in many instances when he had to perform some stiching on the child and knew he could operate more effectively if the child was resting and comfortable after his unfortunate accident.

The small child is seated on the operating table and his right hand is placed, palm down, in his lap. A fountain pen is opened and a small drop of ink is caused to fall on the back of this right hand. He says, "Look hard at the ink spot because it is going to slowly start to come up and it will come closer and closer to your forehead."

After the hand starts to raise, he continues, "Now the harder you try to get away from the ink spot the faster and faster it will move towards your face and when you feel your hand touching your face you will close your eyes and your head will become heavy and tired and you will go to sleep". In rare instances it has been necessary to urge the hand with the ink spot to move upwards, but just the very minimum assistance from the hypnotist's forefinger has been sufficient.

After the child's eyes close and his body falls back, the physician then speaks with reassurance that he will rest and feel fine and have a good appetite for the Ice Cream he will soon receive and that he will be able to follow all instructions.

Check-point: The hypnotist must wait until he sees the child's hand begin to rise.

You Do As I Do Technique

Age category: Three to eight years of age.

Dr. Kashiwa has developed this technique which he uses on small children. He sits the child on the examining table in his office and says, are going to do as I do. We will play a game and then you will feel no pain. Hold your finger like this and when I count to 'three' touch your nose." He then counts, "One, two, three". He touches his nose and waits for the child to do the same. When they both have their forefingers poised on the tip of their noses, he says, "When I count 'three' his time you will touch the top of your head. One, two, three."

Dr. Kashiwa touches the top of his head and the child imitates the action but he is corrected as the physician says, "Not here, but right on top." This is done to show the patient that he has an exact spot in mind and that the instructions must be followed precisely. Thus if the technique fails to induce hypnosis at first, it is possible for the therapist to try again, saying, "You see, you did not follow me exactly and you did not touch the right spot and now we must try it again until you do it correctly."

After the child has touched the top of his head, Dr. Kashiwa says, "Put your hand down and look into my eye. Not that eye, but this eye. Now I will count to three and you will close your eyes and you will feel very sleepy." Sometimes the child's manner indicates that he has been influenced and Dr. Kashiwa says, "Now you feel fine and you feel no pain."

On other occasions, when it is difficult to determine if a state of hypnosis has been induced, he sometimes presses his hand firmly against

188

the child's hand which is resting on the examining table and he says, "When I take my hand away, your hand will feel very light and it will go up in the air." When Dr. Kashiwa removes his hand, the child's hand rises and this "test" is usually all the asurance Dr. Kashiwa needs before he operates.

Check-point: When the child touches his nose as the hypnotist does the same.

Hypnotizing A Sleeping Person

Age category: Three to sixty years of age.

When you realize that a person who is hypnotized is actually awake, you can understand more readily that before a person who is sleeping can be hypnotized he must be awakened to some extent. The hypnotist actually takes the sleeping subject out of his "state of sleep" and puts him into a "state of hypnosis. In order to accomplish this, the hypnotist awakens the subject, but it is done so skillfully and gradually that the subject is not fully aware of the transition period. The hypnotist begins by speaking softly to the sleeping subject and tells him he can hear what is being said but will not be disturbed and will remain relaxed. After some time, the hypnotist says, "When I count to "three' your hand will move down to your side."

This is the point where the hypnotist is able to determine if the subject is following the instructions that he receives. After a pause of a few seconds, the subject either responds by himself or the therapist lifts the indicated hand and moves it for the patient. Thus we see that everything the hypnotist promises, does take place. The hypnotist continues to speak to the sleeping subject saying, "You will find some degree of improvement in the future and you will realize that others are noticing your good qualities and your actions have given them much happiness.

Once again the subject is told, "When I count to 'three' your head will turn so that the left side of your face is resting on your pillow." Another pause of several seconds and then the subject moves his head slowly or else the hypnotist moves the head so that the left side is resting on the pillow and he continues talking. Finally the hypnotist tells the patient to move an arm or leg and he responds voluntarily. It can them be suggested that he go into a deeper "hypnotic state" by complying with another movement. In such a "hypnotic trance" the patient can be questioned and at the end of the session he can be told that he will revert back to a condition of natural sleep after the hypnotist has counted to 'seven' and left the room.

Obviously, this technique can only be used upon someone who is familiar with the hypnotist and someone the hypnotist can properly visit while asleep.

Check-point: When the child moves his arm or head as directed. Thereafter, he can be considered to be in a "hypnotic state" and the "hypnotic prescription" could effectively be administered.

Back-Against-The-Wall Technique

Age category: Six to twelve years of age.

I have developed and used the following technique with great success when called upon to hypnotize small children. I know several dentists who prefer to use this induction techniquqe in a room adjoining the room containing the dental chair and dental instruments. After hypnosis has been induced, the child is told that at the count of 'three' he will open his eyes, go into the next room, sit in the dental chair and then close his eyes and go into a deeper sleep.

In this techniqque the position of the hypnotist is almost as important as that of the subject and it is rather unusual since the hypnotist is seated and the child stands. I try to select the largest and most comfortable chair available. I turn the chair so that it is facing a wall. I place the chair about two feet from the wall. I sit with my body down in the chair as much as possible and I extend my legs out from my body and I spread them apart. I invite the child to stand in between my exxtended legs with his body touching the wall. I ask the child to bring his heels up to the wall and stand erect and then I extend both my arms and spread them apart slightly, thus he can see that I have prepared myself to catch him when he falls forward.

Having talked to the child previously to develop a feeling of rapport and having offered to improve his ability as a student and as a participant in school sports, I now say, "Please stand with your back straight up against the wall. When I count to 'three' I want you to close your eyes. One, two, three."

"Now, when I count to 'three' I want you to try to bend your body at your waist. You will find that your body will become rigid and stiff and you will feel like a little wooden soldier. The harder you try to bend over the more rigid your back will become. However, even though you find that you can not bend over, I want you to keep right on trying. You will try to bend over so hard that you will just fall into my arms and then you will fall asleep. One, two, three."

That is all there is to this technique. An older person may be able to reason he has difficulty in bending over because he is standing so close to the wall. I have found that these simple instructions were all that were needed in almost every instance. Sometimes the child promptly moves forward and falls into my lap. I lift his rigid body and cradle him in my arms as I give him the hypnotic prescription. Sometimes I see a smirk on the the lad's face as he moves forward, confident he has the ability to bend over and then the smirk changes into a look of puzzlement as he realizes that he is not able to move forward without losing his balance and falling. When the child simply stands still, I continue to urge him forward by saying, "You feel so rigid and still and straight, but you must try to bend over. You bring your body forward and you feel your body getting heavier and heavier and you are falling forward as you try so hard to bend your rigid body."

Check-point: When the boy is standing straight up against the wall, I ask him to close his eyes when I count 'three'. If he does not comply, I know it is an indication that he does not want to be hypnotized at that time. Usually this is due to his parents being in the room. I have always found it effective to dismiss the parents saying, "You will have to leave us alone as I want to talk to this fellow on a man-to-man basis."

Hole-In-Top-Of-Head Technique

Age category: Eight to fourteen years of age.

The child is seated in a firm chair and asked to close his eyes. He is then asked to imagine or "play" that he has a hole-in-the-top-of-his-head. The hypnotist says, "Now when I count to 'three' I want you to play like you can look up through the hole in the top of your head. One, two, three. While you are trying to look at the ceiling through the hole in the top of your head I am going to count to 'three' and this time you will find that your eyelids will become tightly glued together. The harder you try to pull your eyelids apart the tighter they will become. One, two, three."

When the patient is trying to look at the ceiling through the imaginary hole in the top of his head and is also trying to open his eyes, he will find that his eyelids feel stuck together and he will be unable to open his eyes. This is true because it is impossible for us to open our eyes while our eyeballs are turned upward. The hypnotist should keep the subject's attention focused on the top of his head and if necessary, tap the top of the head gently as he says, "Keep looking through the hole in the top of your head and try to pull your eyelids apart."

After there has been some effort shown, the child is told that he is happy and contented to feel his eyes closed and he will feel so rested and tired he will no longer try to open his eyes but rather will enjoy knowing that he will become stronger and more capable in the future.

Check-point: The hypnotist can look at the child's closed eyelids and see if the eyeballs are turned upwards as directed.

Eyes Stuck Together Test

This technique can also be used as a most effective "test". In the midst of the hypnotic session I have had a subject open his eyes and say, "Look, I can open my eyes "

I explain that he can do so since we were not concerned about his eyes being open or closed. If I have noted a change in his respiration and felt he had been responsive, to some extent, I then proceed with the "hole in the top of the head" technique and I have always been pleased to find the subject respond by going into a deeper hypnotic state after he found his eyes apparently stuck together.

The Hypnotic Couch

Age category: Eight to sixteen years of age.

When hypnotizing small children in the presence of their parents, Dr. Kashiwa prefers to use some form of equipment. This is effective in showing both the patient and the parents that the physician is well equipped for this type of therapy. He will mention the "psychiatric couch" which is known to be an essential part of the psychiatrist's office and then he introduces his "hypnotic couch". This is actually a small foam rubber pad about three feet wide and five feet long. The pad is three inches thick and is enclosed in a heavy white cloth that can be removed and laundered. This pad is kept in place against the wall in the examining office by the use of several brackets that turn easily and allow the pad to be removed and place on the office floor.

The young patient is instructed to remove his shoes and stand on the pad near one end and with his back turned to the length of the pad which is obviously provided to support his body when he falls. He is told to stand with his feet together and his hands at his sides. The hypnotist says, "When I count 'three' I want you to close your eyes. One, two, three. Now I will count to 'three' and you will feel yourself swaying like you are standing on the deck of a small boat. One, two, three."

When the swaying is observed, the physician says, "When I count "three" you will feel the movement of the boat become greater and your swaying will be more forward and backward rather than from side to side. One, two, three. Now when I count 'three' you will feel yourself falling back and I will catch you. One, two, three." When the child falls, his body is supported by the hypnotist and brought down gently to the pad upon which he is allowed to rest during the entire hypnotic session.

Check-point: As in the previous technique, the check point is to see the child close his eyes promptly at the count of 'three'. If he does not comply, the parents are dismissed and the hypnotist endeavors to establish a greater degree of rapport.

Corner Of The Room Technique

Age category: Fourteen to Twenty years of age.

The subject is asked to stand with his feet together and his hands at his sides. He is told to look at the far corner of the room. This is explained to him as being the point where the two walls meet the ceiling. The hypnotist stands at the left side of the patient and he points with his out-stretched left hand towards the far corner of the room. The hypnotist rests his right arm around the shoulders of the patient. He is thus able to support the falling body and also feel if the body is responsive or resisting.

The hypnotist looks directly at the left side of the patient's face as he points with his left forefinger towards the far corner of the room. He says, "When I count to 'three' I want you to look at the tip of my finger."

After the patient changes his gaze from the far corner of the room to the finger tip, the hypnotist says, "When I count 'three' this time you will close your eyes and your eyeballs will roll upwards and your head and body will feel rigid and stiff and you will fall back." While saying this, the therapist slowly brings the tip of his left forefinger towards the patient's eyes. As the finger nears the patient's face the hypnotist says, "One, two, three." If the patient is resisting it may be necessary for the hypnotist to pull his right shoulder back slightly as he speaks to him after the eyes are closed.

Check-point: The performer is looking at the left side of the patient's face as he wants to see if the patient does shift his gaze slightly from the far corner of the room to the tip of the left forefinger.

The Silent Technique

Age category: Sixteen to twenty six years of age.

Perhaps one of the most useful techniques, aside from the eye-to-eye technique is the "silent" technique. It has proven to be extremely valuable to me when I demonstrate hypnosis in Japan since I can not speak the language understood by the subject and also it is so unusual that it can be effectively used on about ninety nine per cent of the patients, who are in the proper age category.

After explaining that I will hypnotize the person without saying a word, I indicate by gestures that I wish the individual to rise from his chair and stand in front of me with his feet close together. I place his hands at his sides and then I indicate with a little pressure that I want him to hold his hands closely to his body. As he complies, I nod to indicate that he has been following my unspoken instructions, properly.

Moving to his side, I gently close his eyelids and then pause for a moment and look to make sure that he is keeping his eyes shut. I move around so that I am standing directly behind him and I then bring up my two hands so that they are along side his head and I very gently touch his temples. I touch his temples very lightly and then I quickly withdraw my fingers. Once again I touch his temples but this time I gently indicate that I want him to fall backwards since I exert a minimum of pressure against his temples in that direction. I again remove my fingers for a pause of several moments and then I return them to the subject's temples with the same mimimum backward pressure. This is continued until the subject falls backward.

As the subject falls, I hold his body at a forty-five degree angle and command him to stiffen his body. I then say, "When I count 'three' you will stand up, with my help, but you will feel as heavy and as tired as you feel now. One, two, three."

Once the subject is back in an upright position, I step to his left side with my right arm around his shoulders, in order to support his body as he may often sway and appear unsteady on his feet. I now say, "When I count 'three' your head will feel heavy and tired and will begin to fall slowly down towards your chest. One, two, three." As the head begins to nod and then move downward, the patient's respiration can usually be seen to change and this is the indication that he is entering the 'hypnotic state'. At this time I either proceed with the rigid arm 'test' or merely deliver the hypnotic prescription.

The silent technique can be explained in this manner. First of all it is not actually accomplished without any words being spoken. The statement that the subject will be hypnotized without the hypnotist saying a word is heard and understood by the subject as well as by any audience that might be present. That rather remarkable statement serves to impress the subject, and when the hypnotist stands behind him, the subject is puzzled and bewildered. He wonders what will take place and what he will be expected to do. It is impossible for him to reject any of the suggestions given to him by the hypnotist, he thinks, as the suggestions are not spoken, He can not challenge the therapist after the session, saying, "You said this was going to happen but it did not happen."

The unusual situation causes the subject to be extremely alert and concious of the least change in his condition. As soon as he receives the slight indication at his temples that it is desired for him to fall back, he begins to think of falling and this in most cases, is enough to cause him to fall.

Check-points: Aside from the eye-to-eye technique, this is one of the most valuable techniques as it is so easy to learn and it affords so many good check-points. The first check-point is felt by the hypnotist as he places the subject's hands firmly against his body. If the hands move away from the side of the leg, this can be considered to be a negative reaction. The subject will either sway back slightly after the first indication at his temples that a backward movement is desired or else he will deliberately pull his body forward and that is a most dramatic negative indication. The hypnotist continues with the un-spoken suggestion at the subject's temples and when the subject does fall back, he will either rest on the back of his heels or bend his knees and thus his body will be supported by the hypnotist while his feet are still resting flat on the floor. This is another negative indication. Finally, the subject is told that he will stand in an upright position, **with the help of the hypnotist,** and thus we find him either bringing himself erect or holding his body straight and allowing the therapist to bring him forward.

Reflex Technique

Age category: Fourteen to thirty years of age.

One of the simplest and almost infallible techniques for inducing hypnosis is so effective since the first portion provides the subject with a strange feeling or "phenomena" which is the result of a natural reflex action. Timing is an important factor as the induction must move smoothly from one step to the other

The subject is asked to stand facing the hypnotist with the right side of his body about one foot from a wall. The hypnotist is standing with the left side of his body about one foot from the same wall in the room. They both hold their hands down by their sides and the subject is told to follow all instructions. He can see the hypnotist mirroring the movements that he is asked to make. The subject is asked to press the back of his right hand firmly against the wall. He can see the hypnotist pressing the back of his own left hand against the wall. The subject is asked to take two steps to his left side when the hypnotist counts 'three' and he sees the hypnotist take two steps away from the wall as they move in unison.

The hypnotist says, "When I count 'three' you will feel your right hand begin to grow lighter and start to float up in the air." This happens as a natural reflex action and is encouraged by the subject watching the hypnotist raise his own left hand. Actually this first portion of the technique can be considered a "trick" designed to help you gain the subject's confidence.

Immediately after the subject's hand rises, the hypnotist says, "When I count 'three' you will point at my toes with your right forefinger. One, two, three" They are then standing facing each other about seven or eight feet apart, pointing at the other's toes. The hypnotist continues, "When I count 'three' this time your right hand will begin to move upwards and I want you to continue to look at whatever part of my body your finger is pointing toward. One, two, three." The hypnotist then starts to slowly raise his left hand with the extended forefinger and the verbal suggestion along with the visual suggestion of the therapist's rising left hand is usually sufficient for the subject to respond and when his hand starts to rise this time you know it is not as a reflex action but that it is a real response to the hypnotic suggestion.

As the subject's hand rises, the hypnotist says, "When your finger is pointing at my face, your eyes will close." The hypnotist has his own left hand raised by this time and he is staring intently at the patient's eyes. He waits for the subject to close his eyes and if after a few moments there is no response, it is acceptable for the hypnotist to step forward and with his two forefingers, to gently close the eyes that are staring at him with such a fixed gaze.

The hypnotist continues, "When I count 'three' this time, you right hand will come down and when your right forefinger is pointing towards the floor, your body will fall forward and I will catch you. One, two, three." The physician steps forward and prepares to catch the falling body. He says, "When I count 'three' you will stand up straight, with my help, but you will still feel as heavy and as tired as you feel now. One, two, three."

As in the other falling techniques, the hypnotist then stands at the side of the subject, with his right arm around the person's back to support him, and says, "When I count to 'three' your head will become heavy and tired and will begin to slowly move down towards your chest. One, two, three." When the subject's head does begin to nod and move down towards his chest, the hypnotist watches for a change in the patient's respiration as this is the "check-point" he can depend upon most often.

Check-points: When the subject's right hand rises upwards as the result of the reflex action caused by his pressing his right hand so intently against the unyielding wall. If there is no reaction at this point, the hypnotist must suggest another position since he may wish to attempt another induction technique after speaking to the patient briefly in order to increase the feeling of rapport. The second check-point is to see the right hand with extended forefinger rise up. This indicates that the response is entirely due to the visual and spoken suggestions. The third check-point is for the subject to close his eyes as directed. If the patient does not close his eyes, the hypnotist steps forward and closes the eyes for him. This action can be responsible for the successful induction of hypnosis. If the subject re-opens his eyes, the hypnotist explains again that the induction of hypnosis is a completely voluntary act and involves the fullest co-operation of the patient. At this point, the negative response would cause the hypnotist to dismiss the remainder of this induction technique and perhaps stand next to the subject and speak the intended prescription before asking him to open his eyes at the count of 'seven'.

Eye-To-Eye Technique

Age category: Sixteen to sixty years of age.

This technique has been carefully explained in Chapter Two of this second section.

Check-points: The primary check-points are first, the resistance you feel when you turn the subject's hands palm upwards in his lap. Secondly, when you ask the subject to look into your right eye. Third is when you ask him to close his eyes. Fourth is when you see if his eyeballs are turning upwards and fifth is when you see his head begin to nod.

The secondary check-points can be used in all the various induction techniques. After the subject's head has fallen forward, the hypnotist says, "When I count 'three' your head will come up, **with my help.**" He then puts his right hand under the patient's forehead and counts, "One, two, three." At this point he pauses briefly in order to determine if the subject is about to lift his head without assistance or not. When the therapist finds he must gently raise the patient's head, this is considered an affirmation that the individual is responding to the hypnotic instructions. The final and usually the most conclusive check-point is when the subject opens his eyes after the hypnotist has said, "Seven."

The individual who has not been influenced will open his eyes promptly as it really does not take much effort to do this. The patient who has been successfully hypnotized, to some extent, will open his eyes slowly and blink several times and often sit with a fixed stare for a moment and in other ways indicate that he is making an effort to "bring himself back to the present situation."

Eye-To-Finger Technique

Age category: Sixteen to sixty years of age.

The "eye-to-finger technique" can be used easily in semi-darkness and when the hypnotist and subject are seated side by side. The hypnotist holds his right forefinger directly in front of the patient's face and says, "Please look at the tip of my finger and listen to my voice. When I count 'three' I want you to allow your eyes to close, your eyeballs will roll upwards and your head will feel heavy and tired. One, two three."

When the hypnotist sees the subject's head nod or begin to fall, he says, "Now, when I count to 'three' your head will begin to slowly nod and move down towards your chest." If the response is not apparent, the therapist can increase the effectiveness of this technique by saying, "You will notice that your head is moving very slowly and it seems to you that your head has a great distance to travel."

Check-points: He looks intently at the patient's eyes and he can then observe if there is a steady, fixed gaze and if the eyes close promptly at the given command. Of course, he also places the subject's hands in his lap with the palms upward.

Eye-To-Pencil Technique

Age category: Sixteen to sixty years of age.

Those who prefer to have the subject look at the tip of a lead pencil instead of at their finger feel that this way the attention is focused on a more exact point. The subjects who have a pre-conceived idea that some device is necessary for the induction of hypnosis will find the "eye-to-pencil technique" more acceptable. The hypnotist speaks in the same manner as in the "eye-to-finger technique."

Check-points: These are exactly the same as in the "eye-to-finger technique."

Eye-To-Crystal Ball Technique

Age category: Sixteen to sixty years of age.

In some intsances, the "eye-to-crystal ball technique" is effective when the subject feels his attention is held by the fascinating crystal. If the crystal ball is rather large and properly introduced, it will be impressive and cause some older people to respond more quickly than in the previously described techniques. The hypnotist speaks in the same manner as in the "eye-to-finger technique."

Check-points: The check-points are the same as used in the "eye-to-finger technique."

Swinging Object Technique

Age category: Sixteen to sixty years of age.

Asking the subject to watch a shining swinging object is one of the classic induction techniques associated with hypnotists and so might prove to be effective when used on an individual who has seen such a method used by a hypnotist in a motion picture or on a television show. The movement of the subject's eyes from side to side is expected to cause fatigue and create a desire to rest the eyes by closing them as instructed.

The hypnotist says, "You will hold your head still and allow your eyes to rest upon this shining object and you will continue to watch this shining object until I count 'three'. When I count 'three' your eyes will close, your eyeballs will roll upward and your head will feel heavy and tired." From this point, the hypnotist continues exactly as in the "eye-to-eye technique."

Check-points: The check-points are the same as in the "eye-to-finger technique."

Dry Lips Technique

Age category: Fourteen to seventy five years of age.

If I find the subject un-responsive to the "eye-to-eye technique" I always attempt to induce hypnosis with the "dry lips technique".

The hypnotist says, "When I count 'three' your lips will feel very dry and parched and you will feel thirsty and have a great desire to swallow. One, two, three." There is a pause of several seconds and often the subject will pucker his lips or in some other way indicate that his lips do feel uncomfortable.

The therapist then continues, "When I count 'three' this time, you will open your mouth, take a breath of a air and swallow it and you will feel like you had a sip of water. One, two, three. Now, when I count 'three' you will run your tongue over your lips and your lips will feel better, your mouth will feel. better and your throat will feel better. One, two three."

On a great many occasions I have seen the subject hesitantly push his tongue out through slightly opened lips and then I have seen his respiration change and his head begin to nod as his entire manner indicated his responsiveness to this induction technique.

Dentists will find this "dry lips technique" of great value since the patient who feels thirsty and parched will have a minimum amount of salivary secretion. They first induce hypnosis by another induction technique and then tell the patient that his lips feel dry and his mouth is parched and he feels thirsty and has a great desire to swallow. They then proceed to do their dental work on the patient's teeth and before asking the patient to open his eyes, they remove the uncomfortable feeling by telling the patient to swallow a breath of air and then run his tongue over his lips and feel the improvement.

Check-point: The check-point here is to see the patient run his tongue over his lips when he is instructed to do so.

Rigid Arm Technique

Age category: Eight to fifty years of age.

This is a most effective "test" when used with young boys or men who are conscious of their muscles and pleased with the idea that by exerting a great deal of effort and thus straining their muscles they will be increasing their strength.

The hypnotist says, "When I count 'three' I will raise your right arm in the air, but it will not disturb you. Your head and body will feel just as it does now. One, two, three." The therapist then picks up the patient's right hand and arm and gently raises it into the air. This is done to show the subject that the hypnotist is concerned about him and is considerate as he proceeds with this induction technique or "test" if it is presented after some other induction technique has been used with some degree of success.

The hypnotist continues saying, "When I count 'three' I want you to try to bend your right arm at the elbow." The instructions must be carefully worded and presented in a precise manner as otherwise the subject may insist later that he was never asked to attempt to bend his arm.

The therapist then says, "One. Close your right hand very tightly, digging your fingers into your palm. Two. Push your right fist out, away from your body, until you feel your elbow lock into place." Here it is important to wait and see if the patient is indeed pushing his fist away from his body to the fullest extent. If the effort does not seem complete, the hypnotist will urge him to increase his voluntary co-operation, saying, "You must push your fist way out from your body. This is like everything else in life, the more you put into it the more benefit you will get out of it.

"Three. Your right arm feels like a huge massive solid bar of steel."

If the subject makes a great effort and appears to be about to bend his right arm, somewhat, the hypnotist stops the movement and says, "That is very good. I want you to be aware of the great amount of effort that was required." At this point I want to remind the student of hypnotherapy that he did not tell the patient that the right arm could not be bent. Thus he need feel no embarrassment over what might at first seem to be a failure. On the other hand, the subject is very likely to find it most difficult to bend his arm as we can not exert pressure in two directions at the same time and he can not pull his arm in towards his body if he is also pushing his fist away. The subject will usually strain his arm and show that he feels the rigidity that is desired and implied, but not as yet, expressed in words.

The hypnotist says, "You notice the rigidity and strength in your arm and you will also notice the increased strength and power in your shoulder muscles as well as in your arm muscles. I want you to notice that the harder you try to bend your arm the more rigid it becomes. However, even though you can not bend your arm, I want you to put forth a great deal of effort as this will be a strain to your muscles and thus bring about an improvement in your muscular tone and muscular co-ordination.

"When I count 'three' I will raise your left arm into the air, but it will not disturb you and your head and body will continue to feel just as it does now. One, two, three." The left hand is very gently and slowly raised into the air as the hypnotist watches intently to see if the patient opens his eyes or makes an attempt to bend his right arm.

"When I count 'three' this time, I want you to try to bend your left arm at the elbow. Your left arm will feel more rigid that the right. It is important for you to notice and be aware of this difference. One. Close your left fist very tightly. Two. Push your left fist out, away from your body until your elbow locks into place. Three. Your left arm feels more rigid than your right.

"When I count 'three' your arms will slowly come down to your sides and your head will fall slowly down to your chest and you will feel a great sense of exhaustion, just as though you had been working in a gymnasium for several hours. After your arms are down you will be able to unclench your fists and the rigidity will completely disappear from your arms.

Check-points: The first check-point is to see if the right fist is tightly clenched. You can look at the knuckles to see if this has been accomplished. The second check-point is to see if the right fist is thrust as far as possible away from the body. The third check-point is to see if the subject is making an effort to bend his right elbow. If these first three checkpoints are negative, it is still possible that this technique might induce hypnosis as the difference between the left arm and the right arm is called to his attention.

Hand Rising And Floating In The Air Technique

Age category: Sixteen to thirty five years of age.

I have used this technique exclusively with girls and young women as I can suggest that the lightness of the hand will help to make their entire body lighter and more buoyant in the future. Thus I present the idea that ultimately the subject will feel lighter, with more poise and appear more beautiful.

The hypnotist says, "When I count 'three' I will move your right hand but it will not disturb you, your head and your body will continue to feel just as it does now. One, two, three." The therapist very gently and slowly lifts the right hand and carefully turns it over so that it is with the palm down and then he lowers it so that it rests lightly on the patient's knee.

"When I count 'three' your right hand will begin to feel as though it is full of a light type of helium gas. It will seem to be without any bones or muscles and it will very slowly start to rise up into the air. This is a very pleasant feeling and you will notice that the higher it goes the lighter it will get. One, two, three." The hypnotist then waves his hand over the subject's right hand as this gentle breeze will be noticed and cause a greater degree of attention to be focused on that hand. Sometimes a great deal of patience is required as some individuals will respond more slowly than others. After a bit the therapist can urge the right hand upward by calling attention to the fact that the left hand feels so very heavy and tired and the right hand feels different.

"You notice how the hand feels so very light and pleasant. This is a very pleasant floating sensation and it makes you feel so restful, just as though your hand were floating on a cloud." If in two or three minutes this does not have the desired effect, I then slip my right forefinger under the patient's right wrist and gently exert enough pressure to move the hand and thus urge it to respond. I continue to raise her wrist with my right forefinger as I speak and if the hand begins to move of it's own accord, that is fine, otherwise I raise the wrist myself and thus fulfill the promise I made that "her hand would rise up into the air."

Of course, it is to be expected that the right hand will slowly move and rise up, of it's own accord, and then the left hand is gently turned over and it is also caused to rise up into the air.

Check-points: The check-point is the resistance that can be felt as the right hand is turned over. A negative indication at this time will often be the moving of one or more fingers on the left hand and this is a sign that the attention is being focused away from the right hand.

Expanding Chest Technique

Age category: Ten to thirty years of age.

While this has long been a favorite technique for me to use with small boys, I have been extremely pleased on several occasions to find it to be a most effective induction technique when used on young men who were between the ages of twenty and thirty and were athletically inclined.

The hypnotist says, "When I count 'three' you will take a deep breath and fill your lungs full of air. One, two, three. When I count 'three' this time you will allow the air from your lungs to go out through your lips but your body will remain the same and your chest will remain the same. One, two, three. When I count 'three' this time you will take another deep breath and fill your lungs full of air. This time you will have a much greater capacity than before. One, two, three. I want you to hold this breath as I know that you will feel the difference as your shoulder muscles will feel stronger and more powerful and your pectoral muscles in your chest will feel stronger and you will feel like you have a huge chest, much larger than before. When I count three this time, you will once again allow the air to leave your lungs, but your chest will remain up and your shoulders and the entire upper portion of your body will feel stronger and more powerful. One, two three."

The inceasred amount of oxygen coupled with the hypnotic suggestions regarding the large chest and increased lung capacity will often be sufficient to induce an hypnotic state, especially when the individual is most desirous for such physical improvement.

Check-point: This is when the subject takes his first deep breath. It must be apparent that he is indeed filling his lungs with air as he raises his chest. Otherwise, he is told that hypnosis can only be induced as the result of voluntary co-operation on his part and that he must consciously follow all the instructions.

Hypnotizing In The Dark

Age category: Eighteen to fifty years of age.

When speaking to a patient in darkness or semi-darkness I prefer to suddenly place my right hand over his eyes, thus making him aware that he is in total darkness and the technique is somewhat similar to the "shock technique" as the abrupt movement is always a suprise.

The hypnotist says, "When I count to 'three' your head will begin to feel heavy and tired and will begin to move down toward your chest. One, two, three." Once the head begins to move, the right hand is slowly lifted away from the face and the therapist then proceeds with either the "dry lips technique" or the "rigid arm technique" or the "hand rising technique".

Check-point: The check-point is when the subject's head begins to slowly move down towards his chest. If this response is negative, you are in the same position as you would be if the first five check-points of the "eye-to-eye technique" were negative. The "dry lips technique" or the "rigid arm technique" would then be applied in an effort to induce hypnosis rather than as a "test" to make the patient aware of his hypnotic condition.

Hypnotizing Over The Telephone

Age category: Sixteen to sixty years of age.

Of course the hypnotist and the subject must agree that there is a valid reason for the hypnosis at that moment and under the unusual induction conditions. Thus it can certainly be expected that all instructions will be followed. The patient is asked to sit on a firm chair, with his feet flat on the floor and with his eyes closed. The hypnotist says, "When I count to 'three' your head will begin to feel heavy and tired and your chest will feel heavy and tired. One, two, three. Now, with each breath you take you will notice your chest getting heavier and heavier."

The "dry lips technique" is almost a necessity at this point as the subject needs to know that he can feel "a difference". When the individual is present in the same room as the hypnotist he has confidence that the therapist can see the changes in his condition.

If the subject has been hypnotized previously, it is only necessary to tell him that he will feel as heavy and tired as he felt on the last occasion when he had been hypnotized, but that he will still be able to hold the telephone to his ear.

Check-point: The subject is told to breath into the mouthpiece as he feels his chest grow heavier. The labored breathing becomes quite audible.

The Shock Technique

Age category: Sixteen to sixty years of age.

The shock technique is perhaps the most dramatic method of inducing hypnosis. It has it's greatest value in that it can be used most effectively when the patient is in a condition of shock. In Chapter Thirteen of the first part of this book we find that Dr. Kashiwa has used this technique in several emergencies.

The hypnotist jumps at the patient, throws his hands towards the subject's face and shouts, "Sleep"!

This technique can not be practised by the beginner, but in an emergency it's value can not be denied.

Check-point: The patient will fall and his body will become rigid.

Hypnotizing A Person Who Is Sitting Next To A Hypnotized Person

Age category: Sixteen to sixty years of age.

This technique has it's greatest value when working with mental patients or those who might, for one reason or another, resist the idea of hypnosis. It is dependent upon the fact that there is a "sympathetic response" between two people who are sitting together. Thus the hypnotist is able to speak to the hypnotized person and bring about several changes in his breathing and rigidity in his arms and the person sitting beside this subject is likely to be greatly impressed.

We know that a person who is hypnotized looks so different from the way he feels. He looks so helpless and seems to be moving as in a "trance". When the hypnotist points dramatically at the subject who has watched his neighbor respond to the hypnotic instructions and says, "Now you will close your eyes and your eyeballs will roll upwards and your head will feel heavy and tired", he feels certain that there is no escape from the physician's "hypnotic power".

Check-point: The movement upwards of the patient's eyeballs when he closes his eyes.

Red or Bench Technique

Age category: Sixteen to sixty years of age.

This is a most effective induction technique, but because of the rather intimate position between the hypnotist and his subject, it is usually used only for the treatment of mental patients or when the therapist is hypnotizing his own wife.

The patient is seated on the edge of a bed or low bench. The hypnotist stands with his right leg between the subject's knees and the subject's hands are turned palms upwards and these are placed well back in the lap. This induction technique is similar to the "eye-to-eye technique" except that the hypnotist is so close to the patient that the patient's body is forced to assume a most uncomfortable position. Also the patient's body is off balance as it is supported by the hypnotist.

The hypnotist supports the subject's body with his left hand as he points toward his right eye with his right forefinger and says, "Please look into this eye and listen to my voice. When I count 'three' your eyes will close, your eyeballs will roll upwards and your head and body will feel heavy and tired. One, two, three."

The fact that the patient is sitting on the edge of the bed, makes it easy for him to accept the idea that he will fall back. Once he has closed his eyes, the therapist slowly removes his left hand from the subject's back and then the subject must feel his body grow heavy as gravity pulls him down. The subject is allowed to fall back down on the bed or bench and the hypnotist keeps his hand around the upper portion of the subject's back. At this point there is usually a change seen in the patient's respiration. The hypnotist says, "When I count 'three' you will sit up, with my help, but you will still feel as heavy and as tired as you feel now. One, two, three."

The hypnotist then raises the patient back into a sitting position and says, "When I count 'three' your head will feel heavier and will begin to slowly move down towards your chest. One, two, three". This time the respiration change should be more apparent and it would then be proper to use the "dry lips technique" or the "rigid arm technique" or the "hand rising and floating technique."

Check-point: All the check-points of the "eye-to-eye technique" are used as this technique is so similar.

Hospital Cart Technique

Age category: Eighteen to sixty years of age.

This is an extremely effective induction technique as the hypnotist has the advantage of gravity and also he can move his position to best suit the responsiveness of his patient.

The patient is placed on the hospital cart in order to be moved into the operating room or the delivery room in the case of childbirth. The hypnotist stands on the left side of the cart and he has the patient sit up. His legs are extended straight in front of his body and the therapist rests his right arm around the subject's body, with the right hand on the subject's right shoulder. The patient's hands are placed palm upwards in his lap and his head is turned considerably to the left as the physician says, "Please look in my right eye. When I count 'three' your eyes will close, your eyeballs will roll upward and your head and body will feel heavy and tired. One, two, three."

When the subject has closed his eyes, the hypnotist can feel the body slowly move back and rest against his right arm. He then says, "When I count 'three' this time your head and body will begin to fall back. One, two, three."

When the patient has fallen back onto the cart, it is then likely the physician might use the "hand rising technique" or the "rigid arm technique" as the patient's hand in the air can be used as a re-assuring check-point throughout the operation.

Check-points: The same check-points as in the "eye-to-eye technique."

Arm Chair Technique

Age category: Forty to eighty years of age.

This is a most effective induction technique for older persons as they can be comfortably seated and the hypnotist in this technique is in a less dominating and therefore, more acceptable position.

The patient is seated in a comfortable arm chair and the hypnotist sits in a firm chair that is placed on the left side of the arm chair and is turned so that when the therapist is seated, he is facing the left side of the patient. The two chairs are as close as possible and thus the hypnotist is able to rest his right arm around the subject's shoulders as he holds his extended left forefinger about fifteen inches in from of the subjects face.

The hypnotist lifts the patient's hands and gently turns them palm upwards and allows them to rest in the patient's lap. When the patient is seventy years old or more, they often sit with their hands on the arm rests of the chair and I have found it is best not to disturb them by moving the hands. Otherwise, this provides an effective check-point as well as creating a feeling of helplessness.

The hypnotist holds his extended left forefinger in front of the subject's face as he says, "Please look at my finger. When I count 'three' your eyes will close, your eyeballs will roll upward and your head and body will feel heavy and tired. One, two, three."

The therapist does not look at the extended left forefinger. He looks intently at the left side of the patient's face and thus he can see if the patient does respond by closing his eyes as directed. When the eyes are closed, the hypnotist waits until he sees the subject's head begin to nod. He then says, "When I count 'three' your head will begin to slowly move down towards your chest. As your head begins to move it will seem to you that it is moving very slowly and that it has a long way to go. Also, you will notice that your chest will get heavy and tired and with each breath you take, your chest will seem to get heavier and heavier. One, two, three."

The "dry lips technique" can then be used either as a "test" or as a supplemental induction technique.

Check-points: The turning of the hands palm upwards affords the first check-point. Secondly, the closing of the eyes at the count of 'three'.

Flickering Candle Flame Technique

Age category: Sixty five to eighty five years of age.

The patient is seated in a comfortable chair and is asked to gaze at a flickering candle flame that is placed about three feet in front of his face. Dentists have found this to be a most effective induction technique as they have the small gas burner available as part of their office equipment and the patient need not move from the dental chair as the office is darkened and the burner is lit.

After the patient has been allowed to look at the flickering flame for a minute or more, the hypnotist says, "When I count 'three' your eyes will close, your eyeballs will roll upwards and your head and body will feel heavy and tired. One, two, three."

After the eyes are closed by either the patient or the therapist, and the head is seen nodding, the therapist says, "When I count 'three' your head will begin to slowly move down towards your chest. One, two, three."

Check-point: The palms are turned upward and the nodding of the head after the eyes are closed afford two effective check-points. In this technique it is not significant if the hypnotist finds that he must close the eyes for the patient.

Eyes Open Technique

Age category: Sixty to eighty five years old.

In rare instances the patient is likely to refuse to close his eyes. I have found this can be overcome by the use of this technique.

The hypnotist asks the patient to look at his extended left forefinger. The hypnotist says, "When I count 'three' your head will grow heavy and tired and your body will grow heavy and tired and as you look at this finger you will find that with each breath you take your body will grow heavier and heavier. One, two, three."

The therapist watches for the respiration to change and when this is apparent, he can close the patient's eyes.

Check-point: It is important to see that the patient does keep his eyes on the extended left finger and does not allow his gaze to wander.

Carotid Artery Technique

Age category: Sixteen to forty years of age.

The "carotid artery technique" is recommended for use only by members of the medical profession. It should not be used on a patient who has a weak heart condition.

The subject is seated at the end of an examining table so that he can fall backwards on the table. The physician's left hand is placed behind the subject's head in order to support it. The therapist presses the right thumb and index finger against the vagus nerve and carotid artery on each side of the Adam's apple at about the level of the cricoid cartilage, leaving the larynx free from pressure so that breathing is not obstructed. The pressure is firm but not too strong.

At the same time that pressure is applied to the throat, the left thumb and second finger may be pressed firmly against the neck just below the mastoid, behind each ear. It will be found that pressure on a small spot just behind the lobe of the ear quickly produces a slight dazed feeling.

As pressure is applied with both hands at the same time, the hypnotist whispers into the ear of the patient, "Close your eyes when I count 'three' and rest. One, two, three. Breathe deeply and feel your body grow heavy and tired. Your body will feel so heavy you will feel that you could go right to sleep but you will hear everything I say."

Check-point: The eyes must be closed voluntarily by the patient as the hypnotist is using both hands in this induction technique.

WILSHIRE SELF-IMPROVEMENT LIBRARY

ASTROLOGY

BRIDGE

BUSINESS, STUDY & REFERENCE

CALLIGRAPHY

CHESS & CHECKERS

_____HOW TO WIN AT CHECKERS Fred Reinfeld 7.00
_____1001 BRILLIANT WAYS TO CHECKMATE Fred Reinfeld 10.00
_____1001 WINNING CHESS SACRIFICES & COMBINATIONS Fred Reinfeld 10.00

COOKERY & HERBS

_____CULPEPER'S HERBAL REMEDIES Dr. Nicholas Culpeper 5.00
_____FAST GOURMET COOKBOOK Poppy Cannon 2.50
_____HEALING POWER OF HERBS May Bethel 5.00
_____HEALING POWER OF NATURAL FOODS May Bethel 7.00
_____HERBS FOR HEALTH—HOW TO GROW & USE THEM Louise Evans Doole 7.00
_____HOME GARDEN COOKBOOK—DELICIOUS NATURAL FOOD RECIPES Ken Kraft .. 3.00
_____MEATLESS MEAL GUIDE Tomi Ryan & James H. Ryan, M.D. 4.00
_____VEGETABLE GARDENING FOR BEGINNERS Hugh Wilberg 2.00
_____VEGETABLES FOR TODAY'S GARDENS R. Milton Carleton 2.00
_____VEGETARIAN COOKERY Janet Walker 10.00
_____VEGETARIAN COOKING MADE EASY & DELECTABLE Veronica Vezza 3.00

GAMBLING & POKER

_____HOW TO WIN AT POKER Terence Reese & Anthony T. Watkins 10.00
_____SCARNE ON DICE John Scarne 20.00
_____WINNING AT CRAPS Dr. Lloyd T. Commins 10.00
_____WINNING AT GIN Chester Wander & Cy Rice 10.00
_____WINNING AT POKER—AN EXPERT'S GUIDE John Archer 10.00
_____WINNING AT 21—AN EXPERT'S GUIDE John Archer 10.00
_____WINNING POKER SYSTEMS Norman Zadeh 10.00

HEALTH

_____BEE POLLEN Lynda Lyngheim & Jack Scagnetti 5.00
_____COPING WITH ALZHEIMER'S Rose Oliver, Ph.D. & Francis Bock, Ph.D. 10.00
_____HELP YOURSELF TO BETTER SIGHT Margaret Darst Corbett 10.00
_____HOW YOU CAN STOP SMOKING PERMANENTLY Ernest Caldwell 5.00
_____NATURE'S WAY TO NUTRITION & VIBRANT HEALTH Robert J. Scrutton 3.00
_____NEW CARBOHYDRATE DIET COUNTER Patti Lopez-Pereira 2.00
_____REFLEXOLOGY Dr. Maybelle Segal 7.00
_____REFLEXOLOGY FOR GOOD HEALTH Anna Kaye & Don C. Matchan 10.00
_____YOU CAN LEARN TO RELAX Dr. Samuel Gutwirth 5.00

HOBBIES

_____BEACHCOMBING FOR BEGINNERS Norman Hickin 2.00
_____BLACKSTONE'S MODERN CARD TRICKS Harry Blackstone 7.00
_____BLACKSTONE'S SECRETS OF MAGIC Harry Blackstone 7.00
_____COIN COLLECTING FOR BEGINNERS Burton Hobson & Fred Reinfeld 7.00
_____ENTERTAINING WITH ESP Tony 'Doc' Shiels 2.00
_____400 FASCINATING MAGIC TRICKS YOU CAN DO Howard Thurston 10.00
_____HOW I TURN JUNK INTO FUN AND PROFIT Sari 3.00
_____HOW TO WRITE A HIT SONG AND SELL IT Tommy Boyce 10.00
_____MAGIC FOR ALL AGES Walter Gibson 10.00
_____STAMP COLLECTING FOR BEGINNERS Burton Hobson 7.00

HORSE PLAYERS' WINNING GUIDES

_____BETTING HORSES TO WIN Les Conklin 10.00
_____ELIMINATE THE LOSERS Bob McKnight 5.00
_____HOW TO PICK WINNING HORSES Bob McKnight 5.00
_____HOW TO WIN AT THE RACES Sam (The Genius) Lewin 5.00
_____HOW YOU CAN BEAT THE RACES Jack Kavanagh 5.00
_____MAKING MONEY AT THE RACES David Barr 10.00
_____PAYDAY AT THE RACES Les Conklin 7.00

—SMART HANDICAPPING MADE EASY William Bauman 5.00
—SUCCESS AT THE HARNESS RACES Barry Meadow 7.00

HUMOR
—HOW TO FLATTEN YOUR TUSH Coach Marge Reardon 2.00
—JOKE TELLER'S HANDBOOK Bob Orben 10.00
—JOKES FOR ALL OCCASIONS Al Schock 10.00
—2,000 NEW LAUGHS FOR SPEAKERS Bob Orben 7.00
—2,400 JOKES TO BRIGHTEN YOUR SPEECHES Robert Orben 10.00
—2,500 JOKES TO START'EM LAUGHING Bob Orben 10.00

HYPNOTISM
—CHILDBIRTH WITH HYPNOSIS William S. Kroger, M.D. 5.00
—HOW YOU CAN BOWL BETTER USING SELF-HYPNOSIS Jack Heise 7.00
—HYPNOSIS AND SELF-HYPNOSIS Bernard Hollander, M.D. 7.00
—HYPNOTISM (Originally published 1893) Carl Sextus 5.00
—HYPNOTISM MADE EASY Dr. Ralph Winn 10.00
—HYPNOTISM MADE PRACTICAL Louis Orton 5.00
—MODERN HYPNOSIS Lesley Kuhn & Salvatore Russo, Ph.D. 5.00
—NEW CONCEPTS OF HYPNOSIS Bernard C. Gindes, M.D. 15.00
—NEW SELF-HYPNOSIS Paul Adams 10.00
—POST-HYPNOTIC INSTRUCTIONS—SUGGESTIONS FOR THERAPY Arnold Furst . 10.00
—PRACTICAL GUIDE TO SELF-HYPNOSIS Melvin Powers 10.00
—PRACTICAL HYPNOTISM Philip Magonet, M.D. 3.00
—SECRETS OF HYPNOTISM S.J. Van Pelt, M.D. 5.00
—SELF-HYPNOSIS—A CONDITIONED-RESPONSE TECHNIQUE Laurence Sparks ... 7.00
—SELF-HYPNOSIS—ITS THEORY, TECHNIQUE & APPLICATION Melvin Powers 7.00
—THERAPY THROUGH HYPNOSIS Edited by Raphael H. Rhodes 5.00

JUDAICA
—SERVICE OF THE HEART Evelyn Garfiel, Ph.D. 10.00
—STORY OF ISRAEL IN COINS Jean & Maurice Gould 2.00
—STORY OF ISRAEL IN STAMPS Maxim & Gabriel Shamir 1.00
—TONGUE OF THE PROPHETS Robert St. John 10.00

JUST FOR WOMEN
—COSMOPOLITAN'S GUIDE TO MARVELOUS MEN Foreword by Helen Gurley Brown   3.00
—COSMOPOLITAN'S HANG-UP HANDBOOK Foreword by Helen Gurley Brown 4.00
—COSMOPOLITAN'S LOVE BOOK—A GUIDE TO ECSTASY IN BED 7.00
—COSMOPOLITAN'S NEW ETIQUETTE GUIDE Foreword by Helen Gurley Brown 4.00
—I AM A COMPLEAT WOMAN Doris Hagopian & Karen O'Connor Sweeney 3.00
—JUST FOR WOMEN—A GUIDE TO THE FEMALE BODY Richard E. Sand M.D. 5.00
—NEW APPROACHES TO SEX IN MARRIAGE John E. Eichenlaub, M.D. 3.00
—SEXUALLY ADEQUATE FEMALE Frank S. Caprio, M.D. 3.00
—SEXUALLY FULFILLED WOMAN Dr. Rachel Copelan 5.00

MARRIAGE, SEX & PARENTHOOD
—ABILITY TO LOVE Dr. Allan Fromme 7.00
—GUIDE TO SUCCESSFUL MARRIAGE Drs. Albert Ellis & Robert Harper 10.00
—HOW TO RAISE AN EMOTIONALLY HEALTHY, HAPPY CHILD Albert Ellis, Ph.D. ... 10.00
—PARENT SURVIVAL TRAINING Marvin Silverman, Ed.D. & David Lustig, Ph.D. 15.00
—SEX WITHOUT GUILT Albert Ellis, Ph.D. 7.00
—SEXUALLY ADEQUATE MALE Frank S. Caprio, M.D. 3.00
—SEXUALLY FULFILLED MAN Dr. Rachel Copelan 5.00
—STAYING IN LOVE Dr. Norton F. Kristy 7.00

MELVIN POWERS MAIL ORDER LIBRARY

____HOW TO GET RICH IN MAIL ORDER Melvin Powers 20.00
____HOW TO SELF-PUBLISH YOUR BOOK Melvin Powers 20.00
____HOW TO WRITE A GOOD ADVERTISEMENT Victor O. Schwab 20.00
____MAIL ORDER MADE EASY J. Frank Brumbaugh 20.00
____MAKING MONEY WITH CLASSIFIED ADS Melvin Powers 20.00

METAPHYSICS & NEW AGE

____CONCENTRATION—A GUIDE TO MENTAL MASTERY Mouni Sadhu 10.00
____EXTRA-TERRESTRIAL INTELLIGENCE—THE FIRST ENCOUNTER 6.00
____FORTUNE TELLING WITH CARDS P. Foli 10.00
____HOW TO INTERPRET DREAMS, OMENS & FORTUNE TELLING SIGNS Gettings ... 5.00
____HOW TO UNDERSTAND YOUR DREAMS Geoffrey A. Dudley 7.00
____MAGICIAN—HIS TRAINING AND WORK W.E. Butler 7.00
____MEDITATION Mouni Sadhu 10.00
____MODERN NUMEROLOGY Morris C. Goodman 10.00
____NUMEROLOGY—ITS FACTS AND SECRETS Ariel Yvon Taylor 5.00
____NUMEROLOGY MADE EASY W. Mykian 10.00
____PALMISTRY MADE EASY Fred Gettings 7.00
____PALMISTRY MADE PRACTICAL Elizabeth Daniels Squire 7.00
____PROPHECY IN OUR TIME Martin Ebon 2.50
____SUPERSTITION—ARE YOU SUPERSTITIOUS? Eric Maple 2.00
____TAROT OF THE BOHEMIANS Papus 10.00
____WAYS TO SELF-REALIZATION Mouni Sadhu 7.00
____WITCHCRAFT, MAGIC & OCCULTISM—A FASCINATING HISTORY W.B. Crow 10.00
____WITCHCRAFT—THE SIXTH SENSE Justine Glass 7.00

RECOVERY

____KNIGHT IN RUSTY ARMOR Robert Fisher 5.00
____KNIGHTS WITHOUT ARMOR (Hardcover edition) Aaron R. Kipnis, Ph.D. 10.00
____PRINCESS WHO BELIEVED IN FAIRY TALES Marcia Grad 10.00
____SECRET OF OVERCOMING VERBAL ABUSE Dr. Albert Ellis & Marcia Grad Powers . 12.00

SELF-HELP & INSPIRATIONAL

____CHANGE YOUR VOICE, CHANGE YOUR LIFE Morton Cooper, Ph.D. 10.00
____CHARISMA—HOW TO GET "THAT SPECIAL MAGIC" Marcia Grad 10.00
____DAILY POWER FOR JOYFUL LIVING Dr. Donald Curtis 7.00
____DYNAMIC THINKING Melvin Powers 7.00
____GREATEST POWER IN THE UNIVERSE U.S. Andersen 10.00
____GROW RICH WHILE YOU SLEEP Ben Sweetland 10.00
____GROW RICH WITH YOUR MILLION DOLLAR MIND Brian Adams 10.00
____GROWTH THROUGH REASON Albert Ellis, Ph.D. 10.00
____GUIDE TO PERSONAL HAPPINESS Albert Ellis, Ph.D. & Irving Becker, Ed.D. 10.00
____GUIDE TO RATIONAL LIVING Albert Ellis, Ph.D. & R. Harper, Ph.D. 15.00
____HANDWRITING ANALYSIS MADE EASY John Marley 10.00
____HANDWRITING TELLS Nadya Olyanova 10.00
____HOW TO ATTRACT GOOD LUCK A.H.Z. Carr 10.00
____HOW TO DEVELOP A WINNING PERSONALITY Martin Panzer 10.00
____HOW TO DEVELOP AN EXCEPTIONAL MEMORY Young & Gibson 10.00
____HOW TO LIVE WITH A NEUROTIC Albert Ellis, Ph.D. 10.00
____HOW TO MAKE $100,000 A YEAR IN SALES Albert Winnikoff 15.00
____HOW TO SUCCEED Brian Adams 10.00
____I CAN Ben Sweetland 10.00
____I WILL Ben Sweetland 10.00
____KNIGHT IN RUSTY ARMOR Robert Fisher 5.00
____LAW OF SUCCESS Napoleon Hill (Two-Volume Set) 30.00
____MAGIC IN YOUR MIND U.S. Andersen 15.00

———MAGIC OF THINKING SUCCESS Dr. David J. Schwartz 10.00
———MAGIC POWER OF YOUR MIND Walter M. Germain 10.00
———NEVER UNDERESTIMATE THE SELLING POWER OF A WOMAN Dottie Walters . . . 7.00
———PRINCESS WHO BELIEVED IN FAIRY TALES Marcia Grad 10.00
———PSYCHO-CYBERNETICS Maxwell Maltz, M.D. 10.00
———PSYCHOLOGY OF HANDWRITING Nadya Olyanova 10.00
———SALES CYBERNETICS Brian Adams 10.00
———SECRET OF OVERCOMING VERBAL ABUSE Dr. Albert Ellis & Marcia Grad Powers . 12.00
———SECRET OF SECRETS U.S. Andersen 10.00
———SECRET POWER OF THE PYRAMIDS U.S. Andersen 7.00
———SELF-THERAPY FOR THE STUTTERER Malcolm Frazer 3.00
———STOP COMMITTING VOICE SUICIDE Morton Cooper, Ph.D. 10.00
———SUCCESS CYBERNETICS U.S. Andersen 10.00
———10 DAYS TO A GREAT NEW LIFE William E. Edwards 3.00
———THINK AND GROW RICH Napoleon Hill 10.00
———THINK LIKE A WINNER Walter Doyle Staples, Ph.D. 15.00
———THREE MAGIC WORDS U.S. Andersen 15.00
———TREASURY OF COMFORT Edited by Rabbi Sidney Greenberg 15.00
———TREASURY OF THE ART OF LIVING Edited by Rabbi Sidney Greenberg 10.00
———WHAT YOUR HANDWRITING REVEALS Albert E. Hughes 4.00
———WINNING WITH YOUR VOICE Morton Cooper, Ph.D. 10.00
———YOUR SUBCONSCIOUS POWER Charles M. Simmons 7.00

SPORTS

———BILLIARDS—POCKET ● CAROM ● THREE CUSHION Clive Cottingham, Jr. 10.00
———COMPLETE GUIDE TO FISHING Vlad Evanoff 2.00
———HOW TO IMPROVE YOUR RACQUETBALL Lubarsky, Kaufman & Scagnetti 5.00
———HOW TO WIN AT POCKET BILLIARDS Edward D. Knuchell 10.00
———JOY OF WALKING Jack Scagnetti 3.00
———RACQUETBALL FOR WOMEN Toni Hudson, Jack Scagnetti & Vince Rondone 3.00
———SECRET OF BOWLING STRIKES Dawson Taylor 5.00
———SOCCER—THE GAME & HOW TO PLAY IT Gary Rosenthal 7.00
———STARTING SOCCER Edward F Dolan, Jr. 5.00

TENNIS LOVERS' LIBRARY

———HOW TO BEAT BETTER TENNIS PLAYERS Loring Fiske 4.00
———PSYCH YOURSELF TO BETTER TENNIS Dr. Walter A. Luszki 2.00
———WEEKEND TENNIS—HOW TO HAVE FUN & WIN AT THE SAME TIME Bill Talbert . . 3.00

WILSHIRE PET LIBRARY

———HOW TO BRING UP YOUR PET DOG Kurt Unkelbach 2.00

LIBROS EN ESPAÑOL

———CABALLERO DE LA ARMADURA OXIDAD Robert Fisher 10.00
———CABALLERO DE LA ARMADURA OXIDAD (con cubierta gruesa) Robert Fisher 20.00
———CARISMA—CÓMO LOGRAR ESA MAGIA ESPECIAL Marcia Grad 10.00
———CÓMO ALRAER LA BUENA SUERTE A.H.Z. Carr 10.00
———PRINCESA QUE CREÍA EN CUENTOS DE HADAS Marcia Grad 10.00
———RECETAS DE LA PRINCESA QUE CREÍA EN LOS CUENTOS DE HADAS M.Grad . . 15.00
———SU PODER SUBCONSCIENTE Charles Simmons 10.00

Available from your bookstore or from Wilshire Book Company.
Please add $2.00 shipping and handling for each book ordered.

Wilshire Book Company
12015 Sherman Road
No. Hollywood, California 91605

For our complete catalog, visit our Web site at www.mpowers.com.